DREAMS OF DIFFERENCE

Dreams of Difference

THE JAPAN ROMANTIC SCHOOL
AND THE CRISIS OF
MODERNITY

KEVIN MICHAEL DOAK

University of California Press

Berkeley • Los Angeles • London

University of California Press
Berkeley and Los Angeles, California

University of California Press, Ltd.
London, England

© 1994 by
The Regents of the University of California

Doak, Kevin Michael
    Dreams of difference : the Japan Romantic School and
the crisis of modernity / Kevin Michael Doak.
        p. cm.
    Includes bibliographical references and index.
    ISBN 0-520-08377-6 (alk. paper).
        1. Japan—Intellectual life—20th century.
    2. Romanticism—Japan.   3. Nationalism—Japan.
    I. Title.
    DS822.4.D63   1994
    952.03'3 — dc20   93-5626
                                                          CIP

Printed in the United States of America
9 8 7 6 5 4 3 2

To Therese,
with special thanks for our past,
and to Anatole and Emile,
with special hopes for your future

Contents

Acknowledgments

So many people have helped me along the way that it is impossible to acknowledge them all. But special thanks must go first to Harry Harootunian, Tetsuo Najita, Norma Field, and Bill Sibley; without their encouragement and assistance this study would never have taken shape. Many colleagues at Wake Forest University have been generous with their support and critical suggestions, and I would particularly like to thank Michael L. Hughes, Phil Kuberski, Alan Williams, and Yuri Slezkine, now of U.C., Berkeley.

My debts on the other side of the Pacific are equally large, and I would like to acknowledge the help I received from Watanabe Kazutami, the late Maeda Ai, Itō Takashi, Tanisaki Akio, Oketani Hideaki, Romano Vulpitta, Yoshimura Chikai, Yanai Michihiro, Sugimoto Hidetarō, Nagai Jun'ichi, Etō Shigehiro, Aoki Toshio, and Kishi Masaki.

Financial support for this study has included a Fulbright fellowship, a grant from the Joint Committee on Japanese Studies of the Social Science Research Council and the American Council of Learned Societies with funds provided by the William and Flora Hewlett Foundation, and a grant from the Mrs. Giles Whiting Foundation. I am grateful to the Center for East Asian Studies at the University of Chicago for research support. Special thanks also to Mrs. Kuki and the entire staff of the East Asian Library at the University of Chicago. Wake Forest University gave me a Z. Smith Reynolds junior faculty research leave and financial support for the indexing costs, and Tokai University generously allowed me the use of office space and access to its many fine facilities during the final revision stage.

The book profited greatly from the suggestions of two anonymous readers for the Press; I am especially grateful to them and my editor Betsey Scheiner, whose sharp critical eye has improved on my work immeasurably.

Finally, I would like to thank Therese C. Doak for all her help, from criticism of many earlier drafts to extra help with the household chores, but mainly for just being there. It seems only fitting, if insufficient, to dedicate this work to her and to our two sons, Anatole and Emile. May they live in a better world.

Prologue

Nationalism, Romanticism, and the
Problem of Modernity

In the last decade or so, there has been a great deal of renewed, critical attention to the problem of nationalism and, particularly, to the ways in which nationalism relates aesthetics to broader questions of politics and political ideologies.[1] For those interested in intellectual history, this is an especially welcome development, as it reminds us once again that ideas about culture, art, and identity are not always completely private matters, devoid of historical and ideological value, but that they also intersect with public issues, at times yielding profound and disturbing results. Romantic nationalists may provide one of the best examples. A central claim of nearly all romantics is that they themselves are above the nasty world of political struggle and intrigue. Romantics and their apologists like to suggest that their interest in the expression of an individual consciousness cannot be reduced to the mundane world and its more base concerns with power and domination. Yet, of course, romantics (like all of us) do live in a mundane world, and the texts they produce can always be recontextualized as essential data within a historical project that does indeed have political significance. To establish that romanticism has a political or historical significance in spite of the protestations of romantics to the contrary does not require that we scrutinize the intentions of those making the claims or accuse them of bad faith. But it does mean that rather than accepting romantic claims at face value, we should interrogate the intertextuality of such arguments, in relation both to other, similar arguments and to the specific, historical and political context in which they occur.

Such is the purpose of this study. Through a close reading of the claims made by a group of romantics (the Japan Romantic School, or Nihon Rōmanha) during the 1930s and 1940s, I believe that one can get a sense of the political and cultural significance of the group. But since one of their central claims is the specificity of the Japanese experience, it may be helpful to bring into the discussion, when appropriate, comparisons with how Japanese romanticism, nationalism, and cultural exceptionalism have been found to intersect with other, non-Japanese, discourses. I do not mean to suggest that there are not aporia in the historical field, what Ernst Bloch refers to as "nonsynchronicity," which always resist full disclosure within narrative modes of explanation.[2] Rather, I hope to show that the historical significance of these romantics is best located by focusing on the contradictions between the universality of the human experience as promised by the discourse on modernity and the particularity of specific experience as represented through culture. This approach should help to reveal the modern character of the Japanese romantics who, ironically, joined in the modern denunciation of modernity itself as the root of all evil.

But a general statement on the modernity of the romantic movement does not answer the question of why this particular discourse appeared in Japanese history when it did and how the events of that time influenced the subsequent development of the discourse. One cannot adequately explain the problem by suggesting the accident of individual birth, as if history were determined by great men who just happened along. Consequently, it is not my intention to present an intellectual biography of the romantics; instead, biographical information is provided only when it seems especially germane. And a class-based analysis of the membership rosters of the Japan Romantic School cannot fully explain either the production of nationalism within the school or its popularity for those who read the members' work.[3] Of course, information on the varied backgrounds of the authors whose works are discussed below was generally not available to those who read, and were influenced by, the romantics' journal in the 1930s. Moreover, if the romantics considered themselves a "school," one may accept this self-definition to the extent that they created a public space through their writings that allowed for a discussion of the issues in ways that redefined and ultimately transcended the intentions of individual members. Given my focus on the impact of the Romantic School on Japanese intellectual discourse and given the social and historical nature of the Romantic School itself, it seems that a full explanation of the school's formation in the mid-1930s can only be found within the intellectual context that preceded it and out of which it developed.

Rereading the claims made by this group in the 1930s within the context of an ongoing debate on modernity, one finds that its historical origins were not in the period of wartime madness, when something "went wrong."[4] Rather, they predate the immediate prewar years and ultimately may be traced to the moment in the late nineteenth century when Japan had just emerged from the experience of the Meiji Restoration to confront the question of modernity. Leading Meiji politicians and intellectuals as diverse as Fukuzawa Yukichi (1835–1901), Iwakura Tomomi (1825–1883), and Natsume Sōseki (1867–1916) discussed many of the same concerns that the Japan Romantic School later expressed regarding the possibility of preserving a distinctive cultural difference within the modern world. An early attempt at critically assessing the effect of modernity on culture was made forcefully and systematically in the 1880s by the Min'yūsha and Seikyōsha intellectuals.[5] Consequently, a brief discussion of the early Meiji forms of nationalism may be helpful in understanding the conceptual similarities and historical differences between them and twentieth-century forms of Japanese nationalism.

Since the very foundations of Meiji society were grounded in an experience of the dominance of the West, it is not surprising to find the first attempt to come to terms with the strong attraction to, and subsequent reaction against, Western models of society in the Meiji years. One might begin with the "freedom and people's rights movement" (*jiyū minken undō*) of the 1870s and 1880s, which drew on Western natural rights theories to argue for inclusive notions of the national community. But most studies of Meiji nationalism emphasize the formation of Min'yūsha (Society of Friends of the Nation) by Tokutomi Sohō (1863–1957) and his journal *Kokumin no tomo* (The nation's friend); Tokutomi's organization came into existence at the same time as, but in opposition to, the Kokka Gakkai (Association for Research on the State), which began publishing its own journal in 1887. The cardinal difference between these groups rested not so much on the acceptance or rejection of Western social theory (both were attracted to Spencer's

theories on progress and social evolution) but on whether
"nation building" (*kokumin keisei*) should take precedence over
"state building" (*kokka keisei*).[6] While Tokutomi argued that it
should, the Meiji state and its ideologues continued to give priority to building a state that would impress Western diplomats into
revising the unequal treaties that threatened the Meiji state's
autonomy.

Tokutomi's attempt to redefine the national community from
within Western social theory was almost immediately criticized
by those who saw it as lacking a basis in Japanese native tradition. In their own journal, *Nihonjin*, members of the Seikyōsha
(Society for Political Education) group such as Miyake Setsurei
(1860–1945) and Kuga Katsunan (1857–1907) suggested as early
as 1888 that the essential problem was not the redefinition of the
goals of Westernization but an overemphasis of Western theories
that failed to account for native identity. As Ishida Takeshi suggested recently, their attempt to restore a sense of traditional
identity to the national community through the concept of "essence of the state" (*kokusui*) may well have been the earliest expression of the sense of cultural crisis that accompanied the Meiji
state's specific use of Western modernization for the purpose of
industrialization.[7] Kuga, in fact, centered his concept of nationalism on the people (*kokumin-shugi*) in a way that suggested a continuation of Tokutomi's struggle to define a more central role for
the people in the new state; his version of nationalism, with its
allowance for Western science alongside Eastern morality, seems
quite similar to the Japan Romantic School's use of European
cultural discourse in developing its own brand of ethnic nationalism.

Yet the differences between these Meiji nationalists and the
cultural and ethnic nationalism of the romantics in the 1930s were
profound, reflecting the historical difference between the two
periods Japanese society. The members of the "new generation"
that came of age in the 1880s began their search for a national
identity within the context of the Meiji experiment in national
development and state building and sought to retain notions
of progress within their reappropriations of culture.[8] Within the
broader context of modernization, they felt themselves caught between indigenous culture and the West, but none of them com-

pletely rejected Western culture and concepts of progress. As
Carol Gluck's penetrating analysis of the language of Meiji nationalism shows, such terms as *kokka* and *kokumin* were not that far
apart in their ultimate goals: these "invocations of nation included
the effort to draw all the people into the state, to have them thinking national thoughts, to make *kokumin* of them, new Japanese for
what was called 'the new Japan.'"[9]

It might be useful to see how Yasuda Yojūrō (1910–81), the
acknowledged leader of the Japan Romantic School, conceptual-
ized the differences between his group and Meiji forms of romanticism. In a sweeping essay on the "spirit of Meiji" (1937), Yasuda
expressed his respect for Kitamura Tōkoku (1868–94), Masaoka
Shiki (1867–1902), Okakura Tenshin (1862–1913), and Takayama
Chogyū (1871–1902) for their participation in a general resistance
to the "utilitarian literature" of the newly arisen Meiji bourgeoisie.
The weakness of Meiji romanticism, he notes, stemmed from its
historical context, which coalesced after the Sino-Japanese War
(1894–95) with the desires of contemporary political elites to promote a new, modern state in Japan. Takayama fought against this
tendency, as witnessed by his attempt to distinguish his "Japanism" (*Nihonshugi*) from the "essence of the state" (*kokusui*) of
Shiga Shigetaka (1863–1927) and the Seikyōsha intellectuals. But
his incipient attempt to distinguish between a concept of the nation centered on the people and one expressed in the state was
absorbed by the general celebratory spirit that followed the Russo-
Japanese war (1904–5), Japan's first military defeat of a Western
state. Consequently, Yasuda sees the Meiji period as an incomplete
project, and one of the tasks of the Romantic School "to reflect on
Meiji culture and its most superb aspect—its poetry, songs, and
literature"—a cultural accomplishment that Yasuda consciously
situates in opposition to the modern Meiji state.[10]

The "Meiji spirit" stemmed from an awareness that anything
was still possible in Japan's modernization, but by the 1930s modernization was complete enough to present "modernity" as an
object of criticism. In the subsequent turn to ethnic concepts of
national identity, it soon became clear that the difference between
indigenous culture and the West remained only as a memory that
now had to be produced. The problem of how best to represent the
past was intricately caught up with the ways in which post-Meiji

Japan experienced modernity. There was no single, definitive understanding among the members of the Japan Romantic School of what "modernity" meant. Modernity was defined in a variety of ways (and therefore often tended toward obscurity): at times it represented a foreign influence—the West; at other times it referred to the Meiji state and its ideology of "civilization and enlightenment"; and at still others it referred to the reality of Japanese culture in its only existent (if decadent) form. It is impossible to reduce the conceptual polysemy of this key concept to a stable definition and still retain an accurate sense of what the romantics were about. In fact, much of the dramatic appeal of the Romantic School rested on its ongoing attempt to define modernity and culture through the production of critical texts. Consequently, I have tried to allow the sense of ambiguity and overdetermination that the romantics experienced to come through in my own text in order to gain a better approximation of the complex historical and cultural processes that ultimately yielded a more reductive—and tragic—sense of modernity.

Nevertheless, there were some critical points of agreement in the romantic critique of modernity. All commentators agreed that modernity signified a new historical consciousness in Japan. This new consciousness brought them very close to Jürgen Habermas's recent definition of modernity as "the consciousness of an epoch that relates itself to the past of antiquity, in order to view itself as the result of a transition from the old to the new."[11] Along with this highly self-conscious awareness of a transition into something new, modernity generally involves a belief in the infinite progress of rational knowledge, which is often expressed by a confidence that historical progress provides the most accurate, formal representation of the movement of time. Habermas reminds us, however, that such analyses frequently overlook the fact that modernity also gives birth to a romantic spirit that seeks to free itself from all historical ties.[12] In Japan, modernity had become sufficiently "indigenized" by the early twentieth century to produce a host of complex and ambiguous responses to it. Much of the appeal of the Japan Romantic School lay in its attempt to confront the legacies of modernity in Japan, even if the members of the school could not always agree on what those legacies were.

Here, a few words on why the romantics turned to nationalism in their critique of modernity may be helpful. Benedict Anderson has contributed greatly to our understanding of the problem of nationalism by distinguishing between "official nationalism," which is centered on the state and imperial expansion, and "popular nationalism," which spreads among the masses and often is regarded as a threat by the state.[13] Japanese historical experience provides us with two comparable variants of nationalism. The "official" form of nationalism (*kokka-shugi*) has been studied exhaustively.[14] Yet this focus has not yet answered the complaint raised by Harry Harootunian at a symposium on Japanese nationalism some twenty years ago that "there is a striking yet silent agreement in all of these studies that in going beyond an inherited tradition of discourse the concept of nationalism has failed to yield an operational method adequate to organizing and examining *specific experiences*."[15] I believe that part of the reason for the inability to grasp the specific form of Japanese nationalism is the failure of many historians to consider "ethnic nationalism" (*minzoku-shugi*) as seriously as they have "official nationalism."[16] But it is ethnic, or "popular" nationalism (the word for ethnicity, *minzoku*, denotes a "tribe of the people") that the romantics turned to in their critique of modernity.

The focus on ethnic nationalism led to ambivalent relationships not only with the West but also with the Japanese state and its official nationalism. Very little interest is expressed in the early issues of the Romantic School's journal in condemning Western culture. On the contrary, the pages are sprinkled liberally with discussions of Goethe and Napoleon, *Sturm und Drang*, translations of Schlegel, and the like, alongside poems and essays on contemporary Japanese writers. One easily gets the impression that the writers were members of the young, bilingual intelligentsia that Anderson saw as the vanguard of popular nationalism among colonized peoples elsewhere.[17] When political issues appear in the journal, they are often treated with characteristic romantic disdain. A good example is Yasuda's essay "Bourudouin shushō," ostensibly a discussion of British Prime Minister Stanley Baldwin's remarks on parliamentary monarchy but actually a carefully crafted critique of Japanese "official nationalism" (*kokka-shugi*) for its subordination of "humanism" (not to mention the emperor) to political expediency:

I have come to understand that since the Meiji period our own nation of Japan has never yet gone beyond the Bismarckian forms of a late developing country....

... When even nation-states throughout the world no longer hold one's loyalty, the Japanese literary world, particularly in the present, gains its ethical significance.[18]

It is hard to appreciate Yasuda's argument fully without the entire context of the essay, as his critique is lodged within a rather wide-ranging, and at times cryptic, discussion of literature, history, and current affairs. But here one can already begin to see how some proletarian writers, especially those who were imprisoned, might find the romantics' moral condemnation of the modern Japanese state compelling.

The modern origin of such "ethnic revivals" has been supported by the findings of Michael Hechter and Tom Nairn, who argue in their studies of ethnic movements in Britain that ethnic movements "should be viewed as a product of economic development and capitalist industrial expansion, and not as some regrettable deviation or culture-lag of modernization."[19] While not all ethnic movements are explicitly romantic in orientation, some are, and Nairn's study of Welsh national movements reveals the role that a romanticization of culture can play in establishing national identity. Anthony D. Smith is quite persuasive in suggesting the limitations of this model of "internal colonialism" for all ethnic movements and in criticizing Hechter and Nairn for what he believes is an overemphasis on economics, which reduces ethnicity to a transitional phenomenon that will eventually pass away when modernization has completed its course. An ethnic "revival," Smith points out, "is at one and the same time an attempt to preserve the past, and to transform it into something new, to create a new type upon ancient foundations, to create a new man and society through the revival of old identities."[20]

The Japanese romantics made clear—clearer, in fact, than the Meiji nationalists discussed above—the artificial nature of "ethnicity" or "culture" in modern Japan and, hence, the need to consciously produce within the context of the modern world what will appear as native, traditional, and pure. This emphasis on the artificial nature of Japanese tradition separated the Japan Romantic School from such Meiji romantics as Kitamura and Takayama.

As Karatani Kōjin points out, "It is important to note that the Japan Romantic School did not think, as the Meiji romantics did, that the *Man'yōshū* was more natural or more original [than later works]. Rather, they praised it for its artificiality, as a kind of decadence."[21] The choice was not either modernity or culture, but both: for if romanticism was an offspring of modernity, it carried with it an Oedipal fantasy.

The immediate problem facing the later romantics was how to produce a memory that belonged irretrievably to an earlier generation. They reflected soberly that, as inhabitants of a modern world, they had much more in common with their contemporaries in Europe and America than with their own premodern ancestors. This realization gave rise to a sense of loss and longing, which Marxism traces to the alienation present in modern capitalist societies between production and existence or, as German romantics saw it, between politics and culture. The sense of loss was especially strong during the years of "Taishō democracy" when interest in politics and political action increasingly became defined in terms of culture.[22] This problem was not peculiar to Japanese discourse but was widely shared in the 1920s by most modern societies. The loss of immediate access to tradition in modern society, and to an unmediated culture free from state intervention, may well define part of what it means to be modern.[23] For the Japan Romantic School, this experience of loss was not solely due to Japan's specific modern transformation. Nevertheless, it suggested the possibility of a more thorough analysis of the general problem of the origins and nature of modernity, while simultaneously suggesting certain possibilities for a new, cultural politics. According to this analysis, the Japanese were singularly well placed to grasp the historical nature of modernity. Unlike the Europeans and Americans, for whom modernity had produced what must have seemed a universal condition, the Japanese could see from their own experience that modernity was originally a specific historical development rooted in the culture of the Other. Because of the distance in time and space that separated their own experience of modernity from that of the Europeans, many Japanese intellectuals hoped to recover the historical origins of modernity and, quite possibly, to redefine it. From this distance, modernity no longer appeared as a decisive break with premodern European history, but only as a minor shift that was firmly rooted in a long, cultural tradition. Indeed, much of the excitement and promise that accompanied the announcement of the formation of the Japan Romantic School may have stemmed from an expectation that it would expose the historical and cultural roots of modernity that the Europeans had suppressed, or at least forgotten.

Yet a sustained romantic critique of modernity did not begin until the late 1920s and early 1930s. The reasons for this timing might be sought within broader historical events that were transforming the globe after World War I. In fact, I argue that the resurgence of interest in romanticism and ethnicity in Japan during the 1930s was closely related to the questioning of modernity that was occurring throughout Europe in the years following World War I and the Bolshevik Revolution. There is a substantial body of literature that suggests that the postwar period was, in many ways, a time of radical rethinking of the universal values so readily accepted before the war. Eric Hobsbawm even calls this period the "apogee of nationalism."[24] Benedict Anderson offers a succinct explanation of the transformation:

> The First World War brought the age of high dynasticism to an end. By 1922, Habsburgs, Hohenzollerns, Romanovs and Ottomans were gone. In place of the Congress of Berlin came the League of *Nations*, from which non-Europeans were not excluded. From this time on, the legitimate international norm was the nation-state, so that in the League even the surviving imperial powers came dressed in national costume rather than imperial uniform.[25]

While one is naturally suspicious of sweeping explanations of a "Zeitgeist," those who accept the principle that thought has its own historical conditions have reason to believe a close relationship existed between the emerging nationalism of the interwar period and a renewed emphasis in the intellectual and cultural circles during the 1920s on identity and specificity at the expense of universal values.

This is not merely a retrospective view. In a highly influential essay that appeared in *Kaizō* in June 1933 called "The Philosophy of Anxiety and Its Transcendence," Miki Kiyoshi drew from the contemporary French literary critic Benjamin Crémieux to suggest that the years from 1918 to 1930 were best grasped as a period of transition. Crémieux had written two years earlier in his "Inquiétude et reconstruction: Essai sur la littérature d'après-guerre" that the war had reduced the idols of the nineteenth century, particularly the concept of the individual or individual rights, to ashes. He held that, in the aftermath of the war, those who had experienced social chaos found it increasingly difficult to trust in the objective existence of the external world and began to accept the reality of life only to the degree that it was a life that they themselves had imagined or invented. Miki locates the emergence of a literature and philosophy of "anxiety" (*fuan*) within the tradition of Karl Jasper's "boundary situations," which rejected the certainty of objective, social knowledge in favor of the subjective intent of the individual who exists within a "boundary situation."[26] In concise terms, he shows how "a man who has lost faith in society or has been precluded from taking social action will necessarily be driven further and further within himself."[27] Miki warns of the dangers in placing the same trust in relative values that were earlier accorded absolute truths, and he seeks to prevent this "spiritual" crisis from being transformed into a "cultural" crisis, concluding that romanticism could be discounted as a possible result of this "spiritual" anxiety.

Miki's refusal to recognize the attraction culturalism had in the early 1930s stemmed at least in part from his insistence that this spiritual anxiety was merely an "internalization" of Marxist anxiety over class divisions in society. Consequently, he tried to separate intellectual anxiety in Japan from what Crémieux discussed in Europe by insisting that in Japan this anxiety was felt only sporadically until 1932, when the proletarian literary movement came under attack. In fact, a number of intellectual developments in the 1920s contributed to the cultural crisis of the 1930s.

Foremost among these was the Shinjinkai (New Man Society), an organization of mainly Tokyo Imperial University students that was founded in December 1918. As Henry D. Smith shows, the Shinjinkai was imbued with strong populist principles from its very inception, especially through Asō Hisashi and his clique. Asō was a Russophile who responded to the Bolshevik Revolution of 1917 with enthusiasm and found in Turgenev's *narodniki* an answer to the Japanese rice riots of the summer of 1918.[28]

Although Smith argues that the Shinjinkai struggled with defining its own identity as a student organization, it seems fair to suggest that at least part of its appeal for many Japanese university students in the 1920s rested on its discovery of populism as a new form of collective identity. In a similar way, Donald Roden uncovers a fascination with gender ambivalence in urban Japan during the 1920s and locates it within the context of a modern "backdrop of moral as well as scientific relativity, of *'dissolving certainties'* about the beautiful, the righteous, and the evil, and of a fundamental tension between man's instinctive nature and his existence in a 'civilized' social order."[29] There is a vast distance between the gender ambivalence of the theaters and cafes of urban Japan and the political writings and other activities of elite students at a premier university. Yet both seem to provide evidence of an underlying concern in the 1920s with the source of individual identity and with reconceiving that identity in new and unpredictable ways.

As the 1920s drew to a close, a broad spectrum of Japanese intellectuals began to offer powerful, theoretical models of how identity might be reconceived in nonindividualist terms. Central to this effort was the role played by the Marxists and non-Marxists who wrote in the journal *Shinkō kagaku no hata no moto ni* (Under the banner of the new science) from October 1928 until December 1929, when the journal ceased publication. Led by Miki and his close friend Hani Gorō, the journal attracted many followers of Fukumotoism's theoretical purity after its condemnation by the 1927 Comintern thesis, but the editors noted from the outset their "desire to consider all non-Marxist developments in New Science and to represent them as well."[30] The writers for the journal shared a commitment to developing a new theoretical position that, rejecting the basis of modern science in a universal nature, would synthesize knowledge instead around the principle of nature as a societal category. The influence of the Marburg philosophers was present in their writings, as was that of Heinrich Rickert, Wilhelm Dilthey, and Georg Lukács. Miki was especially interested in these European theorists, for he felt they held the key to returning human agency to the scientific process and thereby restoring values to the forefront of sociological analysis. The objective was not merely a knowledge that was reliable, but also one that was useful; or as he puts it (citing Giambattista Vico), "we find in nature only what we can produce."[31] Those who shared in the New Science project generally agreed that the production of knowledge should not be reduced to culture, and they tried desperately to distinguish their own socially based identities from a cultural identity, but they did contribute to a fundamental shift in the structure of discourse away from questions of individual identity toward a theoretical foundation for collective identities.[32]

If this brief outline offers a partial explanation of the gradual move toward collective notions of identity, toward class consciousness on the left and nationalism on the right, it also foregrounds the specific problem of politics and culture that provided the immediate matrix for the Japan Romantic School. At the same time that Miki was searching for a "New Science," the proletarian literary movement was enjoying its heyday. The standard accounts all mark the high point of proletarian literature as the period from the suicide of Akutagawa Ryūnosuke (1892–1927) on July 24, 1927, to the murder of Kobayashi Takiji (1903–33) at the hands of the police on February 20, 1933. Akutagawa's suicide is especially significant. Yoshio Iwamoto suggests that it was a harrowing sign that the "established literature," in particular the "I novel," was becoming increasingly marginalized by "revolutionary changes in Japanese literature."[33] Yokomitsu Riichi's attack on the "Ego" and the "cultural renaissance" (*bungei fukkō*) that overtook literary discussions from 1932 to 1935 are discussed in detail in Chapter 5, but here it suffices to suggest how the turn to "cultural production" (*bungei*) and the attempt to supplant individual identity with various forms of collective identities that often rested on "culture" (*bunka*) were both intricately involved in a movement to uncover the unlimited possibilities of the subjective artist.

When Kurahara Korehito (b. 1902) returned from Moscow, where he had attended the Fifth General Meeting of the Profintern in August 1930, he brought with him instructions that "a Marxist consciousness must throb in every corner of a work."[34] Almost immediately, the proletarian movement was transformed to emphasize "culture." The All-Japan Federation of Proletarian Arts (NAPF) was incorporated into the newly formed Japan Proletarian Culture Federation (KOPF) and its major journals, *NAPF* and

Senki (Battle flag), were subsumed into *Puroretaria bunka* (Proletariat culture). But KOPF's attempt at a cultural revolution from the left proved short-lived. Its activities soon were declared illegal and, with the arrest in March 1932 of Kurahara, Kubokawa Tsurujirō (1903–74), Nakano Shigeharu (1902–79) and Tsuboi Shigeji (1897–1975), Kobayashi and Miyamoto Kenji (b. 1908) went underground. Clearly, leftist literary and cultural organizations were coming under increasing pressure from the police, and to debate culture from a proletarian standpoint involved certain risks. But within the proletarian movement itself, internal debate raged: if culture was to be politicized in line with the Profintern's directions, what role if any remained for literary creativity by Japanese artists? Moreover, given the implications of the attack on universal nature that theorists like Miki had articulated, how could theories of class consciousness emanating from the Soviet Union succeed as cultural criticism in the context of growing nationalist pressures at home?[35] As we see in Chapters 4 and 5, these questions were particularly important to Kamei Katsuichirō (1907–66) and Hayashi Fusao (1903–75), who began to move away from the proletarian movement and to embrace romanticism under the banner of the "cultural renaissance."

The Japan Romantic School contributed to this "cultural renaissance." But the romantics were not alone, nor were they esoteric, in their concern with Japanese culture. Although not all of those concerned with the cultural conditions of modern Japan embraced ethnic nationalism, or even state nationalism, the problematic of the status of culture in modern Japan was widely perceived as an urgent, indeed critical, issue, and it received a wide variety of responses. Generally, this cultural movement led to a reassessment of Fukuzawa Yukichi's position, announced in the newspaper *Jiji shinpō* on March 16, 1885, that Japan must "leave Asia" and "enter Europe" (*datsu-A nyū-Ō*). Fukuzawa simply meant that if Japan, as an independent state, were to survive in the context of increasing encroachment by Western states on Asia, it would have to promote Western culture at home and adopt "Western" policies toward its own Asian neighbors, principally China and Korea. Implicit was not only support for the policies that eventually led to the Sino-Japanese War and the annexation of Korea, but also a painful sense of cultural loss among those who believed that cultural authenticity was sacrificed in order to preserve state autonomy.

But it was the reversal of Fukuzawa's formula, a new call for "reentry into Asia and an abandonment of Europe" (*nyū-A datsu-Ō*), that characterized the renewed concern with culture in the twentieth century. This concern reached its zenith during the 1930s, but it was inspired and guided by the early twentieth-century work of Okakura Tenshin. In a work published only a few years before the outbreak of war with Russia (*The Ideals of the East*; 1902), Okakura outlined in English and for Western consumption a broad aesthetic theory of Pan-Asianism best capsulated in his opening statement that "Asia is one." Of course, some Asians were more Asian than others, and the Japanese retained to a greater degree than any of their Asian neighbors the "historic wealth of Asian culture."[36] In spite of Okakura's stress on the religious, aesthetic, and humanitarian aspects of Pan-Asianism, the timing of his work, coming as it did in the years immediately preceding the "respectable" war with Russia, certainly did little to discourage those in the 1930s who saw an inevitable connection between cultural particularism, nationalism, and political forms of revolt against the West.

Gondō Seikei (1868–1937), Inoue Nisshō (1886–1967), and Tachibana Kōsaburō (1893–1974) were a few of the traditionalists who emphasized the connection between cultural criticism and national, political action. Moreover, they shared a generally utopian view of society, which they located in an agrarian form of Asian communalism. Like Yasuda, they hoped to dislodge the emperor from the state and to restore him as the foundation of a new society in which representative politics would be abandoned in favor of a popular union of the emperor and the people (*kunmin kyōchi*). Yet, unlike Yasuda, they did not shy away from political action, including violence and terrorism, in attempting to realize their utopian dreams. With Gondō's and Inoue's involvement in the assassination of former finance minister Inoue Junnosuke and businessman Dan Takuma in early 1932 and Gondō and Tachibana's involvement in the assassination of Prime Minister Inukai a few months later, these men demonstrated that their ideas carried a serious political weight in the uncertain and highly charged atmosphere of the 1930s. The personal consequences of their terrorism were less evident though: although Inoue and Tachibana were arrested and imprisoned for these acts, both men were released by 1940.

Within the political context provided by men such as Gondō, Inoue, and Tachibana, cultural discourse was serious business even when the political implications of an intellectual's work were not immediately obvious. A good case in point is the philosophy of Nishida Kitarō (1870–1945). Nishida is usually described as a representative intellectual of Taishō-period "culturalism," and indeed there is evidence that he often protested against attempts to apply his philosophy to concrete historical and political problems. Nevertheless, applied it was, and "Nishida philosophy" became the intellectual foundation for the "Kyoto School" philosophers and their justification of the state and its war policies in the 1940s. Therefore, a brief discussion of some of his key philosophical concepts may reveal alternative dimensions of the nationalist and culturalist discourse within which the Romantic School operated.

Implicit in Nishida's thought was an attempt to transcend the limitations of modern philosophy, particularly through his concept of the "place of Nothingness" (*Mu no basho*). This concept can be seen as an attempt to limit the syncretic power of Western thought by situating it within a transexistential context. That is, in arguing that absolute identity could only come about through a "self-contradictory" process, Nishida sought to reintroduce the alterity of the "East" as a means of decentering or defamiliarizing Western thought. As he notes in his introduction to "From Doing to Seeing" ("Hataraku mono kara miru mono e"; 1927), there was much to learn from Western culture but, he asks, "is there not, deep down in the Oriental culture fostered by our ancestors over thousands of years, something that sees the form of the formless, something that hears the voice of the voiceless? Our minds can never cease looking for such a thing, and it is my hope to provide a philosophical basis for this kind of demand."[37] Because Nishida's thought came quite close to mysticism, one discusses him only with a great deal of peril. Rather than attempt to provide a complete accounting of his thought, it may suffice to conclude with the words of one of his students and critics. In a critique of the Kyoto School published in September 1932 (which Nishida praised for its accuracy), Tosaka Jun (1900–1945) points to the romantic character of Nishida's philosophy, which he defined as "a logical symbolism" in a "transhistorical system of hermeneutic categories," concluding that it was, ultimately, "a type of aestheticism."[38]

While it is hard to contest a characterization of Nishida's philosophy as a form of aestheticism or romanticism, there was an important difference between the Kyoto School's brand of nationalism and that of the Japan Romantic School, which is evident in the work of Tanabe Hajime (1885–1962), another philosopher closely associated with the Kyoto School. Tanabe developed his theory of "species" (*shu*) "around 1935, when the question of whether 'Japan' could be identified in ethnic terms cast a pall over the minds of all."[39] He drew several of his key concepts from Nishida's philosophy, particularly what he called "the absolute, dialectical method," but sought to connect them more closely with the knowable, actual world. By introducing the concept of "species," Tanabe hoped to clarify the relationships among the subjective individual, the human race, and the state. As he later described it, this was "an attempt to investigate theoretically the concrete structure of state society.... My motive was to take up as a philosophical issue the problem of ethnic nationalism (*minzoku-shugi*), which was emerging at the time and, while criticizing the liberal thought that had dominated us for so long, to negate the so-called totalitarianism that is based merely on ethnic nationalism." But as he went on to say, and support in his various writings, the solution to the "dialectic" between the rational individual and irrational claims of ethnicity was to be found in the synthesis provided by the moral state.[40]

A more in-depth analysis of the contribution of the Kyoto School in the attempt to "overcome the modern" must await the Epilogue, since these arguments gained prominence in the early 1940s, after the Japan Romantic School had already begun to wane in influence. But already two distinct positions in the attack on modernity may be discerned and contrasted with that of the Romantic School. The agrarian radicalism of men such as Gondō came early in the 1930s and was a rejection of, and violent attack on, the modern Japanese state. In contrast, the Kyoto School was engaged in a project that would eventually lead many of its philosophers to conclude that the Japanese state was the vehicle for "overcoming" a modernity that was now largely located beyond the borders of Japan. The Japan Romantic School lay somewhere in between, both chronologically and thematically. In the earlier years, especially in Yasuda's works, there was a strong anti-bureaucratic strain in the essays and poems of its members, which resembled the populism of the agrarianists. Yet, like the members of the Kyoto School, they expressed their antimodern-ism in literary forms, grasping the problem not as one of direct political action but as a crisis in cultural identity. Nonetheless, while some members of the Romantic School such as Kamei and Hayashi seemed to come quite close to a literary expression of the Kyoto School's ideological project, others such as Yasuda were never completely comfortable with the modernity implicit in the state-centered fascism of the Kyoto School.

Closer to the Romantic School's project was the cultural par-ticularism evident in the works of men such as Watsuji Tetsu-rō (1889–1960), Yanagita Kunio (1875–1962), and in a qualified sense, Tanizaki Jun'ichirō (1886–1965). Like Yasuda, Watsuji saw contemporary Japan in a state of cultural decline and sought the solution in a return to an earlier pristine culture, located in the ancient Yamato court (circa A.D. 350–645). His belief in a primor-dial harmonious community, freed from the constraints of politics, rationalism, and utilitarianism, nonetheless did not prevent him from drawing on Buddhism in his quest to distinguish the "spir-itualism" of the East from the "materialism" of the West. Watsuji was active at the same time as the romantics, publishing one of his best-known works, *Climate* (*Fūdo*) in 1935, in the year the Romantic School was founded. While his attempt in that work to trace the origin of determinate cultural traits to geographical causes may have struck many of the romantics as too "scientific," they largely shared his concern with finding spatial constraints to time and historical development. Indeed, for some, his most important con-tribution to "overcoming modernity" may well have been his juxtaposition of "American nationality" (*Amerika no kokuminsei*) to the "Japanese way of the subject" (*Nihon no shindō*).

Yanagita's attempt to develop an ethnography of the Japanese folk (*minzokugaku*) came very close indeed to the Japan Romantic School's vision of ethnic nationalism. Both approaches rejected the state nationalism of modern Japan, although Yanagita's research into the disparity of regional traditions and customs that co-existed with modern nationalism threatened to undermine the notion of a unified nation in modern Japan. Ultimately, how-ever, he settled on a concept of the "abiding folk" (*jōmin*) that effectively functioned to unify all Japanese, if not all Asians, in a view of Asian society as communal and harmonious in opposition to Western society, where class divisions and alienation predomi-nated. Moreover, his rejection of the state's intrusion into the native religion in the form of State Shinto and his belief that archaic dialects, traditions, and beliefs needed to be restored won the respect of many members of the Romantic School, even if they did not always agree with his optimistic view that such ancient practices could be accurately represented by his ethno-graphic methods. His optimism further separated Yanagita from the romantics, for, as Najita and Harootunian have pointed out, it also underwrote his belief that the science of ethnography, coupled with "an earlier concern for agricultural economics ... would enhance the well-being of the country populace in concrete ways."[41]

Finally, a few brief remarks about the novelist Tanizaki Jun'ichirō and the relationship of his writings to the Japan Roman-tic School need to be made. One might think that his nostalgic musings on the receding qualities of a native, Japanese aesthetic style, most eloquently put forth in his essay "In Praise of Shadows" ("In'ei raisan"; 1934) but also represented by his trans-lation into modern Japanese of the *Tale of Genji* (1935–42), would suggest a natural affinity with the writers in the Japan Romantic School. It is true that his writings in the 1930s reflect an appre-ciation for classical Japanese aesthetics, but it was an aestheticism that he never completely accepted. As he confessed at the outset of his "praise" of Japanese shadows, "I know as well as anyone that these are the empty dreams of a novelist, and that having come this far we cannot turn back."[42] While this realism (which was also represented in his willingness to translate the *Tale of Genji* into a modern language accessible to a broader Japanese public, something Yasuda saw as close to sacrilege) ultimately earned him the scorn of some members of the Romantic School, one need not push these differences too far. Certainly, Tanizaki did not lean as heavily toward nationalism as the romantics, but he did contribute to a literature of nostalgia and traditional aesthetics in the turbulent years of the 1930s, when solutions to difficult political problems were increasingly sought in the totalizing power of culturalism.

While the proletarian movement was rediscovering the politicality of literature and culture, another response to the cultural identity crisis of the 1930s was offered by Yasuda Yojūrō. In 1932, when the "cultural renaissance" began, Yasuda was a second-year student in the department of aesthetics of the faculty of letters at Tokyo Imperial University. In March of that year, he founded the journal *Cogito* along with a group of former classmates. The founding members were mainly Yasuda's classmates in the German language course of Osaka Higher School and included Tanaka Katsumi (1911–92), Nakashima Eijirō (1910–45), Odakane Tarō (a.k.a. Miura Tsuneo; b. 1909), Usui Toshiaki (b. ?–d. ?), Matsushita Takeo (1910–38), Funakoshi Akira (b. 1908), and Hige Tsuneo (1909–62), who financed and published the journal. They were later joined by Odakane's younger brother Jirō (a.k.a. Miura Tokio; b. 1911), Itō Shizuo (1906–53), Kurahara Shinjirō (1899–1965), and many others. The journal continued to publish until September 1944. It had close ties with the Japan Romantic School, which included among its members some *Cogito* writers such as Yasuda, Tanaka, Nakashima, Itō, Kamei, Jinbō Kōtarō (1905–90), and Hagiwara Sakutarō (1886–1942). In fact, Yasuda notes in his postwar reminiscences that "our journal *Cogito* and the *Nihon rōmanha* that followed it, shared a common repulsion at the general intellectual trends of the day and grew out of a complete rejection of the literary establishment."[43]

Many critics of the Romantic School, beginning with Kamei, have pointed to the origins of these intellectuals in the Osaka-Kyoto area, the center of traditional Japanese culture, in explaining their focus on tradition and culture. These accounts often remind us, for example, that Yasuda was born to a family with extensive holdings in forested land near the small town of Sakurai near the ancient capital of Nara and received his education in the area until matriculating at Tokyo Imperial University in 1931.[44] Such biographical studies have a particular fascination for many historians and literary scholars, both in Japan and in the West, but they do little to explain the power of the ideas produced by the romantics. The most persuasive arguments contrast the lack of evidence of Yasuda's engagement with leftist movements with the well-known activities of Kamei and Hayashi as if to prove who was more influenced by Marxism and what effect this influence had on their later involvement with romanticism. Of course, lack of evidence does not mean lack of experience, and the jury on Yasuda's experience with leftist movements is still out.[45] In addition, such arguments may confuse Marxist activity with Marxist understanding, ignoring the possibility that Yasuda understood some aspects of Marxism better than those who proclaimed the doctrine loudly in the streets. More important, they gloss over the subtle ways in which certain forms of Marxism and romanticism, particularly in the early decades of this century, often converged on a concern for the possibilities of cultural forms of social criticism.

In a similar vein, attempts to portray Yasuda and the coterie from Osaka Higher School as "traditional" because of their origins in the geographical center of traditional Japan overlook the fact that most of these men were students of German language and culture. It is just as likely, perhaps even more likely, that their interest in German culture provided them with an access to the same kinds of German criticism that Miki and Hani were beginning to introduce to Japan in 1928, the year Yasuda entered Osaka Higher School. Indeed, in his later reminiscences Yasuda suggested that, if anything, the influence he felt from Kyoto was the tradition of European continental philosophy and hermeneutics that underlay Kyoto Imperial University's "humanistic tradition," which stood in clear opposition to the emphasis on politics and elitism that characterized Tokyo Imperial University.[46] That is, the members of the Japan Romantic School greatly resembled the modern professional intelligentsia in other countries that found in historicism

an attractive and necessary framework ... because the crisis in legitimacy under which the old order was sinking demanded that they too find a viable identity and role in the emergent new order. Their secular rationalism meant that they could not simply return to the religious traditions of their respective communities; many of them had been too deeply touched by the vision of global, human

progress to revert to a simple traditionalism. They had to turn elsewhere for their new identity and historical legitimation—to the
"ethnic solution" of the intellectuals.[47]

Yasuda and his colleagues sought to return to the source of this
identity crisis. As the name of the journal suggests, *Cogito* traced
the origins of modern identity to Descartes's famous maxim,
"Cogito, ergo sum." The *Cogito* group saw Descartes's formula
of the knowing subject as the epistemological and existential origin of all forms of modern identity and criticized it for excluding a
Japanese identity grounded in native sensibilities. These writers
saw the Cartesian Ego as an historically and culturally specific
construct and sought to go beyond it to something akin to what
Rabinow and Sullivan have more recently called "a reality before
and behind the cultural world to which that world can be reduced."[48] They wrote with an unsurpassed confidence in their
mastery of Western knowledge, but they focused on modern conventions, particularly the act of literary representation, that had
previously guided all inquiries into knowledge. They sought to
show how representation was not a culturally neutral process that
establishes a natural correspondence between words and things.
Certainly, they themselves relied on representation in their own
literary work, seeking initially to defamiliarize the process of representation as a rebellion against universal culture; ultimately,
however, they were led to an effacement of representation once
again in favor of the natural bonds of cultural nationalism.

In order to produce a new reality from within the conventions of modern culture, the *Cogito* group undertook the historicist project of redefining the relationship between ancient and
modern. By "historicist," I mean that they partook of the "new
historical vision" that Anthony Smith has traced to the early
romantic movements in Europe, which he defines as "a predilec-
tion for interpreting individual and social phenomena as the
product of sequences of events which unfold the identity and
laws of growth of those phenomena.... Its aim is ... to establish,
through detailed historical investigations, the origins, growth
and purpose of particular entities, or classes of entities. In doing
so, the historicist attempts to reconstruct, as accurately and
vividly as he can, the ways of life, attitudes and actions of the

participants in a given period and area."[49] Specifically singling out the ancient classics of Western culture as excess after the modern transformation and as equally distant from all modern cultures, Western and non-Western, the *Cogito* group attempted to reincorporate this cultural loss into a new, broader definition of culture. As the group stated in the editorial postscript of the first issue of *Cogito*, "We have the deepest love for the classics. We love those classics that this country is unable to look back upon. We love the classics as an empty shell. And we love the desire to break that empty shell."[50] Nowhere were "the classics" identified with Japanese tradition. Rather, the members of the *Cogito* group seemed to write as if the cultural distance separating Japan from the West provided the critical distance necessary for understanding the historical use of the Greek and Roman classics in the construction of a modern age. From this distance, they were able to define the essence of modernity as a relentless suppression of the classics of antiquity, leaving implicit allegories with modernity and its effect on Japanese tradition. They accepted the finality of the suppression that had transformed the classics into "empty shells," forms whose content was rendered meaningless, but they refused to surrender the possibility of somehow reintegrating the classics into a new cultural identity.

Since the classics were at least as distant from modern Japan in time as the West was in space, they held no claims of natural contiguity over the Japanese and therefore could serve easily as objects of exoticism and emotional longing. Aware of the artificial nature of any temporal sequence that would establish "true" cultural identity, the *Cogito* group disclosed how the ancient Japanese classics, such as the *Manyōshū* and the *Tale of Genji*, no longer held uncontested, natural claims of immediate cultural identity for modern Japanese. To repossess their own cultural legacy, they agreed it was first necessary to begin with the classics of Western culture (and modernity) and thereby free themselves from the chains of modernity and similitude. As a way out of the "iron cage" of modernity, they turned to the German Romantic School which, early in the nineteenth century, had already tried "to construct, to produce, to effectuate what even at the origin of history was already thought of as a lost and forever inaccessible 'Golden Age.'"[51] For the members of the *Cogito* group, the writings of

Schlegel, Hölderlin, Novalis, and Schelling served as a bridge between the reality of modernity and the lure of antiquity as they sought to uncover specificity within modern culture.

As interest in German romanticism increased, it soon became evident to the members of the *Cogito* group that a more sustained engagement with the romantic project was unavoidable. Thus, an announcement appeared in the pages of the October and November 1934 issues of the journal that heralded the imminent formation of a new group dedicated to the study of romanticism. But two pages long, this "Advertisement for the 'Japan Romantic School'" is signed by Yasuda, Jinbō, Kamei, Nakashima, Nakatani Takao (b. 1901), and Ogata Takashi (1905–38). In the announcement, the authors denounce naturalism and exalt the powers of poetry and songs. They remind their readers that romanticism and classicism are not antagonistic in their aims but take part in a common struggle against naturalism and its belief in the sufficiency of the present moment. For the Japanese romantics, the defeat of naturalism was not merely the goal of rival epistemologies but also a liberation of the senses and therefore a precondition for any investigation into the possibilities and limitations of the production of culture.

This condemnation of literary naturalism included literary realism and was part of an attack on literary modernism.[52] Why the attack focused on naturalism and how the romantics connected it to modernity are important questions that Azade Seyhan's recent investigation into the problem of representation for the Jena romantics has done a great deal to illuminate. With stunning clarity, Seyhan describes the rise of Jena romanticism as an attempt to respond to the modern crisis in representation: "Representation always aims to make the subject or presence present to itself. It strives to present concepts of presence, identity, and being *in their totality*." Yet there always remains a separation between language and what it purports to represent, and this gives rise to "the recognition that some primary presence or truth remains inaccessible to consciousness."[53] In other words, the romantic attack on naturalism rested on a fundamental uneasiness with representations of totality that, by failing to call attention to their own position outside what was being represented, always eluded the goal of total representation and remained mired in logical contradiction. In place of representation, the romantics focused on alternative ways to restore totality through myth, emotion, poetry, irony, and the sublime—all of which ultimately promised greater totalizing power by the very fact of their inconsistent and fragmentary nature.

The belief that certain kinds of artistic practice could produce a radically different form of culture was underscored by the language of the announcement. The romantics make it quite clear that romanticism, as they envision it, is not a simplistic longing for the past. Indeed, the announcement declares that the Japan Romantic School will not be constrained by the conventions of the past or the superficiality of the "vulgar" writers of the present but will attain new heights of artistic and cultural achievement:

> The Japan Romantic School is the present poem of our "youth of the age." We reject everything but the lofty tone of these poems of youth and, untroubled by yesterday's customs, move forward in search of tomorrow's truth. . . .
> The Japan Romantic School pays no attention to history. Rather, the Japan Romantic School excels in all things and is the most pure and beautiful existence. Today, Japan needs such artists and the people require someone who can most acutely sense their demands. We, too, desire and long for what is most exalted and intense. That is the goal of the Japan Romantic School and its present reality. The form of longing is an expression of plunder. In order to protect what is most beautiful, in order to make manifest what is most sublime, this necessary mission to resurrect traditional artists is here an especially noble and urgent method of expression.[54]

The impulse of such language worked to redirect critical thought against a facile acceptance of narrative history as a universal, and irrevocable, means of establishing a modern identity. Yet the romantics did not abandon historical artifice. By emphasizing the unlimited possibilities of youth and by explicitly identifying these possibilities with the Japan Romantic School, the six founding members of the school outlined an agenda for "plundering" history in order to produce a cultural difference based in a large part on the arguments of the German romantics. For, as Seyhan has revealed, the German romantics sought to "exoticize" history by showing how "time, as past, present, and future, could only be conceived in memory and anticipation and synthesized in imagination."[55]

The selection of German romanticism as the mediating discourse in this attack on modernity was by no means an accidental, or even incidental, choice. But neither was it merely the result of a shared, aesthetic taste. The German romantics were seen as rebelling against the same threat of cultural hegemony that many Japanese felt "Americanization" and the "modern boy" (*mobo*) and "modern girl" (*moga*) represented in the late 1920s. According to this view, the German romantics had seen early on that the French Revolution of 1789 represented less the liberation of mankind from the bonds of feudalism than the unification of France and a threat to German independence and national unity. Indeed, when Napoleon's troops brought about the collapse of the Reich and occupied the left bank of the Rhine, German fears seemed fully justified. The Japanese romantics saw their German counterparts as heroic fighters against foreign cultural domination and for the creation of a unified national culture. They found support for this interpretation in Heinrich Heine's *Die romantische Schule*. Heine, who had once written enthusiastically of the liberating influence of Napoleon on German culture, had by the 1830s repudiated this earlier position and come to share Taine's belief that romanticism was essentially a popular movement against the aristocracy (*plébéien occupé à parvenir*).[56] This populism was not identical with democratic aspirations for plurality within unity, however, as it was superimposed with a belief in a folk renaissance. Often identified with Josef Nadler, this view held that romanticism was a return to an ancient Germanic people, a *differentia specifica*, that was historically and sociologically unique.[57] Thus, for Heine the German Romantic School was an attempt at reviving this ancient people through a "rediscovery of the poetry of the Middle Ages, as it had manifested itself in its songs, pictorial and architectural works, art and in life."[58]

Similarly, the Japan Romantic School ultimately joined in a broad, intellectual movement for a "return to Japan" (*Nihon e no kaiki*). This "return," however, could only be intimated through the artificial power of poetry, which the Japanese romantics chose as their preferred mode of expression. In the announcement cited above, the authors specifically identify the Japan Romantic School with the "songs," or poems (*uta*), of youth. But a few months later, when the school published the first issue of its official journal, *Nihon rōmanha* (The Japan Romantic School), the first item on the agenda was the task of clarifying the role poetry was to play in its program:

> In response to these times, we call ourselves the [Japan] Romantic School and, along with a respect for the arts, call for an emphasis on poetic spirit and speak out for the exaltation of the artistic disposition. . . .
>
> We have taken up the lofty tune of the youth of our age and, rejecting faddish and vulgar literature, step forward without regret in the declaration of the noble and liberating action of the artist. We have already heard that poetry lies at the origin and, at the origin of language, it serves to build dreams of spirit in the void.[59]

As this passage suggests, the Japan Romantic School did not share classicism's pessimistic view of the future. While both classicism and romanticism turned their gazes back upon the past and its works, classicism held that the present is only redeemable to the extent that elements of the past can be objectivity grasped and actually relived. Romanticism, however, privileged youth and its enthusiasm for imagining a better future, while utilizing the past as a means of negating the present. Thus, for the Japanese romantics, a "return to Japan" was a necessary element in their projected break from modernity, a move grounded in the historicity of the present but oriented toward the future.

Poetry was the chosen mode of expressing this impossible break from modernity because the Japanese romantics, like their German counterparts, saw poetry as an ideal means of contesting the totalizing powers of modernist representation. As Gaston Bachelard has shown, poetry has a "function of unreality," which opens up forms of knowledge that escape the scientific-rational opposition of subject and object. As "dreaming consciousness," poetic activity escapes from the forward movement of narrative history, and its claim of universal identity, to freeze time in specific "spaces" that can only be appreciated through the topo-analysis of phenomenology.[60] Bachelard's interpretation of poetry as an alternative form of knowledge draws on the German romantics, especially

Jean-Paul Richter, and sheds considerable light on the Japan Romantic School's assertion that poetry is more than a literary form. The romantics and Bachelard would agree that poetry has no past. But Bachelard's work diverges from that of the romantics in his insistence that culture does not inform poetry but rather that poetry originates in a "pure imagination."[61] For the writers in the Japan Romantic School, culture ultimately overtook their poetry and, just as Miki feared, reemerged within their project as a new form of totality that eventually muted the critical possibilities their project had promised.

In spite of all the excitement generated by the formation of the Romantic School, in the end the poetic imagination served as little more than a means for (re)producing a very specific cultural identity. Why this was the case is not easy to explain. Some insight may be gained from Bachelard's suggestion that poetry tends to project considerations of spatial relationships and location. These spatial configurations could easily slide into symbols of ethnic community that in turn might serve as the foundation for a nativism and ethnic nationalism based on a sense of historically shared space. In addition, in his study of nationalism, Anderson suggests how poetry often helps to construct group identities: "There is a special kind of contemporaneous community which language alone suggests—above all in the form of poetry and songs.... No matter how banal the words and mediocre the tunes, there is in this singing an experience of simultaneity. At precisely such moments, people wholly unknown to each other utter the same verses to the same melody."[62] The romantics ultimately settled on this aspect of poetry and began to employ it to suggest a vertical continuity of ancient practices while at the same time highlighting horizontal differences with other countries, especially with the West. Although some members of the school also wrote and translated short stories and novels, prose was always less esteemed than poetry and the critical essay. And the critical essay, as it developed in the romantic tradition, can be seen merely as a different form of poetry insofar as it, too, rejects narrative development in its organization. Like the fragment, it creates a sense of longing and unfulfillment in the reader by calling attention to its arbitrary and incomplete nature.[63] And yet, as we have seen, in so doing it merely attempts even greater powers of inclusion in its representation, incorporating itself and the Other as well. Such writing may be included in Friedrich Schlegel's "transcendental poetry," which Seyhan describes succinctly as follows: "In a proper analogy to transcendental philosophy, this poetry represents 'the producer along with the product' and represents itself in all its representations. It unites 'the transcendental elements and preliminary drafts of a theory of poetic creativity' and is always simultaneously 'poetry and the poetry of poetry'" (the quoted phrases are Schlegel's).[64] Such attempts at representing totality through textual production, whether in poetry, essays, or the occasional novel, served primarily as a means of prefiguring in art the kind of cultural specificity the romantics hoped to achieve in society at large.

Poetry, it should be stressed, was not simply a preferred literary genre but also a deliberately chosen strategy for producing a new subjectivity by representing the world differently. Alongside the imagining of communal identities, another key element in this poetic strategy of producing totality was the function poetry could play in erasing the division between subject and object. Breaking with the even flow of narrative, poetry creates brief scenes of apparently eternal beauty. But as Karatani Kōjin points out, these scenes are not transparent reproductions of an objective nature in the manner of realism, but constructed images of a specific reality that take as the condition of their own possibility the priority of a subjective self.[65] Indeed, the focus on the self, its certainty and effects, is a central theme in romanticism and has been traced to the German romantics' attempt to rethink Descartes's legacy to Western thought that "it is in reconstructing the world ... that the subject constitutes itself *as* subject."[66] Poetry would constitute the world and the subject simultaneously by suggesting that the distinction between the two is an artificial one that can be overcome artificially, thereby displacing the relationship between subject and object that underlies the modern structure of meaning. The romantics saw identity not as the product of a system of signification in which the subject is always decentered but as the moment when "the subject appears fully present to itself in a signified without a signifier, a represented without means of representation."[67] Poetry was seen as the purest form of experience, a method of expression (not representation) that offered the reassuring presence of voice instead of narration. The poetic voice intimated a continuity with the ancient past that, when resurrected in the present, promised to reintegrate the fragmentation of modern life into a new, cultural whole.

Within this broadly shared strategy, there was considerable room for divergent views. Indeed, it would be difficult to imagine it otherwise in light of the sheer number of intellectuals and writers who participated in the Japan Romantic School. From the founding of the school in March 1935 with six members, the membership rolls increased to twenty-two within four months and ultimately to fifty-six members at its strongest (see Appendix A). More significant than the size of the school, however, were the reputation and influence of its leading members. Yasuda, Kamei, and Hayashi were all well-known writers at the time, as were Hagiwara, Dazai Osamu (1909–48), Satō Haruo (1892–1964), and a host of others. Of course, as with any large group, some voices were bound to dominate. Each of the leading voices emphasized its own particular approach, yet all converged in a concerted effort to produce a new subjectivized basis for a Japanese cultural identity. Ultimately, the creative tension between unity and dispersal within the school contributed to a self-characterization of the school as "irony."[68]

Each of the chapters in this book focuses on one of the hegemonic voices, or "moments," in the Japan Romantic School's search for a new basis for cultural identity. The chapters are synchronic, each breaking away from diachronic narrative and moving beyond the layers of history to arrive at a deeper analysis of these claims for particularity. This very well may be a necessary approach if we are to take such alternative histories seriously—that is, if we are to understand the historicity of romantic arguments. It is not my intention to write mini-intellectual biographies, and therefore biographical details have been kept to a minimum. Rather, I have tried to isolate major voices that characterized the tensions within the school. Sometimes, these voices were associated more or less with the name of an individual member, particularly with Yasuda, but even then there was no direct correspondence between the principles and the principal of argument. Internally, each chapter moves in a roughly diachronic manner, a step that risks repetition, or even worse, incoherence, but this may be an unavoidable result of the irrepressible drive to produce meaning historically. In the end, as these critical impulses become embedded in cultural identity, an implicit narrative emerges: the tragic irony of the Romantic School gives way to farce and the triumph of myopia. Finally, in the postscript, I return to a more conventional narrative form in an attempt to suggest briefly how Japanese intellectual discourse in the postwar years has inherited and transformed the issues raised by the Japan Romantic School.

The first chapter describes the attempt by the romantics to articulate an aesthetics that would replace more modern, rational forms of thought. This aesthetics, most closely identified with Yasuda, the acknowledged leader of the Japan Romantic School, would serve as the voice of an ethnic revival, much as Napoleon was seen as the symbol of a newly unified, modern Europe. Drawing on a fundamentally tragic sensibility, Yasuda expressed this aesthetics in his concept of "Japan as irony," which he saw as a means of overcoming the optimism of modernity and its accompanying pride in progress and novelty. But ultimately the emphasis on irony as a form of negative praxis proved impossible to reconcile with any concrete form of social or political intervention and was transformed from a promising critical practice to a latent desire for total culture and, finally, to an aesthetics of death as the ultimate form of totality.

The second chapter introduces the poetics of the Romantic School as articulated by Jinbō Kōtarō and the response to it in the poetic practice of Hagiwara Sakutarō. Jinbō suggested that historical time might be displaced by a "new time" grounded in the spatial relationships of poetry. Hagiwara explored this possibility in his own poetry, in which his disillusionment with the changes of the modern world often took the form of a sense of homelessness and eternal wandering. He made full use of imaginative space in his poetic vignettes, but he refused to settle on the extreme of either the countryside or the city as the home ground of his aesthetics. Although Hagiwara ultimately distilled his disillusionment into the expression "return to Japan," neither he nor Yasuda ever conceived of this return as anything other than ironic.

In the third chapter, this resistance to all forms of definition begins to give way to a clearer sense of direction. Tanaka Katsumi

responded to Jinbō's call for the production of a "new time" by
investigating the possibilities of a transcendental beauty located in
the space of the classics. This transcendental beauty enabled him
to suggest a redefinition of Asia as an aesthetic concept and ultimately brought him to the realization that the true Asia was accessible only to the Japanese. Itō Shizuo, the poet laureate of the
Romantic School, tried to find an answer to what it means to be
Japanese in the workings of language itself. His analysis came
remarkably close to modern understandings of identity, but his
discovery of a "split self" was not an affirmation of a modern,
decentered self. Instead, he developed a poetic anguish over lost
identity, which ultimately sought to replace the decentered self
with a "self" (*watakushi*) that was linguistically and culturally
defined. In the final analysis, this alienation of the self from itself
was transferred to the level of the cultural alienation of Japan from
the world.

Itō's investigation into the problems of the self has close parallels with Kamei Katsuichirō's search for a new subject that would
serve as the basis for a Japanese ethics. Both men were involved
in an attempt to reduce culture to the individual and, from this
individual, to construct a new culture. Kamei's project, however, lacked the ironic qualities of Itō's poetry. At times, Kamei,
Yasuda's chief rival in the Romantic School and the subject of
the fourth chapter, wrote as if he believed that a "return to Japan"
were actually possible. This "return" signified a rejection of Western, class-conflict models of society and developed into a commitment to Japanese ethnicity as a homogeneous whole. While Kamei
did not directly discuss the issue of poetry, his reconceptualization of the ego (*jiga*) as a rejection of the Western individual ego,
was largely indebted to the work of the poets discussed in the
earlier chapters, as it too led to a homogeneous Japanese identity
that was thoroughly poetic in inspiration.

Like Kamei, Hayashi Fusao believed, without a trace of irony, in
the possibility of a "return to Japan." But for Hayashi, the success
of such a return was explicitly connected with the possibility of a
cultural renaissance. He hoped to accomplish this cultural rebirth
through the imaginative reality afforded by historical fiction. In
his fiction he traced the origins of modern Japan to a cultural
encounter with the West that, he felt, had tragically shaped the

outcome of modern Japanese history. By returning to the birth moment of modern Japan and by availing himself of the power of fiction to suggest imaginative alternatives to history, he believed a revitalized Japanese identity based on the unique Japanese emperor system actually could be produced. Yet, in the end, the emperor system provided Hayashi with an internalized principle of difference that enabled his ethnic nationalism to mesh with state nationalism and to more than approximate outright racism, particularly as he projected racism onto "the West."

These five moments, then, constitute the core of the Japan Romantic School and its critique of modernity. Each drew on a particular aspect of the romantic tradition in marking out its own place within the school. Yet none of these moments can be reduced to romanticism as such, or to modernity's claims of universality. Rather, the genesis of the Japan Romantic School is to be found in the intersection between the particular historical situation of Japan in the early twentieth century and the general problem of culture in modern societies. Romanticism provided a discourse with which to mediate between the two, but by no means did it simply provide answers to what, by the 1930s, already had become one of the most enduring traditions of modern Japanese history: the question of a Japanese identity.

Toward an Ironic Praxis

Yasuda Yojūrō and the Aesthetics of Totality

> The person who suspects—rightly—that domination is ever-present in art runs the risk of selling out to the approaching totalitarian tendencies, for he will be inclined to say to himself that things have always been this way and there is nothing he can do about it, forgetting that the illusion that art puts before us of an Other always implies the possibility of that Other, too.
>
> Theodor Adorno, *Aesthetic Theory*

One of the most powerful and lasting contributions of the Japan Romantic School was its claim to cultural difference. As the acknowledged leader of the school, Yasuda Yojūrō was unsurpassed in shaping a systemic view of Japanese culture and its role within the contradictions of an ostensibly homogeneous modern world. Remarkably sensitive to the problems of culture and its production, Yasuda remained firmly confident of the validity of the past in the present, of culture in an era of civilization, and of poetry in an increasingly prosaic world. Decadence was reason for hope, and failure "an ironic victory" for a man to whom Napoleon and the ancient Japanese emperor Gotoba were largely interchangeable. He was acutely aware of the necessity of a broad understanding of the major developments in European history as a precondition for any articulation of difference from it. And yet, in framing this production of cultural difference within the larger discourse on romanticism, Yasuda, it may be argued, had already intimated the ultimate futility of all attempts to "overcome" modernity.

THE TRAGEDY OF HISTORY

The origins of the Romantic School's discourse on difference can be located in the perception of "a sense of ending" that pervaded the brief Taishō era (1912–26).[1] The Taishō years witnessed a renewed interest in problems of defining culture and identity, and Yasuda feared that the production of new cultural identities would be prematurely foreclosed by what he saw as the firm establishment of a complacent, managerial ethics. He found this trend particularly dangerous among university students, especially those in the humanities, whose employment prospects were extremely limited and who were forced to compete for what few openings existed in business and government. For Yasuda, the single-minded pursuit of personal wealth was a perversion of the Meiji tenets of "enriching the country and strengthening the army" (*fukoku kyōhei*). Students, he notes, "were disciplined down to their bone marrow with a smug, home-managerial national ethics."[2] These students were seen as having lost the revolutionary zeal characteristic of the early Meiji years, which had set Japan apart from the rest of Asia, and as having traded in their Asian heritage for the material accouterments of the modern West. The solution was a more humanistic education that would restore meaningfulness to life by moving away from values based on individualism or economic gain. Yasuda's critique of Taishō education is remarkably close to Anthony Smith's insight that

> education ... for historicist intellectuals ... represents something even more than a scientific temper and rationalist outlook. True education is a process of self-fulfillment through self-understanding; and such a process is inevitably a collective or rather communal and historical project. It is a process by which the individual comes to realise his role in the particular historic culture in which he has been brought up, and simultaneously to understand the history and destiny of the community to which his fate is linked.[3]

Thus, the central concern for intellectuals in the Shōwa period (1926–89), Yasuda argues, must be to compensate for this educational failure by producing new cultural forms that will resurrect the ideal of public-mindedness among intelligent and ambitious youth.

In spite of Yasuda's scorn for the excesses of material consumption, he harbored no doubts as to the finality of Japan's modernization. He firmly believed that much of modern culture had finally become accessible to the majority of Japanese during the years of Taishō individualism. But modernity had also become an "ironic victory" for Japan at this juncture. Having achieved unparalleled success in technological and economic development, the Japanese faced the unprecedented problem of assimilating these developments into a new cultural logic that could encompass aspects of both East and West, self and Other. Yasuda was not optimistic about the possibility of such a new, syncretic culture. He understood that the introduction of foreign culture into Japan was irreversible and, more important, had brought with it the loss of Japanese traditions. He agreed with Hagiwara Sakutarō that modern Japan had lost everything but, unlike Hagiwara, he sought to go beyond a mere lamenting of the past to a theory of action, perhaps even a new culture, based on lamentation.

Given Yasuda's reading of the effects of modernity on Japanese culture, it should come as no surprise that he rejected any overt appeal to politics as the basis for a theory of action. In delineating the outlines of his own theory of action in "The Problem of Criticism" (1933), Yasuda agreed in part with Nakano Shigeharu's refutation of the modernist Hirabayashi Hatsunosuke's ideology of fusing politics and art into a new aesthetics of action.[4] Both Nakano and Yasuda, for different reasons, sought to maintain the distinction between the two as separate, if equal, fields of inquiry. But for Yasuda, the separation could only be, at best, a "contradictory synthesis": "The problem may be expressed as a contradictory synthesis of artistic value and political value. The problem may also be framed within the context of the limits of criticism and acceptance. These contradictory values—to speak bluntly—the former may be called a universal value, and the later might be termed a particular, or historical, value."[5] Critical action, then, required an intervention in this "contradictory synthesis" to preserve the possibility of any significant change. Whereas Nakano sought to deny political value to art, Yasuda believed political action possible only within the contradictions of a culturally based art of universal proportions.

By early 1934 Yasuda began to refer to these contradictions as "irony." In an essay on the tragic German poet Friedrich Hölderlin, Yasuda argues that it was Kant's Third Critique that undermined our faith in reason and modernity. Kant openly confessed the failure of his method to establish the relationship of man to nature and God, and thereby gave a candid admission of the failure of reason. In the aftermath of the failure of reason, "pure poets," such as Hölderlin, Kleist, and Nietzsche, who refused to recognize the separation between art and life were able to survive only at the expense of their sanity. However, with the establishment of a capitalist society, livelihood became the supreme concern and was regulated through a system of formal laws. Within capitalist society, where reason prevailed, all change and forms of social difference were underwritten by the irony of "the disintegration that arises from within the absolute, and along with it the painful awareness of that disintegration."[6] The contradictory nature of modern, capitalist society easily lent itself to ironic expression. Irony does not abolish the modern antagonism between art and livelihood but gives expression to this antagonism by "acknowledging and denying in the same gesture the presence/ absence of the organic totality it strives to achieve."[7] Yasuda saw irony not as a means of arriving at a deeper truth, or of self-deprecation, but as a means of suggesting a vague sense of omnipotence through its ability to negate conventional, limited notions of power. In doing so, he certainly ran the risk of substituting text for history and the subject of the work for the work of the subject. Yet while irony dissolved the contradictions of modern society by poetically lamenting the loss of objectivity, it simultaneously sought to disclose that objectivity might actually be grounded in the "truthfulness" of social relativity. In a definitive move, Yasuda ultimately sought to displace irony from the German romantics and their search for cultural relativity in Europe to a nativist context that questioned the applicability of European norms of social organization to Japan.

If Yasuda had misgivings about the way Western culture had been introduced in Japan, he also realized that the longing for an original moment of authenticity was a problem common to Japan and modern Europe. In Europe he located the loss of a sense of the absolute—both political and cultural—in Napoleon's rise to power, a moment that marked the birth of Europe as an entity and, simultaneously, represented its loss of freedom. Napoleon, Yasuda argues, was not merely the "father" of Europe but, as the unifying principal of a "Europe" that had never existed before, he was Europe.[8] Within this historicist vision, the French

Revolution is seen as promising a radical difference from all previous history and standing in contrast to Napoleon's "purity." This, according to Yasuda, is the fundamental nature of modernity: to suggest the possibility of difference through a recognition of the radical purity of an earlier age. But inherent in this nature is a realization that this difference belonged to a lost age and, consequently, is ultimately unattainable. Thus, Napoleon represents the tragic fate of all attempts to assert difference in the modern world. Napoleon's reckless manner of warfare, Yasuda suggests, stemmed from a belief that his battles were not modern calculations of power and wealth but part of a larger war of independence for all "Greeks" who desired freedom and equality. This was a tragic miscalculation that the English did not share. As the last pure, creative man in an impure, modern world, Napoleon failed to understand the finality of the loss of the classical world even after his defeat at Waterloo. Napoleon refused to see Waterloo as the decisive defeat of his revolt against modernity, and instead romanticized it in terms of the defeat of the Romans by Hannibal at the Battle of Cannae in 216 B.C. Cannae, Yasuda remarks dryly, is that fate awaiting all who fail to understand that modernity both gives birth to the universal hero and ensures the complete alienation of such a hero from modernity.[9]

In addition to representing the marginalization of purity and madness, Napoleon's confinement to St. Helena symbolized the alienation of modern societies from the classic ideal of universals. Europe had achieved unity, to be sure, but only at the price of discontinuity with the traditions that had made it great. These traditions had lost their universality through a process of identification with a particular political body, the "New Europe." Napoleon's fate should remind us, Yasuda warns, that a "great defeat" (*idai na haiboku*) always awaits those who attempt to resurrect ancient Greece through Napoleonic means: "What Hölderlin has taught us is the victory of what is called tragedy. In common parlance, this is their glorious day, St. Helena. It is a great defeat. Now we must begin to speak of a tragedy that has greatness."[10] Yasuda means to suggest by this dilemma that, given the paradoxical conditions of the modern world, a military challenge to the nature of modernity is futile at best and ultimately tragic. Victory in battle is possible only if one adopts the most modern forms of warfare and rational calculation; but to do so is to recognize the validity of modernity and to lose the universality of the classical ideals. The only option remaining is to embrace tragedy and defeat as the irony of victory.[11]

There is a double irony to this argument. The loss of universal values occurred at the moment of Napoleon's defeat when the ideal of freedom for all was replaced by an appropriation of the image of the classical world by the English to legitimize their claim to economic plunder. "Universal" no longer signified freedom for all, but the right of the English to expand their economy throughout the world at the expense of others. In essence, the universality of freedom was replaced by the universality of the English currency, language, and culture. Thus, Napoleon's final dream was to escape to the East where, as emperor, he would lead the Indians to freedom from the British crown. The tragedy of this dream, Yasuda concludes, is that it could no longer be accomplished through Napoleonic means but had to wait for Goethe and his fellow romantics' attempt to resurrect the ancient ideal of a universality that encompassed the East as well as the West.[12] Until the return of the original concept of universality, the memory of St. Helena had to be preserved as the tragic fate of the classical ideal of universality in the modern world.

As a means of regaining the classical sense of universality, Yasuda credited the romantics with the important step of discovering a "consciousness of fiction" (*kyokō no ishiki*). This stemmed from a larger concern over the status of nature in the modern world: "Ours is a time of irony; it is a day when all who are great and glorious must think of irony as their own home. It is a day that compels us to remember that. *And while we long for what is natural as our form of expression, as our true attitude we can grasp only what is artificial* [italics mine]. Yet it must be said that our new age makes us aware of this artificial attitude and conscious of its enforcement."[13] *Nature,* as used above, clearly does not refer to Rousseau's sense of nature as a paradise lost. Rather, it corresponds to the hard and unalterable laws discovered by modern physics as the identifying marks of the primordial stuff of the universe: it is essentially a constraint.[14] In contrast to nature, the "consciousness of fiction" is a highly intentional practice that seeks to negate all limitations of objectivity and scientific "truth." In such an ironic view, "truth" reveals its fictitious nature, while fiction gains a practical truthfulness.

Central to the "consciousness of fiction" is the belief that what has been lost must be retained "as if" it were still present. The very act of thinking is, for Yasuda, essentially a longing for a reunion with absolute truth: thus, we "long for what is natural" as the most perfect form of language while speaking as if we already understand nature. Yet here Yasuda is closer to the German philosopher Hans Vaihinger than to Goethe. Vaihinger offered his theory of "As If" (*Als-Ob*) as evidence of the survival of the irrational in modernity. We ought to abandon our fascination with truth for fictions, Vaihinger argues, since fictions have a greater degree of utility. Fictions cannot be mistaken for truth since they are known by all to be false, and this quality of reliability therefore enables them to be used to achieve narrowly designed, intentional goals. For example, even while known to be false, fictions can contradict reality and thereby prove the power of working *as if* true.[15] For Yasuda, the "consciousness of fiction" signifies a romantic attempt not to replace reason with emotion but to maintain the fiction of rationality as the ironic condition of modern Japanese culture.

Only when nature is irretrievably lost can it become the object of longing. But this insight does not necessarily imply a simplistic flight from reason to the sanctuary of the emotions. Yasuda confesses, "Rumor has it that I am a follower of Art for Art's Sake and have escaped from reality, ... [yet] I myself know well how impossible it is to believe in Art for Art's Sake."[16] His criticisms of the Shinkankakuha (New Sensualist) writers reveal his support of Wilhelm Worringer's theories against Theodore Lipps's doctrine of *Einfühlung*, or empathy.[17] He rejects the latter's emphasis on projecting one's own emotions into another's work in favor of Worringer's positing of an "absolute artistic volition" that "exists *per se*, entirely independent of the object and of the mode of creation, and behaves as will to form."[18] For Yasuda, as for Worringer, history can be transcended by an aesthetics that promises to establish a totally artificial world.

Yasuda encapsulates the will to move oneself from the reality of history to the fiction of an artificial world in a call to decadence. Decadence, as Jean Pierrot points out, is intimately connected with a rejection of nature and the identification of art with the artificial.[19] The decadent aesthete abandons hope of a knowledge of anything but the human consciousness and its representations and escapes to the consolation offered by the imagination. Confidence in social progress, and specifically in the efficacy of social science to improve human livelihood, is scorned as the naiveté of youth:

> To say that we have lost our youth is merely to speak of a single historical phenomenon. In other words, the loss of youth is the loss of humanity, which means that the future cannot be known by analogy with existing humanity. That is why I am presently uninterested in anything other than some form of decadence that opposes nature. Why is decadence the way of the future? ... The positivity of decadence is related in the first place to the spirit of an artificial paradise. Here absurdity is not a judgment of truth or falsity, but signifies the ability of the lie, left intact, to jumble things up.[20]

This view of decadence leads to a position that is hardly distinguishable from that of "Art for Art's Sake." But Yasuda repeatedly asserts his belief that decadence, while a temporary flight from the constraints of social reality, is at the same time an attempt to change that very reality. Decadence is for him both a recognition of the impossibility of a return to the past and an attack on the modern historical consciousness that prevents such a return.

Yasuda's theory of irony was formulated within the problematic, ushered in with the birth of modernity, of the ambiguous relationship of universal to particular. While Yasuda believed that the problem was an especially difficult one for the Japanese, who had come to modernity through the particular culture of the Other, he did not believe that this made Napoleon's struggle to maintain the universality of modernity any less meaningful for the Japanese. Rather, when young Japanese students were almost blindly concerned with reaping the benefits of wealth and industrialization, it was high time to realize that "we [Japanese] must defend Napoleon as our own heritage."[21] But this argument involved certain ironies as well. For if the lesson of St. Helena was the defeat of universal values by the forces of history, it was ironic indeed to defend Napoleon's belief in universals as one's own particular tradition. But the alternative was to abandon artificial universals in favor of the lessons of established history, a choice that Yasuda saw as supportive of the European view that Japan was morally and culturally inferior to the West.

TRADITION AS UNIVERSAL

Having elucidated the failure of Napoleon to resurrect a concept of universality that would undergird differences among various cultures in modernity, Yasuda turned to an investigation of the possibility of a universal Japanese culture. This grew out of his recognition that the defeat of Napoleon meant that attempts to establish a spatial concept of universality that ran counter to the new, modern deployment of British political power were doomed. But it also intimated a new direction for the search for universal value. In a world where differences among cultures were becoming increasingly attenuated, the greatest challenge to universal values lay in the division between past and present. Thus, in the midst of the vociferous debate over the validity of "the essence of Japaneseness" in intellectual circles of the mid-1930s, Yasuda argued that it was precisely in ancient Japanese traditions that the best archetype of universality might be found.

Yasuda suggests that all previous universal conceptions signified a world dominated by a single hegemonic power. Instead, he imagines a new concept based on a respect for cultural difference. This conception is an attempt to break out of the "order" within which an international community was conceived and which, although actually representing the political and cultural might of the West, presented itself as sufficient for all forms of difference. Against this "innocent" order, Yasuda offers his own concept of a logic of "sequence" that was essentially Japanese and *therefore* essentially cosmopolitan.

> In the logic of Japan's [mythical] heroes, a natural "sequence" takes precedence over "order." ... "Sequence" allows no deception. For example, the spirit of Greek tragedy originated in "sequence." It was the man of culture who pursued "nature" the furthest. Rather than the artifice that refines artifice into nature and then is expressed in poetry, he esteemed poetry as the expression of nature in artifice. The fate of thinking based on nature and the Way [*dō; tao*] was

decided by sequence. One must not attribute identity to things that
only resemble each other. That sort of logic cannot be allowed here.
The international character of a logic lies in its discovery of individual similarities and differences.[22]

In associating the Japanese logic of "sequence" with ancient
Greece, Yasuda is merely continuing the discussion of Napoleon
he began earlier. Greece, Napoleon, and Japan, on the one hand,
represent the forces that have sought throughout history to protect
cultural differences from the threat of homogenization posed, on
the other hand, by Rome, England, and the West.

As the passage quoted above reveals, Yasuda credits the ancients with a very different concept of nature from the one that
dominates the modern world. Modern man has become separated
from the very source of his being, Yasuda argues, through a re-
bellious insistence on a "knowledge" (*chisei*) of reality that holds
nature to be merely an object. In contrast, the ancients lived in a
time of communion with the gods, a state of being signified by the
word "nature" (*shizen*). This "nature" is not the kind of nature to
which one can return, as if to a place hidden away, but refers to the
lost time when the gods and the Japanese lived together (*dōden
kyōshō*).[23] In such a state of perfect harmony, there was no need for
the mediation of artifice and politics as things ruled themselves.
Nature ultimately indicated a time in which things adhered to
their proper places and a culture of presence (*sono mama*) united
man and the gods. Within this culture of presence, a knowledge of
self replaced a knowledge of things. The ancient knowledge (*eichi*)
of self did not require artificial means of expression as it arose
spontaneously through a poetic apprehension of the world as a
whole. Yet Yasuda is careful to stress that this act of "poeticizing"
the world is not to be mistaken for a withdrawal into the solipsism
of cultural exceptionalism. He cites the nativist Fujitani Mitsue
(1768–1823) to support his view that all ancient poems were
framed within the constraints of a sense of relationality, or in-
tersubjectivity, rather than as an absolute expression of the emotional or linguistic prerogatives of the subject.[24] All poetry of this
age was really a poetry of correspondence (*sōmonka*) in which the
subject matter was of less importance than the awareness of self
and Other that such poetry fostered. Thus, knowledge gained

from poetry was never a soliloquy about objects, but a dialogue between subjects.

Yasuda traces the beginning of the decline of the ancient logic of sequence to a transformative moment described in the *Kojiki*. Yamato Takeru, sent on an imperial mission to subdue the eastern barbarians, approached the deity of Mount Ibuki and, mistaking it for the deity's messenger, "spoke out" (*kotoage su*) to him in a threatening manner. This irreverent language outraged the deity, who then caused a violent hailstorm that dazed Yamato Takeru. Yasuda notes that the proper act would have been for Yamato Takeru to "reverently submit" (*kotodama su*), for this was still a time when the Japanese people and their gods "lived in the same palaces and slept in the same beds" (*dōden kyōshō*). Yamato Takeru paid a high price for his mistake, as he never completely recovered his health and died soon after. But his death offered the best example of the ancient logic of sequence. According to the *Kojiki*, the deceased spirit of Yamato Takeru was transformed into a giant white bird and flew off. The giant white bird landed three times, and at each place a tomb for Yamato Takeru was built. Yasuda insists that although this story might seem improbable to those who approach it with a logic of "order" and demand consistency in the narrative, it is perfectly understandable in terms of the logic of sequence.[25] It is quite acceptable that Yamato Takeru might be buried in three or more graves, since each time the bird landed was a separate event and was experienced as such by those present who witnessed and, more important, truly believed that Yamato Takeru was expressing his choice of burial site. In the logic of sequence, inconsistencies such as this do not appear as problems since they are read separately and in their own contexts. In this way, sequence allows for the expression of individual experiences without reducing them to a single, if coherent, point of view.

Ultimately, Yasuda's search for a universal value in Japanese traditions brought him to the Hakuhō-Tenpyō period (645–794) of Japanese history. During this time Japan was most "Japanese" because the Japanese people were thoroughly imbued with a cosmopolitan spirit; during this time Japan most acutely realized its endemic logic of sequence and difference. "The Hakuhō-Tenpyō period is the single cultural period in our country of which we can feel proud," Yasuda writes.[26] In the early years of this period the

Emperor Tenji announced his intention to turn Japan into a cultural nation and, Yasuda adds, people from all over the world walked the streets of Nara together in peace. Indeed, remnants of the period reveal a great interest in, and influence from, foreign cultures, as Buddhist monks from all over Asia spread their teachings and helped shape some of Japan's finest statues. Toward the end of the period, however, an event dramatically changed the character of Japanese culture. The turning point was the year 784, which marked what Vico might call a transition from the age of the gods to the age of man (and also the year the capital was moved from Nara). According to a ninth-century history, the *Kogo Shūi*, the communal life of the Japanese people and their gods (*dōden kyōshō*) ceased to exist at precisely this point. In 784 precedent was broken when offerings made in the eleventh month were presented not to the god of the high fields (*amatsugami; takamagahara*) but to the god of the sky (*soragami*). Yasuda takes this event as evidence of the alienation of men from the gods and, consequently, the loss of the universal potential of Japanese culture. The fall of man was, he claims, but an ironic victory for man.[27]

Once Yasuda has described the ancient universal traditions, he can hardly remain content with the irony of modern Japanese culture. Indeed, his widely read and often cited *Japanese Bridges* is a frustrated, and ultimately futile, attempt to regain access to those lost traditions. Deftly employing the metaphor of the bridge, Yasuda gives in to the temptation of trying to cross the gulf of time that separates the present from the past. Japanese bridges, he argues, are unlike Roman bridges, which often were situated in the middle of great plains and served as symbols of the power and influence of the imperial palace as much as a means of connecting land masses. Rather, Japanese bridges are frail, makeshift constructs, often no more than a log or two, that spontaneously appear wherever it is necessary to connect two mountain paths or cross a river. Punning on the Japanese word for bridge (*hashi*), Yasuda seeks to show its relationship with homonyms such as the words for ladder, barge, and chopsticks, all of which are involved in the transportation of things. The Japanese bridge, he suggests, serves to connect the "ends of things" (*mono no owari*), again punning on the well-established, aesthetic concept of "the pathos of things" (*mono no aware*).[28] Yasuda seems to hope that he will actually be transported back to the ancient past through this aesthetic analysis of Japanese bridges, or at least regain some remote sense of the culture that gave birth to them.

The attempted return to ancient traditions through architectural remains clearly places Yasuda within the modern, discursive problematic characteristic of romanticism. *Japanese Bridges* may best be understood within the tradition of *Kulturlandschaft*, or culturescapes, that Theodor Adorno dates "from the period of romanticism, more specifically the romantic admiration of ruins of historical buildings."[29] In such culturescapes, it is not buildings, or bridges, themselves that command our attention but rather "the manner in which they give expression to past historical suffering."[30] Yasuda's explication of the inscription on Saidan Bridge in Nagoya, focusing on the pain of a mother who lost her son in battle, certainly shares with European culturescapes a tendency to "bear the imprint of history as expression and of historical continuity as form."[31] Yasuda believed that through the power of "the pathos of things" evoked by Japanese bridges the direction of historical change could be reversed and a connection, albeit an ephemeral one, established with the ancient past.

Yasuda's concern with ancient Japanese traditions could not, however, avoid certain reverberations in his own society. Responding to an article in the March 1937 issue of *Bungei*, Yasuda charges his critics, most notably Aono Suekichi (1890–1961), with failing to understand his project and that of his fellow romantics. To those who accuse him of fascism because of his interest in Japanese tradition, Yasuda replies that fascism can only represent the interests of the dominant culture and its power to destroy other cultures; his own concern for ancient traditions stems from his desire to resurrect this "eradicated history" (*massatsu sarete ita rekishi*).[32] Heretofore, culture always belonged to the class that benefited most from progress and therefore never overcame the "eighteenth century" (modernity). The purpose of the Japan Romantic School, he repeats, is to attain the heights of cosmopolitanism (*sekaisei*) through the construction of a genealogy of Japanese culture.[33] And yet Yasuda's faith in the righteousness of his course of action was shaken enough by this criticism to allow for one minor concession. If his attempt to return to Japan's ancient past is a "mistake," he replies, then so too is Europe's own Renaissance.[34] But underneath this half-hearted justification, Yasuda seems to be beginning to realize the impossibility of avoiding the fact that modern Japan cannot escape from the same principles and standards as the West. Indeed, many of his fellow Japanese knew as much. Yasuda could no longer speak with authority for "Japanese culture" in arguing that Japan was forced to participate in a colonial culture when other Japanese intellectuals, particularly those as skilled and knowledgeable of that culture as Aono Suekichi and Yazaki Dan, vehemently disagreed. Still, he was unwilling to abandon his conviction that this knowledge was being used not to liberate his countrymen but to ensure that they happily enslaved themselves.

JAPAN AS IRONY

To a large degree, Yasuda's despondence over his failure to articulate a coherent basis for a universal value in Japanese traditions accounted for his concept of Japan as irony. Not only did the project contain inherent contradictions, but it was severely criticized by people who had little difficulty in revealing the romantic and anachronistic underpinnings of his argument. While Yasuda did retreat a bit from his more sanguine visions, he did not completely abandon the larger critique of modernity he had begun. Indeed, by consigning all "thought" to the same fate as universals, Yasuda offered a critique of modernity that was even more powerful, even while it could only be expressed negatively.

Scholars generally agree that an important shift occurred in Yasuda's thought sometime around 1939. It is not difficult to find a marked tendency in Yasuda's writings after that year toward greater cooperation with official state ideology. Ōkubo Tsuneo attributes this to the success of the Kwantung Army on the Asian continent and especially to rosy reports of the occupation of the Süchow castle on May 19, 1938. Ōoka Makoto argues that Yasuda, as a "celebrity writer" of the time, had a vested interest in perpetuating his influence and rewards, regardless of the cost in ideological terms. Both Ōkubo and Ōoka would accept Matsumoto Teruo's analysis that this new position represented a turn from irony, even while expressed in terms of "Japan as irony."[35] And yet, while there is considerable evidence for all the above views, no one has found reasons for Yasuda's shift within his own textual production.

The key text for understanding how and why Yasuda came to conceive of Japan as irony is his "Why Did Werther Die?" which he published in *Bungakkai* in 1938, the same year that the Japan Romantic School's journal, *Nihon rōmanha*, ceased publication. The two events were related. A conflict that had been building for some time between Kamei Katsuichirō and Yasuda finally came to a head in September of 1937 when Kamei turned over the position of editor of the school's journal to Tomura Shigeru and thereby foreshadowed the demise of the journal less than a year later. Part of the reason for the split was a disagreement over the future of the Romantic School. Kamei still respected Yasuda but criticized what he felt was an excessive concern with the ancient past.[36] To Yasuda, the problem that lay between him and Kamei was simply his own recognition of the unreliability of all conceptual strategies for action—a discovery for which he credited the German romantics and which he believed led young Werther to choose death. Thus, to Yasuda, Goethe's *Sorrows of Young Werther* was more than a love story. As indicated by the throngs of young people during the 1770s who were so influenced by *Werther* as to imitate the hero's dress and suicide, this was a text that crossed the boundaries of fiction and reality. Goethe's ultimate concern, Yasuda argues, was not the dynamics of human love, as the critics maintain, but the death of romanticism and the birth of modernity.[37] Writing at this critical juncture, Goethe was the first and last artist of modernity who was able to articulate what modernity required, but even he could do so only through metaphor and symbol.

Goethe's metaphoric vision revolved around the differences between the hero, Werther, and his friend (and husband of his lover) Albert. Werther is completely given over to passion and, if quite naive, always honest and trusting in his relationships with others. Albert, on the other hand, is smooth and confident, a man who seems competent and loyal but whose motives are never too certain. Werther's sorrows and struggles are not with Albert, however, but with the institution of marriage that constrains his passion for Lotte and the purity she represents. Through an agonizing process, Werther realizes that the only solution is for him to die, and he asks Albert to lend him a pair of pistols. Albert complies, fully aware of what purpose the weapons will serve.

In his discussion, Yasuda attempts to show that Goethe captured something about modernity that had eluded Kant: the use of reason for trickery and deceit. When a reliance on reason overthrew the arbitrary will of the monarch, it also introduced its own arbitrariness under the surface of the rule of law. Honesty and passion were no longer enough, in a world where an absolute authority no longer reigned; in order to survive in this new world, one had to deceive one's closest friend. For those who, like Werther, could not accept the new conditions, there remained only one choice: to commit suicide as a protest of the body against the unreliability of rational concepts. "An increasingly victorious world history knows how to cast gloom when confronted with truly trivial incidents. Criticism and discovery of obstacles were impossible even for Werther, who lacked nothing in education. As a result, Goethe disclosed the shameful contradictions of the new age by criticizing it not with Werther's head but with his body."[38] The "shameful contradictions" of modernity lie in what Yasuda describes as the cowardice of a humanism that clings to life at all costs. In such an age, it is the courage of Werther's act that, by denying the rational fear of death, suggests suicide as the only free choice left to an honest man.

But death also means the end of hope. In the final analysis, Werther dies not because he has failed to change society but simply because he has to die. Living on the edges of two worlds, the modern and the premodern, Werther retains the pride of youth as he has not yet been thoroughly modernized. Yet he can already see that the future belongs to Albert and to modernity, and he refuses to compromise his fate. This belief in fate, Yasuda holds, led Goethe in his later years to a pessimistic reading of the future of modernity and to an interest in the Orient in *Divan*.[39] In this sense, Werther represents the best traditions of the West as well as the death of these traditions. But with the triumph of modernity and the victory of reason and institution over emotion and spontaneity, these traditions are lost once and for all.

Werther's dilemma is not the exclusive property of the West, however, but belongs to every Japanese who has tried to come to terms with the origin of his own modernity. "Japan as irony" is an attempt to capture the nature of the Japanese experience of modernity. Brought out of a feudal society by a revolution that proclaimed a "restoration" of the days of old, modern Japan is a contradiction in terms. Drawing from the lessons of Werther, Yasuda openly confesses his skepticism of the ideology of restoration:

> I believe modern man's *idée* of a restoration of ancient times to be sheer fantasy, simply because there is nothing in the theoretical musings or life of decadent modern man that has a common ground with the adventure, courage, and spirit that supported the naked life on the plains of ancient man. If there were something modern man possessed that could return him to the glory of the earlier era, it would be that which saves modernity from the degrading of culture.[40]

Yet this refutation of the possibility of restoring the past could not lead to a positive program for a course of action directed toward the future. Given Yasuda's belief in the superiority of ancient culture, such modes of praxis were altogether meaningless. Rather, his lamentation signified a pessimistic evaluation of the foundations of modern culture and implied a thinly veiled critique of the Meiji legacy.

In an argument reminiscent of Okakura Tenshin, Yasuda suggests that the Meiji legacy had an unfortunate one-sided focus on achieving respect in the eyes of the world powers. But regardless of the great progress Japan made, the Western nations still regarded Japan as merely a "late-developing nation"; in Asia, however, Japan was the only developed, modern nation. This placed Japan in a unique position in the world. In trading cultural ties to Asia for economic ties to the West, Meiji Japan paid a necessary, but heavy, price for immediate survival. The Meiji leaders failed to return to the ancient harmony of the Hakuhō-Tenpyō period because they became intoxicated with military success (*bu*) and neglected to transform Japan into a cultural nation (*bun*).[41] Thus, the problem for the "transitional period" of post-Meiji Japan was a reconsideration of the role Japan should play as the cultural leader of Asia. Ironically, the result of this attempt to protect Japanese political autonomy from the onslaught of the Western powers was the transformation of Japan into a cultural colony of the West.

Since the Meiji period, Yasuda notes, the Japanese have suffered from a serious disease, one for which there is no cure.[42] The "disease" is the loss of immediate contact with native customs and traditions that formed the "health" of Japanese culture. By labeling it as incurable, Yasuda suggests that, without a critical intervention by Japanese who are aware of their fate, all of Asia will inevitably be reduced, both politically and culturally, to a colony of the West. Still, Yasuda is not ready to accept those seeking to give Japan a new identity under the banner of "Japanism." Such attempts are nothing more than a recapitulation of Western forms of nationalism in Japanese dress and shed little light on the ironic nature of a modern Japan.

In January 1939 Yasuda offered his best assessment of the problem of modernity and Japan in a short essay, "On the End of a Logic of Civilization and Enlightenment." In this essay he traces the various intellectual responses to modernity in Japan since the Meiji Restoration, concluding that Marxism represents the final stage of the response as well as the cultural bankruptcy of criticism. In the wake of the Marxists' failure, the Japan Romantic School sought to reintroduce the concept of culture and thereby become "a night bridge to a new dawn." Yet even the Japan Romantic School could not provide modern Japan with a coherent sense of identity through the production of cultural texts: "The self-praise of the Japan Romantic School, which proclaimed the end of civilization and enlightenment, may be found in its view of irony. . . . But even the overcoming of Japan's logic of civilization and enlightenment was not first started by Japan's self-conscious poets and intellectuals, or by any individual Japanese; it was started by the Japanese people."[43] In the end, Yasuda settles for a criticism of those who, like the Marxists and Japanists, offer rationalist alternatives to his view of Japan as irony, as even he himself cannot offer any positive identification of this "new dawn" without seriously compromising its ironic nature.

From Yasuda's criticism of "civilization and enlightenment," a new imagination of the historical subject emerged. Just as irony had earlier been a problem for the individual in the pursuit of truth (as it had also been for Werther), the idea of Japan as irony signified that the new subject of historical action was best found in the collectivity of Japanese ethnicity. Yasuda foreshadowed this rejection of the individual as capable of meaningful, independent action five years earlier in an article, "Lucinde's Resistance and the Masses Within Me," in which he argues for the interdependency of the self and the masses. The word he chooses for *masses* is *gunshū*, which also serves in Japanese to signify the biological concept of a biocenose, a community of biologically integrated and interdependent plants and animals. It is in this context that the role of the individual comes under question. In this view, the intellectual, as the most powerful model of the critical individual, is merely a member of a community of biologically integrated and interdependent actors who together constitute Japanese ethnicity. The native instinct of the ethnic whole, not the intellectual's concepts, will somehow lead each Japanese to an emancipation from the chains of modernity.

"Japan as irony" signifies both a displacement of the historical subject and a fundamental epistemological shift. Yasuda consigns the "intelligence" that has flourished since the Taishō period to the rubbish heap of history, arguing that it is merely a "situational viewpoint" that can only reflect the status quo. Instead, he is drawn to what he calls "the nonknowledge of the Japanese people."[44] Although Yasuda refuses to articulate what "nonknowledge" (*muchi*) is, he actively mobilizes it as a functional equivalent (and therefore as a negation) of Western knowledge (*chisei*), rather than using it merely as a valorization of the ignorance of the simple peasant. While it certainly shares some characteristics with the latter, Yasuda believes it is essential to attempt to retrieve a vague form of romanticism from this "nonknowledge" and, through romantic irony, to suggest the sense of pain and loss that accompanied the displacement of this native way of knowing from its former preeminence among the Japanese people.

Even while Yasuda argued for a reappraisal of "Japan as irony," it was becoming increasingly clear to him and to others that his view of Japan was anything but ironic. In September 1940, nearly two years after he announced his new interpretation of Japan as irony, Yasuda admitted that his ultimate concern was quite realistic: "The basis of the Japan Romantic School has become a realism called Japan as irony, or the irony of a free Japan that has simultaneously maintained destruction and construction."[45] Indeed, Yasuda's thought had come full circle. In arguing for realism, albeit a "Japanese" one, he failed to prevent irony from enveloping the critical initiative of his own thought. Far from imagining a principle of difference that could distinguish Japan from the modern, Western nations, what he finally achieved was a form of intellectual stagnation that greatly resembled more familiar Western notions of nationalism. But for Yasuda this was merely the result of his analysis of modern culture, which uncovered the unreliability of conceptual approaches to knowledge and sought alternatives in native ways of knowing and feeling.

THE AESTHETICS OF DEATH

Japanese scholars have exerted much effort to pinpoint the cause of Yasuda's turn in the late 1930s and early 1940s to an interest in aesthetics and away from forms of political criticism.[46] Most of them point to his travels in Manchuria and northern China in May and June 1938 as the decisive events in his transformation. Unfortunately, while attempting to protect the problematic of Yasuda's earlier thought from his later association with state propaganda, such arguments neither establish the cause for his intellectual shift nor present a convincing case for his radical break with the earlier concerns. It is far more likely, as Oketani Hideaki points out, that the later direction of Yasuda's thought was quite deeply implicated in his earlier, frustrated search for universal values.[47]

At the same time that Yasuda was beginning to realize the futility of his romantic dreams for a restoration of a universal culture, an ideology of cultural exceptionalism was gaining ascendancy in intellectual discourse. Lacking a critical defense against such an ideology, Yasuda soon became caught up in the process of articulating an ideology with which he himself was not entirely comfortable. This situation was certainly a risk once irony had revealed truth to be fiction and history to be interchangeable with the timeless mores of the ethnic group. Indeed, it was merely an extension of Yasuda's critique of the individual that history ultimately should be replaced by an aesthetics of constant motion (*ruten*), according to which all historical events, even the most hideous, were merely manifestations of a collective sense of human pathos (*aware*).[48] Thus, only six months after his tour of the Asian continent, he was able to write that "Japanese romanticism secretly plants flowers under the eaves of military towers."[49] He saw the role of romanticism not as that of a co-conspirator who worked to cover up the horrors of war but as that of a subversive who would transform the reality of death through the eternity of beauty. Needless to say, political reality was not transformed so easily, nor was the political utility of romanticism so casually avoided.

Yasuda's belief that the act of expressing a dream world could itself bring about the realization of that world was one source of the popularity his writings found among the youths of the early 1940s. His belief was based on a view of Japan as a gemeinschaft society that exceeded the sum of its parts. This "dreamed" Japan was set in opposition to the reality of Japan as irony and could only be realized through the individual's death on the battle-fields: "Yet Japan as irony, the most romantic Japan of this century, has finally shown its face as a result of the war. Look at all values on the battlefield. The moment of life's greatest value is expressed through death. The value of the individual's life is proven through death."[50] Through death, the individual Japanese validated his existence by a radical negation of the modernity in which life took form. Death became attractive as a promise to end the misery of a world in which alienation and irony left little but the ceaseless ennui of repetition. On the other side of life, past dreams merged with present reality in a world where all things were renewed and future possibilities were endless.

Yasuda saw each individual life as a manifestation of the emperor; death brought that individual back into contact with the emperor. "Emperor," however, did not specifically refer to the living Emperor Hirohito but signified a chain of equivalent emperors that had served as the pillar of Japanese culture until Emperor Gotoba's failed bid at restoring imperial power.[51] The defeat by the Hōjō clan of ex-emperor Gotoba and the imperial court in the Jōkyū Upheaval of 1221 represented the end of the rule of culture and the beginning of the rule of politics. Yasuda concedes that the earlier age of harmonious co-existence by the divine and the mundane (*dōden kyōshō*) ended with the death of Yamato Takeru, but he insists that the "flow of the poetry of the ancient throne was not interrupted."[52] Poetry continued as the source of Japanese culture until Emperor Gotoba's defeat. The finality of the defeat of culture was only echoed by the short-lived Kenmu Restoration of Emperor Godaigo in 1334–36. The historical lesson Yasuda derives from all this is clear: the focus on two historical examples of failed imperial restorations serves as a metaphorical reminder to modern Japanese of the farcical nature of the Meiji "Restoration" and the process of modernization that it claims to have initiated in Japan.

But Yasuda is less concerned with a systematic critique of the Meiji Restoration than with the possibilities of a restoration of the culture of the imperial court. He seeks to accomplish this through the production of a "genealogy" (*keifu*) of heroic emperors and poets from Emperor Gotoba to Bashō. This genealogy is a litany of emperors and poets who expressed the ideal of imperial court culture, but were defeated by the rule of politics. Nothing is lost in this history: the vanquished are merely marginalized. Largely synonymous with tradition, the genealogy will replace such Western concepts as "history" through its ability to suspend time in an individual "conception" (*hassō*).[53] "Conception" refers to an individual emperor or poet as a metonymic expression of the whole of the genealogy; the genealogy might be revealed at particular points in time, but it can never be completely comprehended by historical consciousness. Hence, the construction of a cultural genealogy is the first step toward escaping from the modern transformation of culture. Since Emperor Gotoba's failure to restore the courtly elegance and peace that reigned at the center of Japanese culture, Japanese culture has slowly decayed to the point where, in modern Japan, its only unique characteristic is a propensity for copying.[54] This deterioration is merely a logical extension of the transformation that, as early as the thirteenth century, separated culture from its divine origin in the emperor. Since that time, culture itself has been reduced to merely an attempt to incorporate and mobilize various foreign elements as means of displacing the power of the imperial court. Through his act of "rediscovering" the genealogy of heroic emperors and poets, Yasuda seeks to restore the marginalized imperial aesthetics to the center of Japanese culture.

In his view, the tragic marginalization of the imperial aesthetics is based on a fundamental change in the way Japanese appreciated the beauty of their landscape. When the imperial court determined the modality of Japanese culture, the unity of politics and the divine land was expressed as the pathos of things (*mono no aware*). Japanese of the Heian period, for example, enjoyed travel as a means of reaffirming in the roadside scenery the ubiquitous presence of imperial power, as underwritten by the emphasis on the "gaze" (*nagame*) as the foundation of their aesthetics. But between the Heian and the Tokugawa periods, this aesthetics gave way to a new experience of travel as sadness and loneliness. It was best expressed by the poet Bashō, who built a new aesthetics of "desolation" (*sabi; wabi*) around his devotion to the imperial court. While Bashō lamented the absence of imperial culture, he also suggested a means of recovering that culture through its continuity with the older tradition of regarding scenery, not as a stage for historical acts but as an aesthetic extension of the timelessness of the imperial court. Scenery is not a constraint on human possibility, Yasuda argues, but "the history that always exists in our minds."[55]

Yasuda suggests that the possibilities opened up by the Japanese view of scenery are closely connected to the Pacific War. It is time to move beyond intellectual groping for culture to an active realization of it through the war effort: "This is not the time for thinking about the universality of Japanese thought; the present is a time for fighting as [the universality of Japanese thought] has taught us.... Our present mission is not to ponder the universality of Japanese thought but to leave that to be realized as the divine teachings will it: herein lies the significance of the holy war as a holy war."[56] The recovery of the traditional view of scenery is to occur on two fronts: on the domestic front by the intellectuals who articulated an aesthetics of courtly elegance and on the foreign front by those who work toward cultural expansion until "the eight corners of the world are under one roof" (*hakkō ichiu*). The impossibility of ever attaining the "universality" of Japanese thought troubles Yasuda as little as the unlikelihood of military victory. More important is the aesthetic satisfaction of service to the lost imperial cause that the battlefields afford, for after all, defeat is merely "the irony of victory."[57]

Yasuda found the answer to his search for unity and universality in death as the ultimate solution. His death wish may be traced to an earlier fascination with death by the German romantics. Indeed, Lukács points out that "everything the romantics wanted to conquer sufficed for no more than a beautiful death. Their life-philosophy was one of death; their art of living, an art of dying."[58] But, for Yasuda, it was no longer necessary to turn back to the German romantics, since the death wish was expressed best by Ōtomo Yakamochi in the ancient collection of poems, the *Man'yōshū*:

> Across the sea, corpses soaking in the water,
> across the mountains, corpses heaped upon the grass.
> I would die by your side, my lord,
> and never look back.[59]

The citation of this poem by Yasuda in a 1941 essay was not an innocent choice by any measure. This particular poem was often cited in the newspapers and journals during the war years and, set to music, was even played over the radio at the conclusion of the imperial declaration of war. But Yasuda apparently wanted to distance the purity of the classic poem from the ideology of the wartime, modern Japanese state. He had already argued three years earlier that Yakamochi merely was expressing his longing to be near the emperor when he died, not to die for him in a "world historical" struggle with "Western barbarians."[60] Yet given the historical context, Oketani Hideaki is quite right in arguing that it is difficult for contemporary readers to accept Yasuda's attempt to reread the poem as a "polemic against state ideology" by suggesting its poetic meaning lay in an aesthetic tradition that predated the Japanese modern state.[61]

Despite Yasuda's appreciation of Yakamochi's poetry, it was not the ancient poet but the more recent martyr Tomobayashi Mitsuhira (1813–64) who most exercised his imagination during the war years. Yasuda was not merely caught up in the Tomobayashi renaissance of the early 1940s,[62] but found in the nineteenth-century nativist a historical example of how his own "passion for poetry [could be] merged with an interest in contemporary political possibility to produce commitment and action."[63] The "holy war" provided the opportunity to realize what Yasuda had understood from the beginning: that even claims of apoliticality have political goals. Tomobayashi had eschewed political theories of action, but he acted out his thought with his blood, a spontaneous act (*kotodama no fūga*) that reunited thought and action in the Way of the ancestral gods.[64] For his participation in the Tenchūgumi uprising on the eve of the Meiji Restoration, Tomobayashi was imprisoned and finally executed.

Yet it was not merely Tomobayashi's death that fascinated Yasuda. Rather, he found a deep, symbolic political stance in Tomobayashi's acceptance of death as a manifestation of his absolute commitment to the realization of the imperial cause discovered by his teacher, Ban Nobutomo (1773–1846). Ban wrote in his *Mountain Storms at Nagara* (*Nagara no yama arashi*) that the Jinshin Disturbance of 672 was actually a restorationist struggle for power by the court against the bureaucracy. Supported by the Ōmi court, the legitimate heir to the throne, Prince Ōtomo (Emperor Kōbun) sought to return the imperial court to the culture of the ancient gods. But his uncle, Prince Ōama (Emperor Tenmu), and the court at Yoshino were more interested in furthering the set of political reforms, derived from China and outlined by the Taika Reform of 646, that would convert Japan into a Chinese style bureaucratic nation. After a brief, but bloody, battle, Emperor Kōbun committed suicide and Prince Ōama succeeded to the throne as Emperor Tenmu ("heavenly military"). The subsequent success of Emperor Tenmu in securing the implementation of the Taika Reform, Yasuda concluded, began the political use of the court to establish the legitimacy of rational, political institutions—a process that culminated in the Meiji Restoration and modern Japan.[65]

But Yasuda focused less on the development of a centralized state system of government founded on laws (*ritsuryō*) and the unified rule that resulted than on the heroic example of the young Emperor Kōbun, who sacrificed his life and personal ideals for the sake of the nation. Certainly, the lesson of this imperial suicide and of his tragic struggle against a unified, bureaucratic state was clear to Yasuda's readers who, in the early 1940s, could conceive of their own deaths in battle in a similar, heroic light. If even an emperor was willing to die for national harmony in a struggle with foreign models of a bureaucratic state, how much less, Yasuda implied, could one of his people do? To choose death, especially in the service of the imperial army, was not only to realize the harmonious world of the age of the imperial court but also to reproduce the original act of imperial failure and noble defeat, which was repeated again and again throughout the genealogy of heroic emperors and poets. To choose defeat was to choose solidarity with culture over the claims of reason and modernity.

In the end, modernity was, for Yasuda, a time of loss, a time in which one could do little but succumb to a romantic longing for a bygone era, a time when the inherent differences and conflict might be resolved under the umbrella of Japanese culture. It may well have been Yasuda's conceit that he had already transcended modernity that led him to reject an invitation to participate in the 1942 debates on "overcoming modernity." In an article published in June 1942, just one month before the debates were held, Yasuda indicates his dissatisfaction with the journalism and catch phrases that flourish at such debates, which he feels preclude the possibility of any real discussion. He also intimates that the more fundamental problem is a modern way of thinking that appears insincere and frivolous when compared with the ancient, magnanimous way of feeling (*waga korai no gōhō no fukai*).[66] Yet at the same time, his "cowardice" in refusing to experience premodern epistemology in the only way he found possible, through his own death, suggests how well he understood that all such attempts at overcoming modernity end in tragedy. He was not willing to follow fully in Werther's footsteps.

As a founding member and intellectual leader of the Japan Romantic School, Yasuda played a very important role in helping to shape the romantic discourse on Japanese culture. His contribution lay not in his return to the East, for Okakura Tenshin had accomplished this earlier and with more poetic force in his articulation that "Asia is one." But Yasuda was perhaps alone in modern Japanese intellectual history in developing a forceful conception of "Japan" as an aesthetic concept with which to mediate the contesting claims of nature and artifice. Starting with an acute sensitivity to the intimate relationship of politics and art, he sought to produce a space for difference through the production of cultural texts. In the end, however, he could not escape a fetishism of the past that, for all its claims to difference, had more in common with familiar forms of exoticism and escapism. Ultimately, in his attempt to protest the intrusions of the bureaucratic state into the sacred realm of "culture," he merely substituted one totality for another and ignored the agency of the modern state when, ironically, its power over individual Japanese was perhaps at its greatest level ever.

2

Indeterminate Poetics
The Romantic Style

> The poetic mind, in the process it observes in its enterprise,
> cannot be satisfied with a harmonically opposite life, not
> even by comprehending or grasping it through hyperbolic
> opposition.... Thus it no longer can be anything whole and
> unified but, on the contrary, will deteriorate into an infinity
> of isolated moments.
>
> Friedrich Hölderlin, "On the
Process of the Poetic Mind"

As I suggested at the outset, a view of poetry as a revolutionary
epistemology was central to the romantic vision. Poetry was identified as the voice of youth and signified an artistic space in which
the romantics could act on their revolutionary impulses, freed
from the kinds of political demands that confined artistic practice
to certain forms of "safe" art, or even do away with art altogether.
Specifically, the romantics saw poetry as an alternative to the two
major responses to art in Japan during the 1930s. On the one hand,
they rejected the overtly political literature of the Proletarian Literature Movement (from which many of them had only recently
emerged) for its lack of an inspired literary vision as much as for
its political ideology. And yet, while they had certainly grown
disillusioned with the ubiquitous political slogans of the Proletarian Movement, their disillusionment initially represented not so
much a retreat from the concerns of politics as a rejection of its
substitution of base slogans for literary content and the consequent
inability of such literature to offer truly revolutionary possibilities.
At the same time, their rejection of the movement was an implicit
rejection of class as the most significant identity base for literary
production.

Nonetheless, their criticism of certain forms of political literature as bad literature did not necessarily lead to an embracing of

28

all literature that eschewed political concerns. Even though the romantics rejected the Proletarian Literature Movement, they were even more critical of the New Prose Art Movement (Shin Sanbun Geijutsu Undō), which had also formed in the wake of growing disillusionment with the Proletarian Movement and sought to substitute "reality" for class consciousness. "Reality," however, was at least as objectionable as class consciousness, because it reaffirmed the ontological nature of the world and consequently failed to offer any prospect for radical political or artistic change. Thus, in opposition to these two extremes of artistic suicide, art without politics or politics without art, the Japan Romantic School began to propose a concept of poetics as revolutionary.

This was not an entirely new project, as the conflict between poetry and prose has a long history in Western thought. But it was only with the beginning of the modern period that poetry began to signify something other than an expression of human character. This resignification took place toward the end of the eighteenth century with the rise of the romantic movement in Germany. In their rediscovery of neglected traditions (poetry, folklore, the Oriental world), the German romantics were responding to the construction of a new political order in Europe by Napoleonic France, which they saw as a threat to Germanic cultural identity. Thus, we can see how "under the influence of Kant and Schiller, they [the German romantics] presented the idea of infinite perfectibility as an infinite striving toward a state of aesthetic fulfillment where every trace of alienation has been overcome. They saw romantic poetry as an absolutely 'progressive poetry,' involved in a process of constant becoming and endless development."[1] This "progressive" poetry must be understood with a bit of romantic irony. It was seen as progressive only insofar as it was believed to lead ultimately to the creation of a free and unified German nation; it was not necessarily progressive for the individual subject. Rather, for these modern romantics, poetry was a critique of the established division of literature (and thus, thought) into various genres while, simultaneously, it gave expression to a holistic voice that hearkened back to a time when humanity and nature were believed to have co-existed in perfect harmony. In order to progress, one first had to locate an authentic moment in the lost past on which to anchor one's critical vision. This much was well understood by the members of the Japan Romantic School, who drew heavily on the writings of their German counterparts in their own search for ways to overcome the alienation imposed by modernity.

This identification with the German romantics' revolutionary use of poetry was evident even before the Japan Romantic School was formally organized. In the advertisement for the school placed in its sister journal, *Cogito*, it was quite clear that poetry was to be the exclusive property of a young and rising generation of intellectuals who had grown increasingly discontented with the prevailing modes of artistic practice. After first condemning the excesses of vulgarity and superficiality in the established literary circles, the advertisement went on to suggest the vague outlines of the poetry belonging to this new generation, which would solve the problems of the "literary confusion" rampant in the day: "On close scrutiny, one has yet to discover the appearance of a real romantic movement in Japan. At present, the up-and-coming generation is still in its incipient stage, and the existing state of things is lost in confusion and ambiguity. We must intone the poetry of our own generation."[2] A few lines later, the advertisement set out more explicitly what this poetry is expected to accomplish:

> Since the beginning of modernity, a man of letters was a poet of the conscience of the age. . . .
> The Japan Romantic School is the present poem of our "youth of the age." We reject everything but the lofty tone of these poems of youth and, untroubled by yesterday's customs, move forward in search of tomorrow's truth.[3]

Even at this early stage in the Japan Romantic School, poetry, although still vague and ill-defined, was affirmed as belonging exclusively to the young and the future. In looking back to the German romantics as the originators of this revolutionary view and in attempting to emulate their elevation of poetry to a privileged position among the literary genres that would provide the basis for future forms of action, the Japanese romantics were attempting to deal with a problem that was by no means unique to their own culture. They were working well within the bounds of modern intellectual inquiry.

When the school finally started publishing its journal in March 1935, the role of poetry was reaffirmed and more clearly defined. Still associated with the dreams of the younger generation, poetry was located within a history of increasing artistic decadence through the years, culminating in the present age's loss of true art:

> In reflecting on customs in recent literary circles, one finds that there are a number of people who consider the literary arts as expedients to frivolity and skillful lies or as the means to an ugly, vulgar knowledge and who do not dwell in the nobility of the arts but have distanced themselves from the severity of Venus. In response to these times, we call ourselves the Romantic School and, with a respect for art, call for an emphasis on poetic spirit and speak out in favor of the exaltation of the artistic disposition. . . .
> We have all heard that *poetry lies at the origin* [emphasis mine].[4]

Here there are two main points of interest. First, there is a formal statement of commitment to a poetic spirit, not merely as the poetry of the younger generation but as a positive refutation of those who would debase the arts. Second, poetry is placed at the origin, at a point before the separation of words and things, when all was an undifferentiated void. In a time of artistic decadence, then, poetry represents for the romantics a return to that void where one once could rewrite history in accordance with the desires of spirit.

POETRY AS A NEW TIME

The problem of representing the poetic spirit was left to Jinbō Kōtarō who, in a short essay entitled "The Acquisition of a New Time," presented the outline of a general poetics for the Japan Romantic School.[5] In this outline, Jinbō takes issue with the common conceptualization of the Japan Romantic School as "irony" and argues that the ultimate goal of the school was instead a world without irony. The Japan Romantic School, he continues, would oppose the very conditions that required the use of irony in modern Japan through its own "correct critical spirit" (*tadashiki hihyō seishin*), which was essentially poetic: "By 'the Japan Romantic School' I mean a new beginning for poetry. What is 'the Japan Romantic School'? I would like to answer this question through the composition of poems. My hope, as one who has come forth as a poet himself, is that we shall proceed from the acquisition of the new 'space' or 'plane' found in the most passionate poems of our earlier poets to the discovery here of a new 'time.'"[6] By this new logic of "space," Jinbō is suggesting nothing less than the supplanting of narrative history, the logic of developmental time, that lies at the center of modernity.[7] But this is not to come about merely through returning to the past and passively reflecting on the works of the ancient poets. Rather, Jinbō seeks to impose an obligation on the romantics to actively create poems that will represent that ancient space in modern Japan.

How such poems are to be created was the subject of a series of articles that Jinbō had published in previous issues of the *Nihon rōmanha*, which he entitled "A Poetics of the Japan Romantic School."[8] Opening with a declaration that romantic spirit is synonymous with poetic spirit, Jinbō sheds considerable light on what poetry can mean to the members of the Japan Romantic School and to the readers of its journal. While Jinbō's discussion focuses on the possibility of a truly romantic spirit in Japan, it is clear from the opening lines that his concept of poetry is ultimately concerned with the larger question of the formation of culture in modern Japan.

Without an understanding of the history of modern Japanese poetry, he argues, one cannot begin to create the new form of poetry that he hopes will establish a new logic of spatiality. Jinbō describes this history of modern Japanese poetry in terms of a vacillation between the traditional Japanese spirit (which he calls a sensitivity to the seasons of nature) and the mechanistic spirit imported from the West. He sees the mechanistic spirit as gaining the upper hand in Japanese poetic circles in the years immediately following the Meiji Restoration. Jinbō does not deny the authenticity of this poetry or deride it as merely a foreign art form. Rather, this "unreflective" period witnessed the wholesale incorporation of the mechanistic spirit until "it was gradually assimilated within the poet and finally reached a peak as the first [modern] Japanese poem."[9] He does not deny the fundamentally revolutionary character of the Meiji Restoration but instead sees it as ushering in a thoroughly modern period in which the laws of artistic and cultural practice are for the first time dialectical in nature. Along with

Yasuda and other romantics, he does not consider a simple rejection of Western things as a satisfactory solution to the problem of culture in modern Japan but attempts to work out a dialectical method that can overcome the contradictions he finds within modern Japanese culture.

This dialectical method can be seen at work in Jinbō's history of Japanese poetry. Immediately after the appearance of a "mechanistic" poetry in the early Meiji years, the eclectic "New Form Poetry" arose in opposition to it.[10] Although Jinbō concedes that "New Form Poetry" sought the traditional Japanese spirit in free verse rather than in *tanka* or *haiku* and did successfully achieve a free poetic spirit through the use of the Japanese language, he ultimately places it, along with the earlier "mechanistic" attempts at poetry, within what he calls the first stage in the history of modern Japanese verse, a "subjective period." This stage was overcome by an "objective period" characterized by the rise of two countervailing artistic tendencies: one represented by the poetic spirit of the New Prose Poetry Movement[11] and the other by the Proletariat Poetry Movement,[12] which Jinbō argues developed out of the Marxism of Nakano Shigeharu and Moriyama Kei (1904–91) and the "anarchism" of Tosaka Jun and Hagiwara Kyōjirō (1899–1938). Both movements, however, shared an opposition to various aspects of the earlier, "subjective period": "The one began as a criticism of egoistic symbolist poetry, the other arose as a reinvestigation of the 'freedom' that possessed the Populists."[13] In the end, the "objective" stage does not represent for Jinbō a final solution to the problem of modern poetry. Rather, he sees it as merely addressing the same issues as the first stage, only from a different, more "objective" and "realistic" viewpoint, which still leaves open the larger question of culture.

The question of culture as the subject of poetic practice first appeared during what Jinbō calls the contemporary stage in the development of Japanese poetics. This stage is not a literal "swing" back to one of the previous stages but a "transcendence" (*Aufhebung*) of them both. While it rejects the mechanism of the first stage, it also shuns the self-consciously political posture of the second. At the same time, the third stage, in its emphasis on the historicity of the realism of the former two stages, attempts to mark out a new origin for Japanese poetry. This origin should not,

Jinbō warns, be misconstrued as a naive "return to the past," which many think the Japan Romantic School is attempting; it should be understood as a truly new beginning that looks to the future:

> In this sense, [the Japan Romantic School] is what forges together all the elements that lie in chaos in the contemporary poetic world, which exist in me as a new point of departure in Japanese poetic history. It is for this reason that I do not consider the "Japan Romantic School" as deserting the pursuit of realism, nor do I write it off as reminiscent or restorationist, or think of it as one among many remedies for the failings of realism. It is what insists on the prerogatives of the younger generation, which arise when all the many means of salvation have exhausted themselves.[14]

The new beginning shares one important characteristic with the earlier stages: it too must be realized through textual practice. This is an important point; here Jinbō is indicating where the previous attempts at creating a new poetics have failed. The latter stage failed in that the politically motivated poets overlooked the necessity of writing moving poetry, and the former stage was especially guilty of neglecting to consider whose texts were being read and reproduced and why.

This leads Jinbō to indict the previous poetics for their failure to discuss the ontology of language. By this, he is not implying the kind of linguistic analysis of poetic language that Julia Kristeva recently has outlined.[15] He emphatically rejects such rigorous methodologies for their obsession with form and thus for their failure to discuss the question of spirit. Jinbō's emphasis on the spirit existing in language leads his poetics away from concerns over a definition of universal poetry to a definition of "Japanese poetry as something alive today, as [something that] must experience the present, and not as an abstract ideal of a single poet."[16] In order to revive this spirit, which realism has buried beneath mountains of narrative, literary proscriptions, and empirical descriptions, it is only necessary to do away with "methodology."[17] Although what Jinbō means by "methodology" is not entirely clear, the context of his discussion suggests that he is indicating the kind of Marxist approach to literature taken by the Proletarian writers whom he criticized earlier. The problem with this methodology is not only its political orientation (in a sense, this is the least offensive aspect of Marxism for Jinbō) but its privileging of history over literature. Jinbō challenges the historical approach, arguing that if literature must be read historically, then it is also true that history, as a collection of written documents, is nothing more than literature. By thus recouping literature from history, by thus privileging poetry as the most true of all literature, by thus defining poetry as the living spirit inherent in the Japanese language, Jinbō has outlined a poetics for the Japan Romantic School that can claim to escape from the limits of history and bring itself to the brink of a "new time." Whether it could actually do so, of course, rested on the poetic practice of the members of the school.

POETRY AS DESIRE

As one of modern Japan's premier poets, Hagiwara Sakutarō lent a good deal of intellectual strength and public visibility to the Japan Romantic School when he became a member in 1936. Already an established poet and the author of the widely acclaimed *Howling at the Moon*, Hagiwara was twenty years older than the other members of the school and was regarded by many as their teacher.[18] In recent years Asano Akira, an intellectual closely associated with the school, has even gone so far as to suggest that Hagiwara was its central poet.[19] While Asano's claims may be a bit exaggerated, the fact that Hagiwara was a strong supporter of the Japan Romantic School from its inception, even if he did not become a member until 1936, is evident in his praise for Yasuda's *Japanese Bridges*, *Heroes and Poets*, and *An Honorable Poet Laureate* and for Itō Shizuo's *Laments to My Person*. Hagiwara shared Jinbō's assessment that the school represented a "poetic spirit" and offered "three cheers [for the fact that] the emergence of the Romantic School's movement in Japan meant the rise to power in Japanese literary circles of poetic spirit."[20] What Hagiwara hoped to accomplish through the rise of poetry is not immediately clear. Unlike some members of the school, he was not simply calling for a rejection of Western thought in favor of a return to traditional Japanese emotions. Rather, when it is recalled that Hagi-

wara was fond of playing the mandolin and of quoting Baudelaire, his call for a return to Japan appears ironic, at least, and
perhaps can be seen as the result of a lifetime devoted to poetry
as an outlet for the mental anguish of a modern man.

This anguish is first addressed in *The Blue Cat* (*Aoneko*), a collection of poems that Hagiwara first published in 1923 and which,
when the definitive edition of the collection came out in 1936, he
supplied with the English title *The Blue Cat*. In the preface to
The Blue Cat, Hagiwara writes that while the general theme of his
poetry is still melancholy (*yūutsu*), his interests have now shifted
from "sensual" (*kankaku-teki*) melancholy to "philosophical" (*shi-
saku-teki*) melancholy.[21] This transition can best be seen in the
poems in *The Blue Cat* that make up the section called "Intention
and Illusion" ("Ishi to mumyō"). This section, which carries the
subtitle "On Ideas or the World of Images" ("Ideya moshiku wa
imēji no sekai ni tsuite"), is considered by many Japanese critics to
have established Hagiwara as a philosophical poet of modernity.

The nine poems of "Intention and Illusion" are all concerned
with the loneliness of the poet as he wanders through a world
of hopelessness and ennui. They are not written in the pseudo-
classical style of his later works but in the colloquial free style
characteristic of modern verse, suggesting, as one critic puts
it, that Hagiwara is attempting to retrieve emotion (tradition)
within life in a major city (modernity) and, by reintroducing it at
the level of language, to overcome the aporia of lyric poetry in
modern Japan.[22] Hagiwara tries to resolve the tension between
tradition and modernity in the following poem from "Intention
and Illusion":

Is Philosophy Only One Design?

While setting one philosophy to walk
in the shadows of a dense forest
the Buddha sensed a clear blue nature
whatever meditations he brings to life
whatever Nirvana he melts into
it is that kind of beautiful moonlit night he saw.

"Is philosophy only one design?"
the Buddha, while treading on the moon's shadows,
asked this of his gentle soul.

By juxtaposing the gloom of life (suggested by the word *utsu* in "dense," part of the compound *ussō*) with the philosophy of compassion offered by the Buddha to the suffering inhabitants of this life, Hagiwara suggests that the philosophy and meditations of the Buddhists emanate from a deep appreciation of the beauty of nature. Yet, in the second stanza, the power of philosophy to mediate nature is reaffirmed by the doubt the Buddha throws on views that see philosophy as an artificial construct inferior to the authenticity of nature. Only at this point, when the Buddha poses the question of the position of philosophy to himself, do the words "clear blue" (*sōmei*) in the third line echo their Japanese homonym, "sagacity" (*sōmei*), allowing us to read the line as "the Buddha sensed his own innate sagacity" (in having created a philosophy of consolation).

Hagiwara felt that the poetic expression of his philosophical melancholy in *The Blue Cat* provided some consolation for life in the modern city of Tokyo. This much is clear from Hagiwara's own explanation of the meaning of the title, *Aoneko*, which sheds light on the relationship between this collection of poems and the problem of modernity. In the preface to the definitive edition of *The Blue Cat*, Hagiwara writes that the *ao* of *Aoneko* "has the same meaning as the English word 'blue.' That is, I have used it to encompass all the meanings of 'hopelessness,' 'melancholy,' and 'fatigue.' In order to help clarify this meaning, I have had 'The Blue Cat' printed in English on the cover of the definitive edition. In short, it means 'a melancholy cat.'"[23] Whether or not the use of English here helps to clarify anything is hard to say. What "the blue cat" does call to mind, however, is the cat in Natsume Sōseki's novel *I Am a Cat* and Sōseki's use of it to satirize the modern dandies of Meiji Japan. But for Hagiwara there is a positive connotation to "blue" as well: "Another meaning, as one can see in the poem 'The Blue Cat' in this collection, expresses the strong nostalgia I felt for the city when, writing poetry in the countryside back then, I envisioned a large blue cat in the bluish-white sparks from the electrical lines that were reflected in the city sky."[24] This ambivalent attitude toward the modern city of Tokyo—both as the place of exotic forms of amusement and as a cruel and disappointingly materialistic center of commerce—may be seen in the title poem of Hagiwara's collection:

The Blue Cat

It is good to love this beautiful city
it is good to love the architecture of this beautiful city
it is good to come to the capital and pass along these bustling
     streets
in search of all that is valuable in life
in search of all gentle women
this row of cherries that lines the street
are there not innumerable sparrows singing there, too?

Ah! the only one able to sleep in the nights of this big city
is the shadow of but one blue cat
the shadow of a cat that speaks of the history of a pathetic
     humanity
the blue shadow of the happiness we constantly seek.
Just when in search of all our shadows
we think we love this Tokyo even on a sleety day
huddling up against the wall in that back alley there
is that human-looking beggar—what do you suppose he
     dreams of?[25]

Hagiwara finds the city a space where one can spend idle hours
botanizing on the pavement, searching out all sorts of pleasures,
vicarious and real. But such pleasures are dampened by the reality
of an equal amount of misery, again both vicarious and real. His
refusal ever to reconcile these ambivalent views of the city is
supported by an admiration for Charles Baudelaire and what
Hagiwara calls "the mixture of a double image" in Baudelaire's
personality:

> That a man like Baudelaire, who always sleepwalked in the wan
> shadows of a diseased spirit, like the moonlight seen in the dreams
> of an opium smoker, has hidden in the depths of his character such a
> clear, brilliant rationality may be taken to be a pitiful modern mis-
> ery. That is because that clear, brilliant rationality always causes a
> tragic negation and disillusionment of the effects of a deep and
> strange moonlit night. In short, in an everyday life such as that of
> Baudelaire, one finds the mixture of a double image.[26]

Clearly, Hagiwara finds inspiration in Baudelaire, a man whom
Walter Benjamin describes as a "flâneur whose way of living still
bestowed a conciliatory gleam over the growing destitution of
men in the great city ... who still stood at the margin, of the great

city as of the bourgeois class. Neither of them had yet over-whelmed him. In neither of them was he at home. He sought his asylum in the crowd."[27] But if Baudelaire's ambiguous feelings for Paris are a source of consolation for Hagiwara in his own ambi-guity toward Tokyo, a valorization of Baudelaire can also risk an exoticism of the West, something that Hagiwara is not ready to accept. He felt it necessary to relativize his interest in this historical foreigner with curiosity in a mythical demon from Japanese folk-lore, the *Amanojaku*. Hagiwara takes an interest in this trickster because of its reputation for "constantly rebelling against the common things, even against its own thought and tastes *that have already become* general."[28] The ironic nature of this function is subordinate, however, to the even greater irony that Hagiwara feels it is necessary to locate this self-negating doubt (which Bau-delaire also possessed) in ancient Japanese mythology.

Hagiwara's disillusionment with the city and his return to native ground marks the second shift in the development of his poetry and thought. It occurred precisely at the time when he was moving from his home town of Maebashi to Tokyo. Thus, his group of poems "Hopeful Views of the Homeland" ("Kyōdo bōkei shi"), included in his *A Collection of Short Tunes of Pure Emotion* (*Junjō shōkyoku shū*), may be seen as a step toward his later thought in *Return to Japan*. In 1925, the year Hagiwara published *A Collec-tion of Short Tunes of Pure Emotion*, he moved to Tokyo with his wife and two children and began a series of relocations within the metropolitan area, changing residence three more times over the course of the next two years. Although in one sense he saw Tokyo as a liberation from the constraints of life in a small town and took pride in himself as the independent head of his family, he was in fact unemployed and dependent on his father for the paltry sum of 60 yen a month with which he supported his family and himself. Consequently, Hagiwara's first taste of this "liberating" city was heavily flavored with the bitterness of poverty. Only a month after moving to Tokyo, he and his wife began to suffer constantly from influenza, headaches, and nasal catarrh, while his children were afflicted with intestinal catarrh.[29] Hagiwara gave expression to the experience of urban poverty and to a general sense of disillusion-ment with the city in such poems as "Oi Town" and "At the Postal Window."

As one critic indicates, disillusionment led Hagiwara to a position similar to the one Baudelaire captured in his expression "anywhere out of the world," a position from which Hagiwara's poems began to describe scenery from such a spatial and temporal distance that it cannot be identified with either Maebashi or Tokyo.[30] This disillusionment was not, however, an absolute withdrawal into emotionalism, but an ironic form of realism that sought to "relate to the reader, through an insistence on the formal accuracy of details, the vividness of the psychological pressure of the 'external world.'"[31] Hagiwara was compelled to seek refuge in this self-consciously fictitious world as he increasingly found himself caught between his experience of Maebashi and Tokyo, and his romantic hopes for both.

Regardless of how ironic this poem may be, the effect of "Hopeful Views of the Homeland" on those who read it when it was first published must be taken into account in any attempt to establish the historical significance of Hagiwara's poetry. Perhaps the most famous reaction to these poems is that of Akutagawa Ryūnosuke, Hagiwara's neighbor, who is said to have rushed into Hagiwara's study in his pajamas to offer his immediate congratulations.[32] One explanation of this enthusiastic response is that "Akutagawa perceived 'Hopeful Views of the Homeland' to be different from traditional poems of nostalgia in modern lyric poetry and as negating all literary tradition, or at least as giving expression to a split consciousness without embracing any illusions whatsoever of 'modernity.'"[33] This disillusionment in "Hopeful Views of the Homeland" is also evident in Nakano Shigeharu's evaluation of the poems. Nakano discerned a "rage" against modernity in the poems. This rage, which was directed against the petite bourgeoisie, was also turned against Hagiwara, who was himself a bourgeois, and therefore it was expressed "sadly" (*kanashiku*). Nakano was ultimately dissatisfied with this nihilistic rage—which "ridiculed oneself along with ridiculing others"—for going no further than self-criticism, although he did concede that "socialism was on the side of Hagiwara."[34] What both Nakano and Akutagawa recognized in Hagiwara was the disillusionment and loneliness of a new generation of Japanese who were now as ill at ease in the modern city as they had been earlier in the countryside.

Perhaps the most pivotal poem in this collection, and one in which the opinions of both Akutagawa and Nakano seem to be borne out, is "The Great Crossing Bridge," a poem named after a bridge that crosses the Tone River and leads into Maebashi. This bridge, connecting the poet's home town with the capital, becomes the focus of Hagiwara's attention as it belongs to a space independent of both the tradition of Maebashi and the modernity of Tokyo. Having already found the city to be painful, Hagiwara wrote "Alas! To stay in my home town / exhausts the pains of sorrow that penetrate like salt."[35] Hagiwara's rage against the confines of the home town and the coldness of the city turned to this bridge for a suitable means of expression.

> How shall I speak of my present rage and bitterness?
> I tear up my meager books
> and throw everything into the rolling waters of the Tone River.
> A hungry wolf
> I claw the rails and bite my teeth
> yet defenseless before the endless tears
> that roll down my cheeks.

Standing on the bridge between modernity and tradition, Hagiwara finds frustration—frustration with his modern education, frustration with a town where he no longer belongs, frustration with everything, and ultimately frustration with "no thing." Hagiwara's rage has no concrete object because of a "dialectic" that grows out of his disbelief in all that his credulous soul had previously believed. The use of a bridge to capture the sense of a vague longing recalls Yasuda Yojūrō's description of the Japan Romantic School as "a night bridge to a new dawn."[36] Both Yasuda and Hagiwara are signifying their desire to go beyond the alternatives of traditionalism or modernism and their realization that such an attempt is impossible and ironic. For Hagiwara, this means that the valorization of the home town, implicit in his selection of Maebashi as the background for the ten poems in "Hopeful Views of the Homeland," is a necessary, if unsatisfactory, answer to his disillusionment with the city. In other words, "Hagiwara returned to his home town, but that return negated the meaningfulness of just such a return."[37]

Important as "Hopeful Views of the Homeland" was in foreshadowing later developments in Hagiwara's thought, it was not until ten years later that Hagiwara gave public voice to a fuller development of its incipient themes. In 1934 Hagiwara published what some critics consider his greatest work, *The Iceland* (*Hyōtō*; literally, "Ice-Island," but the English title was provided by Hagiwara himself on the cover of the original work), and what all agree is the most important source of his later thought.[38] One indication of the direction of Hagiwara's thought at this time is the fact that in *The Iceland* the more relaxed, colloquial language of *The Blue Cat* has been replaced by a pseudo-classical language, which lends an opaque quality to the poems. But a return to classical language ipso facto does not mean that Hagiwara exchanged the lure of ancient harmony for the pain of modern duress. Rather, "through the rhythm of Chinese grammar and Chinese vocabulary, which cut things off, Sakutarō, more than anything else, was biting back at his own past and present."[39] This interpretation is amplified by the fact that Hagiwara's use of Chinese-style language is especially pronounced in his choice of interrogatives (*gimonshi*).[40] These words, due to their nominal "foreign" status, allow Hagiwara to suggest the possibility of a language exterior to and more perfect than native forms of expression, while at the same time calling into question the very existence of such a language.

Rejecting an intransigent modernism as well as a naive traditionalism, Hagiwara announces in the preface to *The Iceland* that poetry also suffers from the historical crisis of modernity. Just as certain political ideologues have confused the art of politics with the politics of art, so too have poets failed to grasp the essential modernity of traditional Japanese verse: "The idea that poetry as art is the ultimate when all historical development has finally reached its end belongs to the most simple and elementary substance, that is, the pure and simple wonder of poetic passion. (In this sense, the author believes the Japanese *waka* and *haiku* are the future form of modern poetry.)"[41] The reductive nature of this passage will not escape the careful reader. But neither should its essential irony. Hagiwara certainly reduces the artistic qualities of poetry to a "pure and simple wonder," but a wonder that can only arise under conditions of a contradictory relationship between history and art; it is best realized in a thoroughly *modern* form of poetry based on the *waka* and *haiku* of Japan's past.

This ironic return to the past may be discerned in one of the most well-known poems of *The Iceland*, "The Homecoming."

The Homecoming

In the winter of 1929 I left my wife and,
embracing my two children, returned to my homeland.

The day I came home
the locomotive fought a heavy wind.
I awoke by the window alone
as a whistle broke the darkness
and a flame lit the plains.
Are Jōshū's mountains still out of sight?
In the shadows of the night-train's fidgeting lamps
motherless kids sleep with their tears
and each tries to touch the bottom of his private sorrow.
Once again I leave the capital
to find home.
The past touches a lonely valley
and the future those retreating shores.
How much like sand life is!
My courage already drained
I fear growing dismal and old.
How can I come home alone
again and sadly cross the banks of the Tone River?
The train crosses the plains
while beyond nature's lonely force
men rage.

This is not a happy homecoming by any stretch of the imagination. Not only is the traveler in dark spirits, but the night is cold, he has two restive children to look after, and on top of everything else, even nature itself seems bent on impeding the train's progress. Impatient though he may be to see the first signs of the country-side ("Jōshū's mountains"), the traveler harbors no illusions of his home town ("the past touches a lonely valley"), nor can he find solace in the beauty of the countryside ("beyond nature's lonely force / men rage"). Rather, he is aware that life itself is forcing him to ride this train through the darkness that lies between past and present.

Hagiwara's conceit of himself as a wanderer is expressed most clearly in "Song of the Wanderer," a poem in which the visage of Baudelaire occasionally resurfaces to haunt the reader's own sense of complacency and distance from Hagiwara's agony:

Song of the Wanderer

The sun rises above the precipice
while anxiety ducks the overpass.
Behind the railroad fence that continues on
past the never-ending, distant sky
a solitary shadow drifts.

You! Wanderer!
You who come from the past and go toward the future
seeking eternal nostalgia
how can you shift your worries back and forth
like a clock's pendulum?
As though casting a stone at a serpent
one cycle of samsara is broken
and an unwilled loneliness is set free.

More alone than the devil
can you really endure the icy frost of winter?!
With no belief in anything
you have found faith in rage.
Once unaware of the negation of desire
you have now denounced what you desire.
How can you, again exhausted by anxiety,
go back home and be embraced softly and kissed?
You have loved nothing
and nothing has loved you.

You lonely man!
You climb the hill where the sun sadly sets
and wander along the will-less precipice
but you have no home anywhere.
Your home does not exist!

Here Hagiwara captures the essence of the modern condition: a realization of the irretrievable loss and rootlessness contingent on a difference from all previous history and tradition. Like Baudelaire, who also never felt completely at home in the city, Hagiwara strongly rejects the idea of a "home"—whether it be city or country—to which one can return for reassurance, identity, or sense of continuity.[42] In other words, Hagiwara understands that Japanese society in the 1930s is in every sense a modern society. But unlike apologists for modernity, who often seek to fill this loneliness with the comforts of commodity fetishism, Hagiwara finds the pain of modern life accentuated by the presence of such strange and disconcerting objects. The failure of modern commodities to erase his sense of loss lies at the heart of a poem Hagiwara wrote about his short stay in the highly fashionable Akasaka district of Tokyo, where he lived alone in the Nogisaka Club apartments during the winter of 1929.

Nogisaka Club

December has come again.
How cold this winter is!
Last year I lived in a fifth-floor apartment
in a vast Western-style room
I pushed my bed up against the wall and slept alone.
What is it that troubles me?
Already weary of the emptiness of life
must I now starve like some beast of burden?
I have lost nothing
but I have lost everything.
How I seem chased
as I worry and lose my way in the busy holiday streets
and at high noon get drunk on a tavern seat.
A bird flapping its wings at an empty sky
I lose my feelings again in the distant past.

December has come again
How cold this winter is!
Visitors knock on my door
and seeing my indolence pity me, yet
In this vast white-walled Western-style room
lacking coal or hearth
I lie awake alone in my bed
and in broad daylight grow sleepy like a bear.

Like the rest of the poems in *The Iceland*, "Nogisaka Club" is rife with irony. Is the poet really longing for days gone by when he was sheltered from the cold in a large, Western apartment? Is this what Hagiwara means by "my feelings again will disappear into the distant past"? Or is this nostalgia only the product of inebriation, and does not the coldness of the Western room in the second stanza suggest the frustrated possibility of warm human relationships? Instead of giving clear answers to such questions, Hagiwara creates a poetic space in which each possible answer is negated by another, as revealed in the lines, "I have lost nothing / but I have lost everything."[43] Neither the *beddo* of his Western-style room nor the *nokku* of his would-be companions provides Hagiwara with an escape from his loneliness. As his diction indicates, they (Western commodities and Japanese society) are both thoroughly modern. Thus, he creates a cyclical temporality in this poetic space that seeks to overcome his sense of alienation through a challenge to progressive narratives: when December comes the second(?) time, the past is restored in the present and the modern logic of narrative time is displaced altogether. But Hagiwara is still alone.

RETURN FROM POETRY

Hagiwara officially joined the Japan Romantic School in December 1936, two years after the appearance of *The Iceland*. The fact that he waited nearly two years after the school was formed, together with the absence of any articles by him in *Nihon rōmanha*, might indicate an intellectual discord with the other members. But he had been, in fact, on intimate terms with Yasuda Yojūrō and with two of the school's poets, Itō Shizuo and Tanaka Katsumi, since the founding of *Cogito*, a journal to which he did contribute.[44] This is also evident in the manner in which Hagiwara chose to respond to the school's poetics. Beginning with *The Blue Cat*, Hagiwara's own poetry had in many ways anticipated the position articulated by Jinbō for the Japan Romantic School and the conclusions he drew foreshadowed those that Itō arrived at several years after Hagiwara's death.

Ironically, Hagiwara's interest in poetry as a critical voice waned in the years after he joined the Japan Romantic School. The publication in March 1938 of *Return to Japan*, which he had begun writing in 1934, the year that *The Iceland* was published, may be taken as a watershed. After this date, his writings consisted mainly of collections of aphorisms and essays, but the poetry for which he had justly become famous was already written. Thus, *Return to Japan* may be taken as a point of closure in Hagiwara's poetic production as well as in his thought. It has often been claimed that this work is different in both style and theme from Hagiwara's earlier works and, together with his only war poem, "On the Day Nanking Fell," represents an anomaly or a deviation from the natural path of his artistic development.[45] But it should be clear from the above discussion that Hagiwara's privileging of poetry stemmed from his belief in its ability to express better than any other form of writing the discontent he felt with modern life. With *The Iceland*, he had tested this ability as far as possible and, still unsatisfied, abandoned such poetry with his *Return to Japan*.

Hagiwara's dissatisfaction with poetry was already evident in an article he published in *Cogito* only one month after joining the Japan Romantic School. In this article, "On Reading *Heroes and Poets*," Hagiwara goes much deeper than a mere account of his impressions of Yasuda's *Heroes and Poets* to outline his own understanding of the Japan Romantic School and their call for a privileging of poetry:

> The appearance of the Japan Romantic School has raised the cry in Japanese literary circles for the "songs of youth." This refers to the *enthusiasm* for singing out loudly the praises of lost poetry and lyricism in order to regain the happiness of youth. But the reality of this country has stolen away the romance and dreams of youthfulness from all young souls. It is at this point that our Japan Romantic School must sing elegies to youth rather than birthday songs to youth.[46]

The significance of "the reality of this country" was amplified by Hagiwara's suggestion that the Japan Romantic School was not part of a romanticism that belonged to the creative energies of nineteenth-century Europe, but was a "Romantic School during the end of the Japanese century, occurring in the Imperial Year 2590."[47] These two statements taken together seem to indicate that Hagiwara has discarded poetry, if not from a sense of historicity, then at least from an awareness of historical concerns. Poetry has become impossible to write until the larger question of culture is settled.

Thus, when *Return to Japan* appeared in 1938, it not only represented a literary essay by a leading poet but also captured in its title one of the most pressing intellectual issues of its day.[48]

"Return to Japan" became a rallying cry for a broad spectrum of Japanese society including romantics, fascists, government officials, and traditionalists who, in the alacrity with which they seized on it, seemed to have found release from some long confinement. "Return to Japan" may have provided a common theme, but how closely most of these latter-day nativists read Hagiwara's work is another matter.

Unlike the "return" of Kamei, Hayashi, and other romantics, Hagiwara's is an essentially ironic one. "Having searched all the corners of the world, we have finally found that there is no other true home where we can live than our fatherland, Japan," he writes.[49] And yet he is quite cognizant that modernization has so fundamentally and irrevocably changed Japan that the possibility of a unique culture is forever foreclosed:

> But we had been traveling abroad for much too long a time. And now, having returned home, we saw to our surprise that everything was lost: no trace remained of the days of old, the eaves on the houses were all broken, the gardens overrun; not a single memento of what is Japanese was left.[50]

Faced with this predicament, modern Japanese must trace ancient memory and search the corners of "a barren land" in a vain and lonely attempt to find "what is Japanese." We Japanese are, Hagiwara says, "a pathetic group of wanderers."[51] This statement reflects the strong nihilistic tendency in Hagiwara's thought during the late 1930s, when he became increasingly interested in the works of Schopenhauer and Nietzsche, but it is not nihilism alone that accounts for Hagiwara's return to Japan. Rather, his self-definition as a "wanderer" ultimately leads him to discover identity in Japanese ethnicity, much the way, according to Anthony Smith, "the völkerwanderung of the 'dark ages' witnessed a strong, if unfocused and temporary, revival of ethnicity in Europe and the Mediterranean."[52]

Romanticism was not yet dead in Hagiwara, nor was a remnant of poetic spirit lacking in the man who penned the following: "Why is it that even when 99,999 parts of a poem are understood, we still cannot understand the remaining one part? ... This must be attributed to the mystery of literature. Should poetry ever become a form of literature that can be completely dissected, then the romantic image that constitutes the essence of poetry will disappear."[53] Hagiwara may have failed to discover Jinbō's new poetic time, just as he was unable to return to a Japanese space. Neither possibility existed for a man who was acutely aware of the reality of modernity and refused to abandon his dreams of romanticism.

In this sense one may say that Hagiwara's return to Japan was grounded in a critical approach to the problem of modernity in Japan; or, in the words of one critic, "it is precisely the modern which always conjures up prehistory."[54] Hagiwara responded to Jinbō's call for a "new time" by creating a body of poetry in which he wandered between his fascination with the modern city and his attachment to his roots in the countryside. Ultimately he could accept neither. But in expressing his sense of homelessness and his perceived need for an ironic return to a Japan that no longer existed, he sketched the outlines of the process of wandering that was inherited by Tanaka, Itō, and others.

3

Return to Parnassus
The Exoticism of the Self

All poems of antiquity join one to the other, till from ever-increasing masses and members the whole is formed. Everything interpenetrates everything else, and everywhere there is one and the same spirit, only expressed differently. And thus it is truly no empty image to say: ancient poetry is a single, indivisible, and perfect poem. Why should what has once been not come alive again? In a different way, to be sure. And why not in a more beautiful, a greater way?

Friedrich Schlegel,
"Dialogue on Poetry"

In his recently published memoirs, Asano Akira lists Tanaka Katsumi (1911–92) as one of the major poets of the Japan Romantic School.[1] This may seem a rather eccentric estimation to those who remember Tanaka mainly as a founding member of *Cogito* and as a member of the *Shiki* group of poets.[2] Indeed, Tanaka is not usually found in the lists of official members of the Romantic School in literary dictionaries and reference books. But whether or not he formally joined the school (he did not publish in *Nihon rōmanha*), his close association with many of its leading members (he was a high school classmate of Yasuda Yojūrō, whom he joined in founding the journal *Kagiroi*), the themes his work shares with that of other poets in the school (such as Hagiwara Sakutarō and Itō Shizuo), and the boundless praise his work received from many of the members of the Japan Romantic School suggests more than a convergence of intellectual interests. Tanaka's poetry earned him a secure place in the estimations of the members of the Japan Romantic School as a poet who clearly belonged within the intellectual confines of the school.

As early as 1932, when *Cogito* was founded, Tanaka's intellectual interests focused on the idea of classical beauty, which transcended the traditions of East and West. That this was a common concern among all the contributors to *Cogito* hardly needs to be stated again here. But what "classical beauty" meant for Tanaka is not immediately self-evident. The fact that Tanaka's field of study at Tokyo Imperial University was Asian history and that he translated widely from the works of such German romantics as Heine and Novalis for the journal may clarify his concept of classical beauty, especially when it is recalled that much of the modern "rediscovery" of the classical world (and of the Oriental world as well) can be attributed to the works of the German romantics. At the heart of this concern was an aesthetic interest in the problems of historicity and modernity. By envisioning a space outside the constraints of time and the culture of identity, Tanaka was part of a broader intellectual movement that sought to find in poetry a liberation of the senses. His belief in the efficacy of modern lyrical poetry is succinctly described by Saegusa Yoshitaka in his writings on Nakano Shigeharu's rebellion against the dictum "You, don't sing": "This refers to singing of the liberation of the senses, as did for example Heine, or the poets of the Japan Romantic School, and was often an insistence on respect for actual human life."[3] For Tanaka the captor of the senses is historicity, the function of modernity that compels us to place priority on temporality and universality rather than on spatiality and particularity. Thus, it is in response to the entrapment of emotion in time that Tanaka's lyricism seeks out spatial metaphors: "Does not the poetry of Tanaka Katsumi have, above all in its conception, something concrete from which it calls up other images and which invites a delineation of the emotions? It is in regard to this point that a classical quality may be found and a certainty of design may be felt in the lyricism of Tanaka's poetry."[4] Much of Tanaka's poetry is characterized by this tendency toward form and space—a reminder that the classics can only be resurrected in modern times as corpses, that is, as dead shells without a living essence.[5]

The beginnings of Tanaka's search for "something concrete" may be located in his distrust of narratives and the mediation of language that informs much of *Sikang Province*.[6] Tanaka focuses his attention on language, especially language as communicative discourse, while writing poems that present self-contained scenes

rather than such poetic narratives as are found in the work of
Hölderlin. Nowhere is this concern with the futility of a discursive view of language more apparent than in the following poem
from *Sikang Province*:

An Old Station

The road rises toward the valley splendid with fall colors
a broken water wheel and a discarded wheel
quietly the village rests
a crow walks along the street
a knock at the door in search of rest
and a white-haired woman appears
come in, she says with a gesture
have words lost their usefulness here?

With images of broken wheels suggesting the futility of history,
we are led from the paradoxical "road" of narrative language
(paradoxical because it actually takes us down into the valley
even while we believe it leads up) to the space of beauty and rest
afforded by the village. Here, at the end of his journey, the poet
discovers as much to his delight as to his surprise that the mediation of language has been rendered obsolete by the communality
and good-natured character of the village dwellers. More important, however, than the theme of the futility of language specific to
this poem is Tanaka's poetic skill in creating self-referential scenes
such as "An Old Station" throughout *Sikang Province*.

This work, Tanaka's first published collection of poems, drew
universal praise from critics and established Tanaka as a serious
poet whose writing dealt with themes of timely concern. Only one
month after it appeared, the pages of the November 1938 issue of
Cogito were filled with encomiums to *Sikang Province*. Most of the
critics echoed Yasuda's opinion that Tanaka was to be credited for
resurrecting poetry from its demise in the years following Hagiwara Sakutarō:

What has presently turned around the period of poetic decline in
the years since Hagiwara was due for the most part to the merit of
one man, Tanaka Katsumi. It was to Tanaka's credit, more than to
the efforts by any of the geniuses, that a time that understood poetry
as hissing and howling rather than as a song, that saw poetry as

signs and symbols rather than as a tone of voice, was brought back
to the origins of the glory of poetry.[7]

This restoration took place, according to Yasuda, through the
voice of a poet who, grasping history from the vantage point
of lyrical poetry, "always resisted publicly sanctioned space."[8]
Whereas for Hagiwara the subject was preserved as a largely
uncontested unity that wandered between two spaces, the city
and the countryside, for Tanaka a classical space located within
poetry came to take the place of the unified poetic subject.

This classical space may be seen in the following poem, which
Tanaka included in *Sikang Province*:

> *Classics*
>
> Along the strands of Ionia the dolphins play
> in springtime violets bloom in Salamis Bay
> the people of Hellas love blue and yellow
> and all clear colors
> they clap their hands at feasts
> at funerals they bow their heads.

In this apparently trivial poem, the people of ancient Greece do not
come back to us with any great degree of vividness, their alleged
love of clear colors notwithstanding. Indeed, the dolphins and
blooming violets seem to have more joie de vivre than the highly
stylized people, who merely "clap their hands" and "bow their
heads." Tanaka's main interests seem to lie not with the people of
Hellas (the last line even portends their collective death) but with
the poetic space of ancient Greece. Here we see once again that, as
in many of his poems, Tanaka is predominately concerned with
the creation of an artificial and self-contained poetic space.

But "Classics" focuses on a very significant geographical location, an area where Asia Minor meets the European continent. Yet
before we join Funakoshi Akira in finding a "handshake between
East and West"[9] in Tanaka's poetry, we ought to pay careful
attention to the second line, which refers to Salamis Bay, where
Themistocles led the Greek fleet to victory over the Persians in 480
B.C. Even though at least once in the ancient past the West defeated
the East here, Tanaka foresees the coming of springtime as promis-

ing the rebirth of the East as it brings forth the hardy violets, which were once thought dead but were only dormant.

The image of the return of a defeated Asia flits constantly just below the surface of another poem on ancient Greece that Tanaka included in *Sikang Province*. "The Archipelago" shows the influence in title and theme if not in substance of Hölderlin's "Der Archepelagus" and refers to the Aegean Sea, the fabled birthplace of Western civilization.[10]

The Archipelago

What was it that frightened me so?

Losing my step in that violent cove
between the jellyfish and seaweed I saw the gods
virgins with foreheads shining as the evening moon
with crimson tongues all spewn out
seashells with lips like camellias

Like the sunlight shining far and wide
in the twilight many pleasant memories
all come back as in ancient tales
an island, like a shield splattered with blood,
lurks ahead in the dark
from behind the sun shines down
the waves I raise don't even reach his legs
he carries many trees
and has damp shoulders and vertex

There is the dusk surrounding me
and all around me undulates
everything busily working for a return

I set out
twisting and winding my way through that violent cove
so pale, in need of rouge and powder.

This poem recalls the ancient confrontation between East and West in even stronger terms. By claiming to have lost his step in "that violent cove" (*taki no irie*),[11] the narrator suggests that although historical time often is thought to be the only channel to the ancients, it might be conceived better as a treacherous cove that, as water rushes in and out, remains unchanged. Thus, by submerging oneself *in* the water, rather than moving against it, one is able to commune with the ancient gods who "all come back as in ancient tales" and guide one to their ancient, blood-stained tombs, well within sight of their conqueror.

The strong head and shoulders of this conqueror of Asia, perhaps reminiscent of the classical Greek ideal body, serve as a reminder of the contemporary relevance of this ancient struggle and of the need to struggle with history, even while conscious of one's own (or is it really history's?) need for beautification. This call for "beautification" or, more simply put, exoticism, was immediately discerned in Tanaka's poetry by Sakamoto Etsurō (1906–69), poet and member of the Japan Romantic School, who praised Tanaka's *Sikang Province* and raised the question of whether "we Japanese, educated in the graceful poetic taste of *mono no aware*, can only sense the West as exoticism, or [whether we can] ever really delve deeper to arrive at *Wahrheit* [regarding the West]?"[12] Sakamoto's use of the German word for truth was taken from Tanaka's title poem to the collection, "Sikang Province—Dichtung und Wahrheit," a poem that raised the Romantic School's poetics to a new level.

ASIA AS POETRY

If Tanaka felt that modern Japanese could only understand the West as a form of exoticism, the same could also be said of his desire to achieve an identification with China. *Sikang Province* and the title poem of this collection represent his belief that Asia can provide the answer to Jinbō's call for a new historicity. That this historicity is "new," even while supported by an interest in the past, is underscored by Tanaka's highly self-conscious selection of Sikang Province, a symbolic location that in many ways parallels the selection of "the archipelago" as the location for his earlier poem. Sikang was a new province established on the southwestern frontier of China along the old Silk Road in 1928. Thus connecting China to the West, it could easily be read as the geopolitical realization of a "transcendence" (*Aufhebung*) of East and West. This reading is evident in Tanaka's borrowing from Goethe of the subtitle "Dichtung und Wahrheit" (Poetry and truth) to suggest that this poem might itself overcome the contradictions between poetry and truth, fiction and reality. In fact, the poem is little more than a recitation of facts concerning the history, geography, and economic resources of the area, which Tanaka admittedly borrowed from an essay by a Chinese scholar named Ch'en Chung-wei. The following excerpt from the lengthy poem should yield a sufficient sense of Tanaka's interest in this part of Asia:

> *Sikang Province—Dichtung und Wahrheit—*
>
> Lying between the Yalung River and the Brahmaputra River
> a plateau 12,000 feet above sea level
> from whence in the second century the Ch'iang descended
> in the seventh century the T'u-yu-hun
> after the tenth century the Hsi-hsia state appeared
> silk and treasures were brought in by horse
> Kubilai gave the land to the monks
> thereafter the Dalai Lama reigned over the mountains and
>   valleys ...
> people came, the Ning-wu, Huo-er-chan, Huo-er-ku, Mu-ke,
>   Luo-luo, Po-i, Yao, and Miao,
> Tibetans came from the west and rebuked them
> the Han came from the east and carried on trade ...
> in 193– I was 22 and at the University of Nanking
> my thinking was wholly disturbed by a certain feeling
> in those days English imperialism had invaded Tibet
> and Soviet socialism had invaded Mongolia and Chinese Turkestan
> (it was a little later when the Tibetan army, under the
> direction of English officers, crossed Sikang and approached
>   Szechwan)
> I enjoined my conscience to build Sikang Province after the
>   Three People's Principles of Dr. Sun Yat-sen
> which was to see that it became a bulwark against the invasions of
>   both large states....
> Eventually my construction plans were realized but
> they were now directed toward the nearby Sikang Province rather
>   than the distant Sikang Province
> because all around us is Sikang Province.

As the idealistic concluding lines make clear, Tanaka attempts to signify through "Sikang Province" a new alternative to the political realities of socialism and capitalism, of the East and the West. His critique of these conflicts extends to include even the agent of conflict, the subject itself, whose replacement as a coherent identity is signaled by the litany of various races that together occupy, or have historically occupied, the space of Sikang Province. But the replacement of the concept of a unified race, so central to the efforts by many states to establish their own "subject(s)," does not in itself put an end to conflict. This is finally intimated by the last line, when all reality is transformed into Sikang Province and "Sikang Province" takes on the form of a poem. Hence, in the conclusion, *Wahrheit* becomes *Dichtung*, *Dichtung* becomes *Wahrheit*. Thus did the exoticism of Asia suggest to Tanaka and his fellow romantics a subject of history that could remain forever free from conflict.

But historical events did not permit such a sanguine view of Asia to remain uncontested for long. As the toll of the bloody war on the Asian continent became increasingly difficult to ignore, Tanaka's dreams of ancient China were forced to undergo a qualitative change. Thus, by 1940 when Tanaka published *A Distant View of the Continent* (*Tairiku enbō*), his interest in aesthetics has lost all of its earlier classical tones and become increasingly caught up with the official war ideology. China, as we can see in the title poem from this collection, no longer signifies a space in the ancient past where the modern contradictions of East and West can be overcome. Instead, as it grows more and more amorphous in description, it comes to represent a "China-for-Japan," signifying the possibility of realizing ancient Japanese desires for wealth and glory.

A Distant View of the Continent

To come each evening to this hill near the great sea
and look out to the west has become my custom of late
the waves always suddenly turn rough after the setting of the
    evening sun.
Among the many murmuring voices I hear
there are unpleasant, complaining voices
and one of them says this to me
"Why do you always look out over there?
Beyond this sea there is nothing but the yellow people
with their five-thousand-year history of bloodshed and lies
building their hamlets and towns
and wriggling around in them every day, quarreling and fighting.
What else is there for you to gaze at?"
At this I raise my eyebrows and answer him this
"Do not ask why and what for
as such questioning is tainted with vulgarity, you know.

But if I must I will answer you.
I do it because there is something our ancestors will and desire
a great desire yet unfulfilled
and this has stirred up my feelings to no end."
Having spoken thus I see in the blue evening haze
numerous pagodas and many Chinese arches, castle towers, and
      the like
come forth in droves, glittering in gold.

No longer can Tanaka hide behind the tombs of ancient history and completely escape the more squalid side of modern China. As others return from the continent with their own experiences of China, such questions, "tainted with vulgarity" though they may be, have become established within the social discourse on China in Japan. Against these views, Tanaka, the student of ancient Chinese history, struggles to reassert a more romantic view of China as a necessary element in the destiny of the Japanese people. But this is merely the beginning of the end of China as the subject and, indeed, of the disappearance of any sense of alterity whatsoever in Tanaka's poetry. It is not the imperial army that forces an end to this alterity, but the *Divine Army*, Tanaka's third collection of poems, which signals the elision of the distance from public space that Yasuda lauded in Tanaka's earlier works.

This death of art may be seen in the following excerpt from "Wind and Flowers" ("Kaze to hana") a poem that, in describing the last moments of a dying child who cries out that "outside the wind is blowing," suggests the death of poetry.

Wind and Flowers

The flowers of the great magnolia tree under
which the child had often played
bloomed that night and the pitiful father heard clearly
"Daddy, outside...."
Having sprung to his feet and closed the shutters
in a wind no one could walk in
the colors of the great magnolia tree were now about to
      rustle and fall.

Tanaka seems to suggest that, like the dying child, he too has exhausted his energies in what has proved to be a vain effort to keep alive the beauty of poetry. But like the father in the poem, he cannot bear to watch the flowers (classical beauty, ancient China, Asia) fall to their deaths. Rather, he chooses to shut himself up within an idealized and utterly solipsistic "Japan," a point of reference from which the difficult questions of the war, politics, and human suffering have been displaced by the question of national identity subsumed in culture.

By 1940 a concept of poetry that allowed for the expression of difference had given way to a concept of a specifically Japanese poetry in which "lyricism is expressed in a form that only indicates the place of the most precise lyricism.... Here one finds the beauty of quiet inactivity that only we Japanese can understand."[13] The journey in search of a "new time" had taken Tanaka from the shores of ancient Ionia to Sikang and finally back home to Japan. But his "Japan" was not the modern Japanese state that was actively engaged in a bloody war in Asia. Rather, Tanaka's search had discovered the quietude of a Japan-as-memory. His plaintive cry "If I forget the road I have traveled in tears, who will know of it?"[14] merely signified his attempt to displace through memory the economic and cultural suffering wrought in Japan by the onset of modernity. At the same time, his method of expressing this memory kept him from understanding the suffering of other Asians, most notably that of the Chinese and Koreans, and foreclosed the possibility of their understanding his view of Asia.

THE NEW WORLD OF LYRICISM

Although Tanaka and Hagiwara made great strides in response to Jinbō's call for a new poetry, Itō Shizuo came the closest to realizing a new poetic subjectivity and consequently came to be recognized as the poet laureate of the Japan Romantic School. Itō began writing his poetry prior to and independent of the Romantic School, first writing for the journal *Ro*, which he founded along with a philosophy student, Aoki Keimaro (b. ?–d. ?), whom he had met at Kyoto University. He also drew on his training in German at Saga Higher School to assist him in his studies of the works of Rainer Maria Rilke, Erich Kästner, and Friedrich Hölderlin. As Itō's later poems bear out, his interest in German scholarship was not limited to questions of beauty and style but stemmed from a consciousness of the dilemma language posed for the mod-

ern subject. His early poetry in particular reveals a painful awareness of the essential alienation of the modern subject, and it may
well have been the poignancy of Itō's expression of this agony in
Ro that caught the attention of Tanaka Katsumi, who first introduced Itō's poetry to Yasuda and the other members of the *Cogito*
group. Not long afterward, a formal invitation to submit poems
for publication in *Cogito* reached Itō from Tanaka and Yasuda.

Itō responded to this invitation on April 28, 1933, by sending
Yasuda the poem "Song of a Hospital Patient." Yasuda published
not only the poem but also an open letter to Tanaka called "Two
Poets" in the November 1934 issue of the journal. In this letter,
Yasuda writes of his high esteem for Itō's poetry, calling it "poetry
of my own soul" and noting that he finds in Itō and Tanaka "the
very same endeavor."[15] But it is Itō's poetry in particular that
interests Yasuda:

> Here, in Itō's poetry, there is nothing but various vague expres-
> sions of being at one's wit's end. In his case, concepts are reduced to
> a vast emptiness, and only the general atmosphere is described. This
> invincible nihility tickles my mind. Perhaps it is my nostalgia for
> "an unknown homeland." I do not know what it is—is it Itō's innate
> physiological gloom? or is it irony? or perhaps Itō's irrepressible
> shortcoming? the dream of someone under pressure? I have no
> idea. What I do know is that it is the ancient grief of Schlegel, the
> songs of Hölderlin's disappointed dream reappearing on such a day
> as this.[16]

This was high praise indeed, coming from a man who in many
ways dominated Japanese literary circles during the late 1930s.
Not only did Yasuda's opinion carry considerable weight with
other intellectuals of the day but, as the editor of *Cogito* and later
of the *Nihon rōmanha*, he was also well placed to ensure a public
forum for Itō's work.

Yasuda was not the only influential voice calling out in support
of this relatively unknown poet. Perhaps of even greater importance in establishing Itō's reputation as a poet of the first order
was Hagiwara Sakutarō who, by the middle of the 1930s, was
certainly one of the most famous living Japanese poets. Hagiwara
was not only one of the earliest of Itō's supporters, but also one of
his most loyal. In 1934, after reading Itō's poetry in *Cogito* for the
first time, Hagiwara sent Itō a letter in which he clearly expressed

his admiration for the younger poet's work. In the letter he notes, "When I first saw Itō Shizuo's poetry in the pages of *Cogito*, I discovered this 'lost lyricism' and, knowing that there was still one more poet in Japan, I was so happy and filled with hope that my heart skipped a beat."[17] Although such unreserved praise for Itō led to resentment and jealousy on the part of some of Hagiwara's loyal admirers and disciples, most notably Miyoshi Tatsuji, many critics at the time agreed with Hagiwara's assessment.[18] So much so, in fact, that in February 1935, shortly after Hagiwara voiced his support of Itō's poetry, Itō received an invitation from Kamei Katsuichirō and Nakatani Takao to join the Japan Romantic School. Itō responded quickly, joining the school and submitting "A Noontime Rest" ("Mahiru no kyūsoku") which was published two months later in the second issue of the school's journal.

Before turning to Itō's poetry, it is important to consider how Itō's work was read by a few of these contemporary critics who prized his work so highly. Such consideration should prove helpful in avoiding the pitfalls of the kind of biographical interpretations that have become standard in studies of Itō's poetry, which have yielded little more than stilted pronouncements on its "difficult style."[19] By focusing first on these contemporary readings, we not only gain an insight into how several of Itō's own colleagues understood his poetry but also should be better placed to recover the historicity of Itō's thought.

Itō's first published collection of poems, *Laments to My Person*, met with sweeping acclaim from the members of the Japan Romantic School immediately upon its publication on October 5, 1935. Hagiwara's praise of the work, which compared its romantic tone with the poetry of the young Shimazaki Tōson, won instant fame for the new poet. Hagiwara took advantage of his position on the nominating board of the Bungei Hanron Prize to award the Second Bungei Hanron Prize in 1936 to Itō's collection.[20] The importance given to this collection may be surmised from the fact that the January 1936 issue of *Cogito* is devoted to commemorating the publication of the work, with articles on Itō's poetry by Tanaka Katsumi, Hagiwara Sakutarō, Nakatani Takao, Aoki Keimaro, Nakajima Eijirō, Jinbō Kōtarō, Yamamura Torinosuke (1909–51), Yasuda Yojūrō, and Momota Sōji (1893–1955), along with a full-page advertisement for the newly published *Laments*.

Tanaka places Itō within the Romantic School's search for a new poetry, arguing that "it seems true that Itō, as a fellow member of the Japan Romantic School, reveals a certain degree of sympathy with Jinbō's movement," although he confesses to a personal sense of frustration with Itō's fascination with "other worlds."[21] Yasuda responds with a reaffirmation of his previous commitment to Itō's resurrection of lyricism, describing Itō's poetry as "lonely lyrical poetry because it inheres not in a pure and simple world but in a diverse, cultural world."[22] But Hagiwara Sakutarō's essay carried the most weight in the literary circles of the day.

In his essay, Hagiwara begins by outlining a history of modern poetry. In it, nineteenth-century French romantic poets such as Verlaine found their own attempts at lyricism frustrated by the ascendancy of the cultural skepticism of the Symbolists and discovered that they could survive only as "wounded souls," decadent romantics who wasted themselves on absinthe and bitterness. Because of its invocation of images of these skeptical Symbolists, *Laments to My Person* is seen as representing the dilemma of art in Japan during the 1930s, a time when, according to Hagiwara, "culture itself had lost its purposiveness and all are groping in a dark age of uncertainty and doubt."[23] But Hagiwara discounts a return to the earlier, naive romanticism, arguing that the conditions of modern society require something altogether new:

> It was the eighteenth-century romantics who truly possessed the pure spirit of lyrical poetry. But society henceforth will not allow the old romanticism. What poetry henceforth must be is a strong, transfigured poetry under tension that, possessing the core of this pure lyricism, can come up from underneath all realistic social conditions and break through the rocks. That is, good lyrical poetry the way it should be is the orthodoxy of this kind of "wounded Romantic School" that is represented by Itō Shizuo and others.[24]

Hagiwara's hopes for Itō's poetry are not founded on a belief that Itō will effect a simplistic reenactment of the poetry of the past. Rather, he believes that, by rejecting the alienating nature of life in modern society while longing for something else, Itō gives the clearest expression possible to the desire of many during the 1930s for a new cultural epistemology.

This skepticism toward the possibility of a return to some previous state of harmony plays a role in the essential ambiguity of

Laments to My Person. At a time when many were calling for a "return to Japan" or bemoaning the loss of a home town, Itō's cynicism may seem out of place. Yet the following poem has more in common with Hagiwara's own troubled homecoming than it does with the simplistic calls for a "return" that were prevalent in the 1930s.

The Homecomer

Nature is unlimited beauty, while its eternal inhabitants
languish in poverty. I have often watched from the shore
the waves roar in
smashing the reef again and again
and scattering into bubbles, ebbing,
each coughing up its froth
those homecomers I constantly see here
are just like those waves
that strangely uniform monologue
I have no sympathy for it
it sounds so terribly commonsensical
"Indeed! There is nothing of beauty in my home town today"
why do they say "today"!
The beautiful home town—
that theirs is truly a vain task
is attested by its glorification in countless ancient poems
that there has ever lived a people amid this nature
whose beauty equaled hers
I cannot believe
yet the fact that, after much suffering and unhappiness,
they all peacefully became a single grave
brought me consolation
and a good deal of happiness

Envoy

I, who have escaped the country,
how could I ever be content with you, City?
I, who have learned poetry,
how could I fail to yearn for you, Action?

Unlike Hagiwara's ironic homecoming, Itō's reveals a valorization of the natural beauty of the countryside. Indeed, even the wretched inhabitants of this home town can only appear to Itō as a part of this nature, as the waves of the sea.

Through this metaphoric substitution of nature for human

agency, Itō is attempting nothing less than a negation of time itself, just as the faceless inhabitants of the home town reproduce themselves in "countless ancient poems" as well as in their "strangely uniform monologue." This program was recognized as early as 1936 by Tsujino Hisanori (1909–37), a brilliant young critic and translator who, in an article on Itō written the year before his own death, suggests that "his [Itō's] self had already completely negated the real world, that is, space. But did it not also try to negate the one other important condition of living beings, namely time? ... That is to say, even though he has already negated space, he feels that time still threatens his self. Therefore, now he wants desperately to dispose of time as he wishes!"[25] But this is not an easy matter. Like Hagiwara, Itō is caught between a rejection of the home town as a hopeless dream of a world prior to the alienation of the self from the world, and a sense of the emptiness engendered by the modern city. The "action" he yearns for is the act of longing for life in the world after this alienation. But he is also aware of the irony that the only ones who can return to such a harmonious life with nature are the dead—those who have lost their individual selves. Thus, Itō is caught in the paradox that, even while longing for life, the self can only realize happiness with its own extinction and the end of time.

Itō encodes this attempt to escape from the constraints of time in the following lines, which close the poem "Song of a Hospital Patient" ("Byōin no kanja no uta"):

> Does this hospital not have that clock
> that so regrettably interrupted my sleep?
> Yes we do, we have it but the method of using it is different
> I am now able to get into a wooden boat alone with my hunting
>   rifle
> and disembark from time to time whenever I wish
> on any of those twelve isles

As Tsujino points out, these lines signify Itō's elevation of the self above the contradictions of self and the world and suggest the conversion of the self into an absolute, a king. Does this not, Tsujino asks, have as an ultimate goal Itō's desire to "create a new world of his own, which will replace the lost real world?"[26]

This new world, then, is not a return to a closed subjective world but is rather a subjective dream of an external world, and it is the belief in this world that finally allows Itō to once again begin to wander in eternal homecoming.

The tension in Itō's thought between the inner and the external worlds stemmed from his earlier interest in *Neue Sachlichkeit*, or New Objectivity. This concept was first introduced into Japan with the publication of Sasazawa Yoshiaki's "The Literature of *Neue Sachlichkeit*" ("Noiu-zaharikaito bungaku") in the June 1930 issue of *Poetry and Poetics* (*Shi to shiron*). By 1932 Itō was already familiar with the poetry of Rainer Maria Rilke and Erich Kästner, reading the latter in an anthology of German poets, *Deutschen Lyrik*, which later became a popular textbook in Japanese universities, and finding the former's *Das Buch der Bilder* imbued with a "subtle metaphoric spirit." Itō admitted that his own idea of a "quiet xenie" was simply an exercise in this spirit.[27] Yet it is important to note that *Neue Sachlichkeit*, as explained in Takeda Chūya's 1931 primer *A Literary Theory of Neue Sachlichkeit* (*Noiu-zaharikaito bungakuron*), was a loosely defined pastiche of recent Germany literary trends, drawing on the works of Rilke, Kästner, Stefan George, Hugo von Hofmannsthal, Bertolt Brecht, and Hans Carossa and encompassing such unfamiliar terms as "new reality," "magical realism," "reality-idealism," and "expressionist or fanatical naturalism."[28] Clearly, Itō had a certain degree of latitude in choosing how he wished to interpret and use this "*Neue Sachlichkeit.*"

Of all Itō's poems, the one that has traditionally been considered most representative of his interpretation of *Neue Sachlichkeit* is "Cinema in the New World" ("Shinsekai no kīnō"). Of concern here is not whether such a meeting as the poem describes between Itō and several of his former classmates actually took place, but what textual strategy Itō gains from the alleged incident.

Cinema in the New World

In the midst of a transfer from Tokyo to Korea
an old friend dropped by my neighborhood
including me, there were three of us former classmates in the
    neighborhood

I took his call because
my buddies were at the cinema showing
in the New World

> I found in my desk my name card from before I was adopted
> and wrote on it the plans for the farewell party
> and told the other two
>
> On the day we four were to meet at the hotel
> I was first
> on the terrace the fan had stopped but it was cool
>
> In the fountain the children who had sneaked in
> floated rubber fish
> on the surface of my plans ...

This poem shares more than a rejection of expressionistic techniques with the *Neue Sachlichkeit* movement. The dry reportage style of the poem is betrayed by the lines "In the fountain ... my plans," where our own sense of familiarity with this world is shaken by a reminder that this is indeed a "new world," no matter how familiar it may have seemed up to that point.

This "new world" is nothing less than the suggestion of a transcendence of the subject-object split by an entirely new reality, much as the new medium of cinema may have seemed to promise to those who first experienced it. Itō's understanding of this fundamental impulse behind *Neue Sachlichkeit* is clear from his reading of Kästner's poem "Sachliche Romanze":

> This poem seems to have no theme worthy of admiration, nor any technique, but the choice of this title shows how the methodology of this approach—which may be called Sachlichkeit-istic or affair-istic—expresses a deliberate mental attitude. Further, and this may be in the author's subconscious, it is believed that the methodology of this approach, as anyone could foresee, demonstrates how close it is to the new romanticism.[29]

With Itō's own poem as well, the title offers the best insight into his understanding of *Neue Sachlichkeit*. Although the words Itō used in the title, *shinsekai* and *kīnō*, may be taken only as the name of a district in Osaka (Shinsekai) and the German word for cinema (*das Kino*), their use together in the title of this poem suggests more. *Kīnō*, although written in the *katakana* script used for transcribing foreign words, echoes the Japanese word for yesterday, "*kinō*," especially as it might be mispronounced by a foreigner. Placed in conjunction with the "new world," it suggests the past of the future, the "yesterday of a new world," as the narrative time in the poem reaches a crescendo with the stillness of the useless fan.

Itō ultimately seeks in *Neue Sachlichkeit* a solution to the cultural chaos in modern Japan. By characterizing the *Neue Sachlichkeit* movement as "affair-istic" (*jibutsu-teki*) he seeks to draw attention to the movement's ability to focus on the "events" (*ji; koto*) and "things" (*butsu; mono*) of modern Japanese society, which have become separated from each other through the mediation of the modern, standard language (*hyōjungo*). His use of German words like *Neue Sachlichkeit* and *Kino* is a part of this effort to express the problem in his own style of "xenie." Itō returns to this problem in his later poems through an investigation of the possibilities of classical language. But already in *Laments to My Person* he is attempting to show in poem after poem how various naive approaches to narrative cannot escape the subjectivity of the author. Such a revelation by itself was not as consequential as Itō's ability to place this fictitiousness in a direct relationship with the conditions of modern Japanese society, which was, in a sense, "truly revolutionary." For as Okaniwa Noboru shows: "The Shōwa period was, in the first place, none other than the time when the Meiji = modern 'natural world' fell apart. Reality became fiction. Or better, it was revealed that reality had always been a fiction."[30] While *Neue Sachlichkeit* did not permit Itō a return to Japan, neither did it prevent him from envisioning a "yesterday of the new world," a moment prior to the hegemony of modernity.

INTERNALIZING THE NEW WORLD

Neue Sachlichkeit led Itō to the conclusion that the separation of "things" and "words" that he found in modern society was not limited to objective reality but occurred also on the level of the subject. Although many of Itō's contemporaries understood Itō's poetry in this light, especially Hagiwara and Tsujino, it was not until Sugimoto Hidetarō's recent study that the biographical emphasis prevalent in the postwar period was challenged by a new focus on Itō's "split self."[31] Sugimoto's simple, but brilliant, insight was that the "my person" (*waga hito*) in the title of the collection did not signify Itō's alleged lover, Sakai Yuriko, as the critics had long maintained. Sugimoto writes:

> No one paid the slightest attention to the fact that both the collection *Laments to My Person* and the title poem in the collection very carefully avoided the diction that the "my person" must be understood as a woman. Biographical intentions spread out everywhere—"like a single swamp." It occurred to me that "my person" appeared as the half-self (*hanshin*) of the "I" (*watakushi*), as a doppelgänger. By focusing on the drama of the "I" that loves another "I" (that is, the "half-self")—an old, new act of giving new names to things, an act that so closely approximates an assault—the faceless poet, exposing himself to the violent storm of metaphors and in the process transforming himself into a pale and ageless magician, revives human suffering and happiness. Even though happiness is immediately imbued with the hues of icy flames like the resignation of stoicism.[32]

This discovery enables Sugimoto to provide a coherency to our understanding of *Laments to My Person* that was lacking in previous studies. Whereas earlier critics selected for consideration only poems that supported their own immediate concerns (or the poems that they could understand) and disregarded the rest, Sugimoto sees the collection in its entirety as a linguistic system of differences unfolding over time. The specific definition of this system cannot be arrived at logically, he cautions, but is a "definition of the realized affair (*jibutsu*) that poetry, in association with other arts (music, sculpture, painting, architecture, dance and ritual) arrived at through itself.... [It is in the experience of this definition of the "realized affair" that] poetry becomes a new experience—for the reader as well as for the poet himself."[33]

The system of differences unfolds as a form of "discursive poetry" composed of a series of continually deferred moments.[34] Sugimoto describes "discursive poetry" in the following manner: "In this unprecedented poetic anthology, one poem calls out to another and the poem called upon calls out to yet another. And while there is not one poem that is not called upon, neither can one find a single poem that responds submissively."[35] Within this discourse, Sugimoto isolates two interdependent subjective positions, neither of which is identical to the poet: the position of the "I" (*watakushi*) and the position of the "half-self" (*hanshin*). With the exception of the last two poems by "an old man" and "(an old man)," each poem in the collection assumes one of these two positions (see appendix B). The "I" is characterized as an anti-poetic and cynical trickster whose own poems are grounded in an unshakable belief in the reliability of everyday life. In contrast, the "half-self" is a romantic dreamer who tries to breathe life into poetry from the world of ideas. And while Itō, as the poet who created both personae, cannot be reduced to either, Sugimoto hints that Itō's sympathies may lie closer to the "half-self."[36]

As Sugimoto's theory does not easily lend itself to summary, it may be best to offer, as an example, his reading of a few of the more important poems in the collection. The first, "On a Clear Day" ("Hareta hi ni") opens the collection:

On a Clear Day

I must tell you
my beloved, my wandering half-self
that one rare fine day
my aged mother
was compelled to return to her homeland
one is not allowed to live
where one desires
your letters from afar
tell me that
you have settled
for now upstream the Chikuma
where at the end of April
in the surrounding mountains and even along the village roads
one meter of snow
still glistens in the sun
waiting for May
and the cherries to open
behind you have seen
a proper apple orchard!
in order to feel love
you say, but you have your orders
together when we were young in our home town
by April we would don our wide-brimmed caps
or walk barefoot along the hot ground under a brilliant sun and
plant a mutant apple tree
that would bear only pale white fruit!
I can guess precisely what it is
that this ordered person my wandering half
you so earnestly refuse to believe in.

In a close, line-by-line analysis of this poem, Sugimoto shows how the poem represents an attempt by the "I" to convince the "half-self" to give up its hopeless dreams of a better world. Even the "I"'s own mother was, after all, "compelled to return to her home-land." But the "I" also knows that the "half-self" is "ordered" by its very nature to continue to wander, so that in spite of all efforts to convince the "half-self" that the familiar home town is not all that bad, the "half-self" will never be convinced that there can be difference in the familiar, a "mutant apple tree" in its own home town.

The half-self's response, and its insistence on the necessity of exotic places in its quest for creative alternatives and poetic possibilities, may be found in the second poem of the collection, "Song of the Prairie" ("Kōya no uta"). Here the "half-self" rejects the overtures of reconciliation and love extended by the "I" in the above poem and renews its insistence on self-reliance and independence.

Song of the Prairie

My imaginary peaks! Do not melt away
your ivory snow
on the beautiful day when I will die
past an unknown spring
in this prairie of stifling sparseness
past this hidden place
of ripened orange branches
fruit of the flowers whose seeds I planted
will these road signs lead the way
for the horse that pulls my corpse, on that near day?
ah, thus your noble white light sends me off
on my eternal homecoming
the shining fruit the laughing spring ...
oh, my painful dreams, then you will finally
find your rest![37]

As the critics generally agree, this image of a postmortem return to the home town is closely modeled after Giovanni Segantini's oil painting "Ritorno al Paese Natio." The "half-self" makes full use of the apparent irony that it will only return to its Japanese home town dead and in a manner reminiscent of a European (foreign) painting. The "half-self" not only rejects the "I"'s invitation to return to its home but also calls into question the validity of any such notion of a home in modern Japan, where a Japanese now can feel as much "at home" with Western art as with native customs. It hopes that even after its death and the dissolution of its own personal identity the peaks of imaginative power will survive to inspire others to seek beauty in ugliness, hope in despair, and life in death. But more immediately, it responds to the "I" by identifying the act of homecoming with death.

Sugimoto's approach is especially helpful in retrieving the historical context of Itō's thought from biographical treatments and in resituating Itō's poetry as a contribution to the Japan Romantic School's attempt to overcome modernity. Itō, like Kamei Katsuichirō in his investigation of the ego in a period of change, focussed his attention on the modern subject and its supposed coherent identity. And yet, although it would be tempting to conclude that his enthusiastic response to Kamei's invitation to join the Romantic School was evidence of his readiness to abandon the painful analysis of the subject in *Laments to My Person* in favor of the collectivity of the school, such a conclusion would be somewhat misleading. After joining the Japan Romantic School in 1935, the year *Laments to My Person* was published, the antagonistic relationship between the "I" and the "half-self" was transferred to the level of the relationship between Itō and the communality of the school. Odakane Jirō, a member of the *Cogito* group and a close friend of Itō, recalls that Itō returned from the party held in Tokyo commemorating his publication of *Laments* thoroughly disgruntled with many of the members of the school.[38] Soon after his return to Osaka, Itō wrote the following poem:

A Refusal [Kyozetsu]

Sitting on a white rock
near a dilapidated temple well
I have erased most of time
clouds arise, pregnant with meaning
and the grass stands tall, silently ...
once again I watch the coming of summer
what will it bring, this change of seasons
which has failed to touch my breast
but now appears before me?
all things in creation, leave me alone
the water in this hidden well dares not
sing of you.

As Odakane points out, in this poem Itō transforms himself into a bottomless well where he is completely cut off from nature. This is not merely an expression of anti-naturalism, or of a vague withdrawal from society, but is a coded "spirit of refusal" whose object the members of the school understood quite well. Yasuda, for one, chastised Itō for his overindulgence in this spirit and attempted to persuade him to soften, if not abandon, it in the future: "Itō, how many friends have you today? Your uncompromising new voice may boast of having few—is that not the contemporary significance of your laments? Even though you went home saying you wished to name your next book of poems *Refusal*, you must not allow yourself to push that word around too far."[39] While Itō did not completely ignore Yasuda's advice, neither did he abandon his resistance to the idea of losing his sense of a critical self, no matter how difficult that may have been within the confines of the Japan Romantic School.

The years from 1935 to 1940 mark a period of tension between Itō and the school as he sought to preserve his own artistic integrity while continuing to write his poetry within the broader framework of the school's declared problematic. Rather than withdraw from the school, Itō worked out a relationship of difference with the school, which provided a degree of sociality to his work that was missing in *Laments to My Person*. But this sociality was not to be achieved at the loss of critical power, for as the contradictions between the school's poetic agenda and Itō's own artistic sense intensified, he attempted to resolve them by appealing to a concept of transcendental beauty:

> When things become unbearable, behold the water flower
>   I fling into the sky.
> The shadow of a goldfish flickers in it.
> When all things turn toward me
> and say, "Die!"
> Everything in my June seems so beautiful.[40]

Implicit in this attempt to construct a personal paradise where one can retreat from the disquieting social world of the late 1930s is, however, an aesthetics that cannot avoid complicity with state ideology. As one critic points out, even while trying to liberate himself from the school, "Itō, who wanted to be a solitary, inde-

pendent [poet], to the contrary has become the positive representative of the spirit of the times."[41] As the war on the Asian
continent was increasingly difficult to ignore in intellectual discourse, many in the Japan Romantic School found just such
poems to express their own fascination with the beauty of death.

This was a crucial moment in Itō's poetic challenge to modernity. In order to avoid a reading that saw his voice of death as
beautiful, rather than beauty as the sublimation of the individual
poetic voice, Itō emphasized this end of the individual through a
valorization of the eternal life of the Japanese ethnic nation. Thus,
in the poems of *Spring's Haste* (*Haru no isogi*; 1943), he seeks to
overcome, once and for all, the ambiguity of modern life. For Itō,
this ambiguity is the result of the imperative function of rationality, which forces one to make a choice and assures one that the
choice will make a difference. By rejecting the parameters of ambiguity and the pain of alienation inherent in choosing one position
over another, he supplants the possibility of action and resistance
with the question of identity. Identity is no longer conceived as a
historical process of self-differentiation from the social but is
merely the intuitive awareness of an ethnically defined set of linguistic skills.

The use of a pseudo-classical language in such poems as "You
and I" ("Nare to ware"), "From Out of the Sky" ("Nakazora no
izuko yori"), and "Shallow Spring" ("Haru asaki") establishes this
identity on two levels: first, between language and the things it
claims to represent; and second, among the individuals who speak
the language. For example, in "Shallow Spring" the arbitrary nature of the process of naming is exposed by an innocent child who
asks his father for the names of two flowers:

> Though you badger me to tell you their names
> what shall I do?
> daddy doesn't know them
>
> I'm at a loss
> my child so the child
> calls them White Flower Yellow Flower
>
> Hearing this, I nod my head
> the answer of a young one's
> endearing mind

> White Flower Yellow Flower
> crying out his song so loudly
> he runs away to the kitchen where his mother is.

In the child's escape to its mother, we find Itō's disillusionment with the inability of the older Meiji generation of modernizers (the fathers) to maintain a unity between words and things, modernity and ethnicity. Fully aware that the process of naming is essentially an arbitrary and fictitious one, Itō envisions an innocent younger generation that, drawing on its forceful desires for new names, would be more consistent with the reality of its own lived experience. This return to the womb is not only a return to origins but also a search for the principle of nurturing that will ground meaning in a renewed sense of direction and future growth. Only at this point can the fictitious process of naming finally be understood and accepted as fiction.

Once this discovery is made, names and ideology immediately lose much of their allure. Like the child in the poem, Itō is enticed by the nurturing power of his own origin, which he finds in the Japanese people. He seeks this origin through the classical language, finding in it not the skepticism that Hagiwara found but an abiding beauty in the life of the common Japanese people (*shomin*). Even while a bloody war is ravaging the lives of these people, Itō's battle becomes a struggle against all forms of thought that might deny him this newly found sense of spiritual wholeness. As Oketani explains, "the war for Itō was the joy and sadness of an everyday life so completely enclosed that no ideology, no formed thought, could be abstracted from his restless and abnormal common life [*shomin-teki nichijō*]."[42]

Clearly Itō's thought had evolved to the point where the kinds of possibilities for resistance and criticism suggested by *Laments to My Person* were completely foreclosed. Itō himself reflected after the war that "my frantic struggle against the dark side of consciousness, such as I carried out in those days, has lost all its fire and has moved on to a simple way of thinking."[43] His earlier vigilance against any attempt to deny the Other within the self had given way to a way of thinking that defined the Other of modernity in the purity of the self. Ironically, this way of thinking not only meant the impossibility of suggesting any plausible alternatives to the modern subject but also suggested the historical meaning of Itō's poetic practice. As Jacques Lacan has shown, there is a moment in the psychological development of the individual when the split self of the mirror stage gives way to a "social I," a "moment in which the mirror-stage comes to an end [and] inaugurates ... the dialectic that will henceforth link the I to socially elaborated situations."[44] For Itō this new way of thinking meant that his poetic vision of an alternative to the modern subject ultimately could only be expressed within the context of a more familiar, and essentially prosaic, modern ideology.

As suggested above, the poetics of the Japan Romantic School was concerned less with questions of literary merit than with an investigation of the problem of culture in the modern age. The poets of the school all shared a critical assessment of the accomplishments of modernity, finding their lives in a modern society filled only with disappointment, disillusionment, and anger. They began by identifying with the German romantics' search for a basis of cultural identity, although seeking it not in the establishment of a nation-state but rather in a cultural voice that they could call their own. This, they felt, had been denied them by the course of their own history, which had placed the economic and military security of the nation ahead of the well-being of its people, or what Itō called the "common people" (*shomin*). But as their search intensified, it became increasingly clear to most that, because the contradictions of the modern condition required comparison with other cultures in order to understand one's own, they were prevented from realizing the kind of cultural identity they had envisioned. They accurately located these contradictions in the modern historical consciousness, which subjected the differences of culture and language to its own overarching laws of development. In the final analysis, they rejected this historical consciousness for its failure to produce a native Japanese subjectivity.

The replacement of history with lyrical poetry opened up certain possibilities within this project. Not only did the privileging of lyrical poetry follow the precedent set by the German romantics, but it also signaled for many a return to a specific, Japanese intellectual tradition. Poetry, in general, had long been seen as a genre proper to the disenfranchised in Japanese history, but lyri-

cal poetry in particular played an active role in countering historicist claims. Saigo Nobutsuna, for one, argues that the historical
function of lyrical poetry and its focus on the nontemporal nature
of mankind was to suggest the possibility of regaining "the self"
as the reservoir of a "lyrical humanity" in a class-divided society.[45] Within this tradition the lyrical "self," whether Hagiwara's "wandering self," Tanaka's "Asian self," or Itō's "self-
alienated self," functioned as an attempt to restore a native sense
of identity within the modern world. Nevertheless, this recovery
of a self within lyrical poetry was not always a simplistic return to
the past. All of these poets took as their point of departure a clear
understanding of the irrevocably modern nature of Japanese society; paradoxically, this understanding led them to seek ways of
overcoming that very modernity. Their emphasis on negations of
modernity and dreams of different worlds was not a longing for
an ancient, historical world but more precisely an envisioning of
"unreal worlds" in the Lacanian sense: "Unreal is not imaginary.
The unreal is defined by articulating itself on the real in a way that
eludes us, and it is precisely this that requires that its representation should be mythical, as I have made it."[46] The members of the
Romantic School represented the unreal poetically rather than
mythically but to much the same end. In giving expression to
the unreal in the very real material practice of poetry, they sought
to suggest certain limits to the "reality" of the modern world—a
"reality" that had failed to account adequately for the question of
culture. Thus, their restoration of lyrical poetry was not satisfied
with a "return to Japan" but sought to create an "unrealistic"
aesthetics of Japan.

Hölderlin, it appears, was right—at least with reference to the
poets of the Japan Romantic School. Having risen up in opposition
to the alienation of culture from meaningful action in modern
Japan, and seeking to regain through their own poetic practice a
native identity with which to replace this alienation, these romantic poets all ultimately grew disillusioned with their task. The
disillusionment was in one sense the result of their realization
that their project itself was marred by an essential contradiction.
In attempting to overcome the reality of modernity, however it
was understood, they found themselves facing two alternatives.
One was the approach taken by the Kyoto School of philosophers,

the Shōwa Research Association (Shōwa Kenkyūkai), and others who articulated a "Japanese" identity secured by the state, a position that functioned merely as the harmonic opposite of that of the West. But the romantics were dissatisfied with modernity itself, including such a "Japanese" rational state, and instead through their poetry tried to overcome the very idea of modernity as a coherent identity. Consequently, their only alternative was to commit themselves to a poetics that would through time "deteriorate into an infinity of isolated moments" and grow increasingly distant from all possibilities of social change.

4

The Ethics of Identity

Kamei Katsuichirō and the Search for a New Subject

> I raise myself to this standpoint and am a new creature,
> and my whole relationship to the present world is trans-
> formed. The ties by which my mind was so far attached to
> this world, and through whose secret tug it followed all
> movements in it, are cut forever, and I stand free and calm
> and unmoved, myself my own world.
>
> Johann Gottlieb Fichte,
> *The Vocation of Man*

Educated at elite preparatory schools, Kamei Katsuichirō matricu-
lated at Tokyo Imperial University in 1926 and enrolled in the
Department of Aesthetics. Although he attended few of his
classes and dropped out of school altogether two years later, his
initial choice of aesthetics as his field of study seems to indicate the
continuation of an earlier distrust of material civilization. At the
tender age of fourteen, Kamei already had written in his school
journal that only "spiritual civilization" was worthy of the term
"civilization."[1] The same critical orientation toward contemporary
society led him to join the Shinjinkai and several Marxist study
groups; although he read Soviet realists such as Lunacharskii and
Bukharin, the degree to which he absorbed the theoretical implications of Marxism is rather dubious. At any rate, in 1928 he was
one of more than a thousand who were arrested on suspicion of
communist ties under the Peace Preservation Law in the weeks
following the March 15 crackdown on the Communist Party. He
was incarcerated in the Ichigaya Correctional Institution for more
than two years. In the fall of 1930 he fell ill and, suffering a lung
hemorrhage, was released after signing a promise that he would
"henceforth no longer participate in any and all illegal political

activities." A week later he returned to his home in Hakodate to convalesce.[2]

Although Kamei greeted the Manchurian Incident of September 18, 1931, with silence, in June of the following year, having waited out the last of his legal problems, he turned to the pen. He accepted a position on the editorial board of the Society for the Study of Marxist Art[3] and began writing articles that showed that, while he had distanced himself from illegal forms of political action, he was still quite active in socialist criticism. In March 1933, at the sixth general meeting of the Japan Proletarian Writers League (NALP), Kamei was appointed to the executive committee and elected to the post of director of education.[4] In addition, he continued writing articles for *Proletarian Literature*.[5] In view of the above, it is rather difficult to take seriously Kamei's postwar reflection that it was Kobayashi Takiji's murder by the police on February 20, 1933, that provided the impetus for his "conversion" (*tenkō*) to Japanism. While the shock of Kobayashi's murder was certainly felt deeply by many intellectuals, especially those involved in the proletariat movement, there was a considerable lapse in time before Kamei's writings began to show any response to it. Certainly by the time of the dissolution of NALP in 1934, Kamei was already beginning to reveal some misgivings about the movement, as can be seen by his absence at the dissolution proceedings for NALP on February 22.

Between Kobayashi's murder and the dissolution of NALP, Kamei published a work that suggested the new direction in which he was already beginning to move. In a short essay of November 1933, "Return to the Homeland," Kamei notes that NALP faced two serious problems: the organization's policy concerning reform, and its failure to investigate the conditions of literary production that arose from the introduction of socialist realism. Kamei argues that while the former was urgent, the latter would require a good deal more time to solve, at least "two or three years until it can be completely and perfectly introduced into Japan, given concrete form and connected with the 'Japanese reality.'"[6] In the meantime, Kamei's prescription is simple, if a bit vague: "We must for the time being return to the homeland of our own flesh and blood. It will be best for us to consider the distant future and then to deliberate carefully on our own political strength and literary temperament."[7] Although "Return to the Homeland" is addressed to the members of the proletariat movement and seeks to address problems endemic to the movement, the article prefigures Kamei's later thought by raising the question of the relationships among politics, literature, and a "Japanese reality" separate from that of the West.

LITERATURE OF A PERIOD IN CHANGE

Nearly a year later Kamei returned to the problem of the relationship between politics and literature in greater depth in his first monograph, *Literature of a Period in Change* (*Tenkeiki no bungaku*). In this work, Kamei not only offers his reflections on and criticisms of the failure of the proletarian literary movement but also suggests the possibility of a new kind of subjectivity. This subjectivity stems from an awareness that beneath the rationality of theoretical discussions on literature is a broader concept of "humanity" that can never be fully encompassed by theoretical frameworks, which continually reemerges to betray all such musings. Even realism, which seeks to enlarge the view of humanity as depicted in psychological novels, is found lacking. Indeed, psychological novels first suggested the hope of expanding the reality of realism through a reinvestigation of "the ego in a period of change" (*tenkeiki no jiga*). Realism, especially as practiced by the advocates of the proletariat movement, has merely focused on changing the external world, while ignoring the fact that the subject of change is each individual author. For Kamei, a new period of change requires the displacement of "the image of the 'pure ego'" by "the consciousness of an active subject immersed in social upheaval." Kamei describes this displacement as drawing on the strengths of realism and psychologism in order to transcend them both.[8]

At the heart of Kamei's critique of realism is a critique of ideology as divorced from the reality of the individual. By "ideology," Kamei essentially means the Marxism understood and practiced by the leftist writers of his day. He likens ideological literature to "iron armor clamped on an emaciated physical body." He concedes the usefulness of this heavy armor during the earlier period of relatively stable capitalism, when class warfare was conducted in a "comparably peaceful manner" yet holds that in a period of change its stark contrast with the physical nature of mankind appears in high relief. As the metaphor of body armor seeks to establish it, ideology is merely a heavy, unwelcome burden, because it has misplaced the locus of the struggle from interiority to exteriority.

> Indeed, rebellion has been pushed further and further toward the outside as if down a single road. Slogans have been screamed louder and louder to the point of fantasy, even today ... but they have finally gone, leaving behind in our hearts an inevitable sense of agitation. Regardless of how crude they were, they may well have been the truth of their day. However, when I reflect on whether those who used slogans were ever able to accumulate with the same degree of alacrity any power of rebellion within their own interiority, any power of reform from the depths of the ego, as [they accumulated] resistance against their seemingly endless exteriority, I cannot but feel an extreme emptiness.

Kamei's criticism of the use of ideology by the leftist writers of his day rests on his displacement of the problems of politics to the problems of literature and mirrors his own move from the social world to the world of the individual.[9]

This choice in favor of the individual and the literary represented for Kamei the best available means of expressing a concept of subjectivity that was able to avoid the narrow restrictions imposed by a politics that threatened to eliminate subjectivity altogether. Reality as conceived and practiced by Kamei's former leftist colleagues was not only a "single road" but one that invariably led to a preordained "happy ending." Thus, Kamei writes that a true author must ask what the real reality [*jijitsu no riaru*] is:

> This sort of rhetorical question must be raised. Can one find even a single figure among Japanese leftist literature who is so filled with confusion (*konmei*) as to lose his own or his class's way? Have not all their endings been, in every sense, happy endings? ... If we can say that the failure to search for a psychology and a reality confused enough to make one lose one's way has brought about the easy adaptation of a type of idealistically given rational solution to the literary work, is that not indeed the drawback to leftist literature? Rather than easily given rational solutions, what is desirable is a deep confusion (*fukai konmei*) that offers no solution. The power to

move people without relying on a text is the image of this confusion. Moreover, is this not the only place where all the reality of a text can be established?

Consequently, Kamei calls for intellectuals and writers to discard their outdated notions of ideology and theory and to face alone the unmediated nature of this confusion. But he is quick to add that he does not intend to make confusion an ultimate ideal but is "merely trying to talk about the nature of what is called the reality of the literary work." To make confusion an ideal would deny its revolutionary power by fixing its meaning within the accepted epistemological order. Instead, the notion of the inexhaustible nature of the literary text provides the basis for a subjectivity (through the reader/writer of the text) that lies outside the previously conceived subject of politics.[10]

In developing this new approach to subjectivity, Kamei drew heavily from the works of Dostoevski, especially from *The Brothers Karamazov*. He believed that this work might hold the key to the problem that had most recently exercised his imagination: the possibility of forming a radically new, revolutionary ego. "What interests me most deeply in *The Brothers Karamazov*," he confesses, "is that, with the increasing power of resistance of the three brothers to the phenomenological existence near them, their rebellion against their very being deepened and became a process capable of forming a new, special ego through inner reflection." This "wonderful process," as he calls it, is essentially a move from rebellion against the external to rebellion against the internal, or the involution of criticism into the subject:

> The intersection of external rebellion and internal rebellion (reflection, the confessions of a passionate soul, illusions) is an endless intersection. Within this intersection the external object that is supposed to be resisted gradually loses its clarity and only then does the oppressive weight of self-rebellion [*jiko hangyaku*] appear, coiled around itself. At the same time, from the depths of this suffering, the ideal of salvation at last becomes real.[11]

Salvation is not a return to the transparent world of clarity and action, or to the clarity and action demanded by the political ideologies, but is guaranteed by the reality of confusion. Kamei finds it first in Dostoevski's discovery of a new ego as he attempts to address the historical problems facing Russian intellectuals in the late nineteenth century.[12]

Kamei believes that, to fully understand Dostoevski's works, one would have to read them in their historical and social context. While Dostoevski held the major problem of his day to be not unfettered rebellion against the external world, but the internal perception that makes rebellion possible, this ostensibly submissive posture was actually "a longing for a better life [by one who had already heard] ... the last words of civilization." One should bear in mind that the "rebellion" that Kamei finds in Dostoevski is not by any means a clear concept, but one that must constantly be placed within the context of "confusion." Dostoevski's self-rebellion is not identical with Kamei's ego but both are based on an attempt at an empirical understanding of their respective social and historical conditions and, thus, at a more complete realization of their own "confused" nature. In Kamei's case, this means that "the author's ego during a period of change ... is established by taking each layer of the historical spirit that in the end makes the ego itself possible and, literally, subjectively assimilating it as if each were the ego's own empirically felt psychological law." Kamei insists on placing the ego within its historical conditions, but only insofar as the ego replaces history as the locus of struggle.[13]

Kamei then raises the problem of "social doubt" (*shakai-teki kaigi*) as an intrinsic part of this empirical spirit. He finds its historical prototype in the Biblical story of Judas's betrayal of Jesus, a problem to which he returns later in his essay on Shestov. In a functional analysis, he argues that Judas's very existence depends on betraying his master: it is what calls our attention to him and is why he must be included in the narrative account of the Messiah. Kamei reads Judas as the "supplement" to the Messiah, arguing that "just as the disciples of Jesus flourish today, two thousand years later, throughout the world, so too do the disciples of Judas.... Had Judas not sold Jesus, would there be a halo around his head, too? No, it was at the very moment that he sold Jesus that he gained his halo." That is, Judas's selling of his master raised the question of whether Jesus might be seen no longer as Jesus the Messiah but as the perversion of Judas the Betrayer. The placement of excess trust in the Messiah by his disciples is pre-

cisely what produced his betrayal and the subsequent disappointment in him. For Japanese intellectuals living in a time of cultural
and political upheaval, the symbiotic relationship between betrayal and loyalty informs any decisive action and thus suggests
the limits of their own egos. Without any reliable basis for social
action, the ego specific to a period of change is a "deformed ego
that wanders in inaction."[14]

The problem of the ego in a period of change is expressed as a
problem of how to overcome the limits imposed on the ego by a
narrow concept of the social and the real. For Kamei, overcoming
these limits must be synonymous with preserving the reality of the
literary work, a reality that is more expansive, more confused, in a
word, more "real" than the reality of social realists or naturalist
writers. Privileging the literary is a means of rejecting praxis,
dialectics, and theory as possible ways of overcoming the stagnation of an ego that has been severely limited by social reality. An
integral part of the literary is an alternative concept of activity,
which Kamei asserts is already present in the ego's awareness of
its own limits. This awareness leads to a strong, active will of the
ego that differentiates it from other attempts merely to describe
the external world within literature, which, in the end, amount to
nothing but vulgar stories *about* the world.

Kamei takes up the question of the active will in a collection of
essays included in *Literature of a Period in Change* called "Willful
Passion in Literature."[15] Here he returns to the problem of the
relationship between politics and literature and insists on a closer
scrutiny of both. He attributes the failure of writers in Japan who
have attempted to write political literature to problems already
deeply rooted in the history of Soviet literature. While adopting
the political stance of Soviet writers, Japanese intellectuals such as
the proletariat writers also uncritically assimilated these problems.
However, Kamei finds two Soviet critics, Kirpotkin[16] and Gorkii,[17]
whose criticism of the lack of passion (*jōnetsu*) in realism offers a
means of solving the problem of Japan's own cultural demise.

In Kirpotkin's eyes, the majority of Soviet writers had a broad
political view, but their artistic materialism was impoverished,
forced, and overly rhetorical. In response to the problem of artistic
creativity, "[Kirpotkin] pointed out the pitfalls of the 'dialectical

materialist method' of production and pushed the special function of art to the forefront ... [and had much to say about] the descriptive world that had discarded the norms, that is, about the author's passion to describe."[18] Without a "passion to describe" (*egaku to iu jōnetsu*), the artist can avoid neither the deterioration of his art into mere reportage nor the loss of his ability to inspire others. Clearly, Kamei finds the young Soviet critic inspiring for the possibility he provides of reevaluating the conventional Marxist understanding of the relationship of base and superstructure. Already implicit is Kamei's desire not merely to reverse the hierarchical relationship between politics and culture but to sever it completely. Here one is left to wonder at Kamei's claim, in his extensive notes, that he has studied Marx's *German Ideology*.

Kamei finds it necessary to supplement Kirpotkin's analysis with that of Gorkii. Gorkii, he argues, is most interested in an author's "passion to experience" (*taiken suru jōnetsu*), which is what has been suppressed, or displaced, by those who see realism as nothing but technique.

> Realism in art—the attitude toward creativity that the artist should adhere closely to reality and seek an objective and truthful artistic expression of it—this spirit of realism as technique already includes within its very words that which protrudes from the domain of creative technique. That which protrudes is precisely what I mean by the passion to experience. Yet the majority of Japanese authors seem to be consciously working to prevent this passion from coming out.[19]

In a classical romantic argument, Kamei tries to suggest the recuperation of a "lost" reality that lies beyond the horizons of orthodox artistic techniques but is absolutely essential to a humanistically complete art. He is driven by more than a mere passion to describe, which he sees as fairly well rooted among contemporary Japanese writers. The need to describe the passion to experience informs much of *Literature of a Period in Change* and helps to account for its apparently ambivalent style.

Kamei insists that these two passions—two different approaches to the same reality—must be kept distinct and separate in order to avoid oversimplifying the conditions of literary pro-

duction. Although earlier critics sought to unify these two positions, Kamei argues that a belief that such a unity does justice to
each individual point of view is but an illusion.

> There is nothing that oversimplifies the problem more than the
> hasty conclusions of critics who insist on unity. Because one may
> neither carelessly substitute the language of logic for the problems
> of praxis nor evade the development of logic with the word
> "praxis," I think it best to see these two passions in perpetual
> rivalry.... I hope that they [Soviet realists] will not be able to offer
> any solution to the problem that everyone seems to want an-
> swered—"what is realism?"—simply because solutions derived
> from *theories* of art are frequently less solutions to realistic things
> and more often dreams about them.[20]

Here, Kamei is merely expanding his earlier argument that the
nature of reality is "in reality" much more one of confusion than
the reality represented by social theorists, proletariat writers, and
champions of literary realism. But he is also setting up the conceptual preconditions for a cultural specificity grounded in Japanese experience that can never be reduced to claims of universality
or even dialectics.

Even if the two passions of description and experience have
already been articulated in Soviet literature, they are yet to be
realized in Japan. Kamei complains that in Japan realism has
gained a good deal of attention while the passion to experience
has been neglected or, indeed, suppressed. By relating the passion
to experience with the conditions that prevent one from writing,
Kamei implies that the unsatisfactory state of contemporary Japanese literature is largely due to the failure of writers to grasp the
meaning of these conditions—yet he himself hardly spelled out
their meaning in clear terms. But he provides a glimpse of what
they are through his analysis of the superficial attempt by many
Japanese writers to avoid their fate of literary paralysis. According
to Kamei, many Japanese authors complain that with the advent of
socialist realism they find themselves unable to write:

> When this indignation on the part of authors that they cannot write
> was expressed through the allegation of the impotence of critics,
> there were many critics who were directly hit by the charge and
> reflected on "political criticism." Thereafter, criticism valorized

the freedom of the author and tried somehow or other to clear up the authors' doubts that they "cannot write" through an encouragement of penetrating everyday reality. *Already those who would mention politics have died out.* Thus, it only seems as though authors have regained their composure and are able to write.[21]

The solution Kamei prescribes for Japanese writers who wish to regain their willful passion is to confront their own doubts about writing and to begin to write from within their experiences of anxiety and doubt. Needless to say, among an author's experiences may be included those that can be called "political," but not in the sense of adherence to an external, ideological structure. Rather, Kamei redefines "politics" in terms of the everyday life experience of each individual writer.

In the final analysis, then, the focus of *Literature of a Period in Change* is not on the passion to describe or the passion to experience but on the interdependence of both and the willful passion [*ishi-teki jōnetsu*] that emerges from the refusal to sacrifice either. Willful passion then becomes the locus of a new subjectivity which, radiating from a new ego that embraces a world of contradictions, experiences each in itself without concern for any logical order or systematic reason. This Kamei calls the "real reality," a discarding of conceptual structures that have outlived their usefulness and no longer fit the reality they claim to represent. Implicit in this new reality is a messianic faith in a "Japanese reality" that is characterized by the ability to encompass a reality of confusion that has eluded Western forms of reality. Describing Tolstoy and Balzac as representatives of the passion to experience and the passion to describe, Kamei goes on to suggest their transcendence by such a Japanese reality. "Only the historical suffering of the Japanese reality, only its consciousness, can in the end be the hope for conquering them [Tolstoy and Balzac]."[22] Even though this argument claims to represent only a literary interest, it best reveals the political implications of Kamei's "willful passion." Yet Kamei insists that the politicality in which he is interested is not the politicality of factions and party affiliations but stems from a belief that the individual artist, as an artist, must never surrender the field of politics to the politicians.

Kamei's reconceptualization of politics in artistic terms is best

expressed in his essay "Political Desire as Artistic Temperament."[23] He draws on Hayashi Fusao's distinction between a
"revolutionist" and a "rebel" to argue that a sincere artist is
incapable of becoming a true "revolutionist" because art places
priority on the honest expression of emotion rather than on the
subjugation of the ego to ideological action.[24] Such an artist constantly struggles against the hegemonic definition of "ideological
action" by creating artistic works that are replete with confusion.
In short, for Kamei the artist is a rebel who appears on the cultural scene after the possibility for a true revolution has already
passed. Clearly he is indicating here his displeasure with the
success of the Meiji Restoration and the modern revolution it
brought to art and culture. Thus, he argues that the artist, by his
very presence in society, protests against the closure that the former revolutionists (now the political elite of the Japanese state)
seek to impose on the possibilities of action: "True activity—political desire as artistic temperament—will ultimately refuse to
recognize, along with Goethe and Heine, that which stabilizes
things."[25] Here we can see what Kamei means by his apparent
paradox that art must be separated from politics while at the same
time a true artist must experience a "political desire." He seeks to
describe a new kind of politics that would be located in artistic
production, especially in the production of certain kinds of literary
texts.

The form that artistic rebellion took for Kamei in subsequent
years is foreshadowed in *Literature of a Period in Change*, especially
in a short essay entitled "On Politics and Literature."[26] Here Kamei responds to Abe Tomoji's assertion that while the politics that
takes place in the conceptual games of intellectuals such as Kamei
may indeed be quite romantic, real politics is not at all a romantic
matter. As might be anticipated from the above reference to
Goethe and Heine, Kamei's response is that romanticism provides
a more realistic politics than Abe's "real politics" because it is
much more aware of the complex nature of "reality." Romantics,
he notes, are unlike the myopic realists in that "while surrounded
by reality, they look not only at reality but also at its possibility
and its future."[27] By the time *Literature of a Period in Change* was
written, Kamei already had found his answer to the problem of
politics in romanticism. By late 1934, Kamei was on intimate terms

with Yasuda Yojūrō and Hayashi Fusao and often referred to them in his writings. In the November announcement in *Cogito* of the soon-to-be-organized Japan Romantic School, Kamei's name was listed among the initial six members of the group. Only two months had passed since *Literature of a Period in Change* was published.

TOWARD A RETURN TO JAPAN

In March 1935 Kamei published an article in the inaugural issue of *Nihon rōmanha* called "Problems of the Romantic Ego."[28] Much of the argument in this article was foreshadowed in his earlier writings on the ego: the need to avoid all forms of reliance, the aversion to formal theory and logic, the rejection of realism and political literature, and the affirmation of the contradictory nature of the ego. Yet there are two salient characteristics of this essay that suggest the new direction Kamei was beginning to take. The first is his apparent need to redefine the problem as one of a "romantic" ego rather than one of an ego of a period in change. This move marks a shift in Kamei's thought from a focus on the solitary individual protesting against closure around social groups to his own participation as a member of a group with a shared purpose—the overthrow of literary forms contrary to its own tastes.

The second characteristic, a move toward a culturally defined collective subject, may be seen in Kamei's study of Lev Shestov's *Philosophy of Tragedy*. Shestov's book was introduced into Japan in 1934 through the publication of a translation by Kawakami Tetsutarō (1902–80) and Abe Rokurō (1904–57). The importance of the text for intellectuals in early Shōwa may be surmised from the translator's preface to the popular edition of 1936:

> Over a year has passed since *The Philosophy of Tragedy* first appeared in Japan. At first, we translators and publishers were quite anxious as to how the work of this eccentric thinker who was almost completely unknown in Japanese literary circles would be received.... But this haughty philosopher's voice captured the fascination of one after another of those who listened to him *until Shestov came to occupy almost a central position in the discussions of our literary circles in 1934....*
> What is the source of Shestov's almost unprecedented ability to

captivate? ... He was most acutely aware of the unreliability of the world view established by the rationalism that has dominated the West since the beginning of the modern age. His contribution was a radical rebellion against the reason that constitutes the basis of rationalism.[29]

Nearly every leading critic of the 1930s felt compelled to address the problems raised by Shestov's *Philosophy of Tragedy*; intellectuals as diverse as Kobayashi Hideo (1902–83), Tosaka Jun, and, of course, Kamei all wrote influential essays on Shestov during this time.

For many of them, the main interest was, contrary to Kawakami and Abe's assertion above, directly related to the dissolution of NALP, which had preceded the first edition of the Japanese translation by only one month. Although Kawakami and Abe argue in their preface that Shestov's real value transcends the problems of "anxiety" (*fuan*) and "despair" (*zetsubō*) (which were seen as hallmarks of his thought), their opinion was not widely shared. Around the middle of 1933 the problem of "anxiety" had surfaced as a serious challenge to writers who still adhered to the principles of activism (*kōdō-shugi*). Miki Kiyoshi's "Philosophy of Anxiety and Its Transcendence" ("Fuan no shisō to sono chōkoku") and Fujiwara Sadamu's "Literature of Anxiety" ("Fuan no bungaku") were but two attempts to respond to this challenge. However, Kobayashi Hideo's "Lev Shestov's *Philosophy of Tragedy*" ("Reo Shesutofu no *Higeki no tetsugaku*") best grasped the challenge to literary activism posed by Shestov's philosophy of tragedy. Kamei's own brief treatment of Shestov in "Problems of the Romantic Ego" is much indebted to Kobayashi's understanding of Shestov's anxiety as a means of refuting the Popular Front and the proponents of activism. But two months after the appearance of this essay, Kamei began the first installment of a longer, in-depth study of Shestov that reveals a serious concern with Shestov and the intellectual problems he raised.

This new attempt to transcend the anxieties of the ego is summed up in Kamei's article "The Living Judas (on Shestov)."[30] In the first installment, Kamei addresses the problem of the negation of God in Shestov's work. Drawing on Nietzsche's *Ecce Homo*, Kamei focuses on the question raised earlier concerning

Judas's betrayal of Jesus. Nietzsche, he argues, proved sin to be a necessary supplement to divinity through his paradoxical argument that only by taking all of the sin in the world upon oneself can one know what it means to be divine. Throughout history, Judas has represented the personification of all evil; Christians have projected evil onto him precisely because they were unwilling to recognize the Judas in themselves. Turning around the orthodox understanding by Christians of Jesus's admonition that those without sin should cast the first stone, Kamei seeks to indicate that, since Christians have been stoning Judas for nearly two thousand years, the divine authority of their Messiah guarantees that all of the world's sin be placed on Judas's shoulders. Ironically, however, Judas became a true martyr through his death, whereas all the good Christians, by their unwillingness to die like their god, have been reduced to followers, not of Christ, but of a "mundane morality" (*nichijōsei no dōtoku*). This, according to Kamei, is the real reason for the popularity of Christianity throughout the world.

Kamei does not raise the issue of Judas's betrayal of Jesus merely to answer theological questions. Rather, his interest in Shestov is in "an unusual soul that emerged during a reactionary period of Imperial Russia."[31] The relationship between Christianity and the power of the Russian state plays an integral part in Kamei's understanding of Shestov's negation of god. The Japanese, he argues, find it difficult to grasp the meaning of the blasphemy of Christ because

> when seen from the entirety of the Japanese religious life, Judas and Christ certainly do not summon much interest. But think of Imperial Russia! What the whole of Russian literature teaches us is how large an influence the close connection between Christianity and state power had on every aspect of everyday life. What does this mean, under these circumstances, to suddenly unfurl the banner of rebellion against Christ?[32]

Kamei's analysis of Shestov begins with an emphasis on the sociohistorical background against which Shestov formulated his philosophy. This was a transitional period, after the defeat of narodnik agrarianism by the capitalist means of production and before a Marxist critique had arisen. Shestov's despair is to be seen in this historical context. Kamei maintains that both Shestov's refusal to accept the validity of social protests based on concepts and the consequently irrational and ahistorical nature of his argument were not due to mental infirmity but stemmed from his conscious decision to reject all arguments for a viable future for mankind. Through his blasphemy of the idols of his contemporaries, Shestov inherited the legacy of Judas's betrayal of Jesus. But Kamei is troubled by two questions: why did Shestov not choose death? how could he, after rejecting all hope, dare to remain on this earth?

The secret to Shestov's ability to face life—to become a living Judas—is summed up in what Kamei calls "a positivity toward evil" (*aku e no sekkyokusei*). Evil, Shestov discovered, is merely the name modernity assigned to all that it had marginalized. The real target of Kamei's attack was the Meiji state, which, one might infer, made a pretext of preventing "evil" from reappearing, even claiming victory over evil under the rubric of "Civilization and Enlightenment." Thus, "evil" is merely what constitutes the most serious threat to the legitimacy and security of the new social order.[33] To Kamei, Shestov appears as a fundamentally "healthy man" (*kenkō na hito*). It would be a mistake, he argues, to confuse the anxiety of Shestov's philosophy with that of other, effete intellectuals who lack the power of social analysis or even of defiance against society. Shestov's anxiety was endowed with a healthy constitution that prevented him from dying *even while he claimed to prefer death*. This healthiness is most evident in what Kamei calls Shestov's "healthy will" (*kenkōtaru ishi*): "Although I argued in the first section of this essay that Shestov negated all social ideals of his time, that is really just the conclusion. His will was fundamentally healthy and his negation of ideals in no way stemmed from a lack of interest in ideals." In support of this view, Kamei points to Shestov's "cool disdain for the individual." He cites a passage from *The Philosophy of Tragedy* where Shestov argues that the duty of nature is not the protection and development of the individual but the perfection of the genus or the species. This is the same argument, he notes, as that of the materialists whom Shestov wrote *The Philosophy of Tragedy* to rebuff. Rather than explain this contradiction, Kamei simply asks, "Is it not his ability to deliberately bring to life one forceful element of this contradiction that proves that Shestov originally possessed a healthy will?"[34]

In the end, Shestov's decision to direct his criticism toward society, even while reluctant to do so, proved the "healthiness" of his philosophy. For the ability to produce a new principle with which to overcome social anxiety is located in "the confusion of one's own language and labor."[35] Kamei is disappointed in Shestov's "composed and meticulous style" but he notes that as long as one struggles with anxiety, there is still the possibility of receiving the gratitude of posterity. Ultimately, however, Shestov went too far and became a personification of anxiety, losing all hope of an eventual return to society. He became the most dangerous of all apostates: one who had emerged from the most powerful of revolutionaries.

Kamei begins the second installment of "The Living Judas" with the longest of the essay's five sections, one entitled "On Egoism" ("Jiga-shugi ni tsuite"). Here he investigates what led Shestov to disavow all forms of intellectual support and to make a clean cut with society. Citing a passage from Goethe's *Faust*, "The Dark Corridor," where Faust exclaims that to tremble with fear is mankind's highest virtue, Kamei begins to reveal what he means by "egoism": "What is egoism? *It is the extraordinary faith that, rejecting 'anything firm enough to give one's body a rest,' rejecting all laws, goodness, and ideals, dares to walk 'the unwalkable path where no one has ever walked before.'*"[36] Kamei describes this faith as a firm resolution, the reckless dream of one possessed by demons, and the consciousness of a genius. Rather than reduce his imagery to one consistent definition, Kamei, in keeping with his argument for the complex nature of reality, chooses to voice a litany of responses.

In order to grasp the nature of this faith, and especially in order to understand the role that faith plays in Kamei's later contribution to "overcoming modernity," it is necessary to supplement this imagery with the following: "Egoism is by no means the defense of those who would adhere to the limits of the self [which was Shestov's failure]; rather, it is the 'highest virtue of life,' which expands one's self and brings one's self into existence at the moment of the greatest crisis, which so many try to ignore and avoid: *it is nothing but a combative will!*"[37] Kamei's emphasis on the solitary and yet dispersed nature of the ego was not new. But through his reading of Shestov, he begins to describe the ego in language that confers on it a clearer sense of mission than it did in his earlier "ego of confusion." In short, this is a move from trembling (*senritsu*) to combat (*sentō*).

The object of combat begins to take shape toward the end of Kamei's lengthy study of Shestov. In the conclusion, Kamei relates an old legend concerning Thales, the father of philosophy, which he found in Shestov's work. The story tells how Thales, fixing his eyes on the secrets of the heavens, fell into a hole. A young Thracian girl who saw his plight laughed and, as the innocent laughter rang in his ears, Thales learned an important, if humbling, lesson: one must above all keep one's feet on the ground.

Kamei does not go so far as to say that Shestov has fallen into the same hole; rather, immediately after relating this story, he raises the question of the relationship of Shestov to the Japanese. He finds the problems of Shestov's time and the problems of contemporary Japanese to be quite different. But Shestov does offer the Japanese two lessons. First, concerning the attitude the Japanese should adopt toward the father of (Western) philosophy, Kamei notes, "we must make this young Thracian girl's laughter our own. We should laugh loudly. This is the main thing I learned from Shestov's fate." Second, in response to the challenge Shestov poses to those who would rely on ideals and hopes for the future, Kamei argues two points. He concedes the illusory nature of ideal worlds in general but adamantly maintains that "our own ideal world is certainly not meaningless: it originates from reality and is constantly being proved." Moreover, he argues, Shestov has confused praxis with theory: "Whether an ideal is fictitious is itself not a problem of theory but a problem of praxis. In the end, people will realize that there is no other way to demonstrate their own convictions than through praxis."[38] Kamei, in the end, sides with Kawakami's reading of Shestov, but not entirely. Kawakami locates Shestov's attack on modern thought in his strategy of always presenting the reader with a dilemma; Kamei locates it in Shestov's attempt to push the fight against modernity to its limits. Rather than join this Russian intellectual, who foresaw the end of modern Western thought, Kamei urges his fellow Japanese to inherit Shestov's "consciousness of adventure" and to overcome Shestov as well: "There is no other way to avoid Shestov than to become his accomplice and destroy him. Declarations that he can be defeated or that he cannot be defeated are all useless. We will never know if we do not take up the fight. And, at that point, the problem is no longer that of just Shestov, but of my attitude toward the reality of Japan."[39] Toward the end of his study, Kamei begins to reveal a new appraisal of Japan as a positive subject capable of overcoming Western thought. The study has shown Kamei the limits of relying on Western thinkers to solve problems that he sees as endemic to "the reality of Japan." The solution to these problems has to come from within the practice of Japanese culture.

Within a year, Kamei found the answer in a work by one of the masters of modern Japanese literature, Shimazaki Tōson. In October 1935 Tōson completed his tour de force, *Before the Dawn* (*Yoakemae*), which he began writing more than eight years earlier; in November he published the novel. The work, Tōson's longest and last completed one, is set in the Kiso Valley in central Japan (present-day Nagano Prefecture) during the turbulent Bakumatsu and early Meiji years. It is, of course, impossible to do justice to as rich and lengthy a work as *Before the Dawn* in so short a space. Nor is this my purpose. Rather, my main concern here is with how Kamei and his contemporaries understood the work within the historical conditions of the mid-1930s. The momentum of critical interest in *Before the Dawn* reached a peak in May 1936 when, only seven months after its publication, the literary journal *Bungakkai* published "A Symposium on *Before the Dawn*."[40] The symposium was attended by many leading critics and intellectuals, including Abe Tomoji (1903–73), Funabashi Seiichi (1904–76), Hayashi Fusao, Kawakami Tetsutarō, Kobayashi Hideo, Murayama Tomoyoshi (1901–77), Shimagi Kensaku (1903–45), and Takeda Rintarō (1904–46). All shared the belief that *Before the Dawn* represented Tōson's protest against the conditions of modern Japanese society. As such, it called for a reflection on the nature of the Meiji Restoration, which had denied the Japanese their own cultural identity within the modern world. Moreover, many credited the work with giving them a critical awareness of their own historical education, which had glossed over many of the negative aspects of the Restoration, especially the price at which it was achieved.[41]

Kamei reevaluated Tōson's work in light of the discussions at the symposium. In his "On *Before the Dawn*," which appeared only one month after the *Bungakkai* symposium, Kamei confesses his new, more positive evaluation of the novel:

> Immediately after the completion of the first half of *Before the Dawn* in 1932, I accepted the opinion of Kurahara [Korehito; i.e., that the work was a failure because it did not select a typical hero of Japanese history] in my criticism of this work, but I am now reconsidering.... Hanzō's family certainly was not an important factor in the Meiji Restoration ... but I believe that the discovery and artification [*geijutsuka*] of a locale, a family, and a personality that had been neglected by all others contributes to Tōson's glory as an author and has a high artistic value. In my own view, the description in literature of a typical character in typical circumstances is something that is determined by the author's discovery and creation and is definitely not merely the mimesis of what emerges as historical social reality.[42]

Thus, *Before the Dawn* represents an example of Kamei's increasing interest in a reality specific to literature, as well as a key to understanding his historical evaluation of the Meiji Restoration and the Japanese birth of modernity.

Before the Dawn may be summed up, Kamei argues, in one word—nature. From the opening line of the novel, "The whole of the Kiso road lies in the mountains," and throughout the work, Tōson intersperses his narrative with descriptions of the luxuriant forests and precipitous gorges that make up the Kiso region. As the Kiso road winds through this verdant growth, it symbolizes both Hanzō's ties to the past and his road to the future. On one level the Kiso road, stretching east to Tokyo and west to Kyoto, represents the major dilemma of Hanzō's time, the choice between East and West. The road offers, symbolically, a choice between a return to the imperial age of the Kyoto court and the politics of the *bakufu* at Edo, as well as a choice between the Eastern culture of Japan and the modernism of the West. As Hanzō wanders along the road between these two poles, the only thing that remains constant is the lush image of nature that surrounds him. But on another level, the road cuts through the chaos of nature and constantly leads Hanzō (and Tōson) back, in Kamei's words, to "the blood ties between his home town and his ancestors."[43] Thus, for Kamei the problem facing Japanese intellectuals is not actually a question of which historical view to adopt but how to realize Tōson's nature in an already thoroughly modern Japan.

What Kamei means by nature can be found in his reading of Motoori Norinaga's nativism as it appears in *Before the Dawn*. This nativism, he argues, is not a simple call for a return to the past but truly a "modern archaism." That is, Motoori's past is not identical with the past of history books and archives; rather, it signifies a "new past" that Motoori himself discovered or, better yet, created. It is an attempt to shed all vestiges of feudal political authority and "return" to the ancient beginning when nothing stood between the ruler and his people. In short, Motoori argues for the replacement of human institutions with nature; in order to accomplish this goal, he devised the notion of "gods" (*kami*). In opposition to the universal, transcendental God of Judeo-Christianity, these gods, Kamei holds, are specific to the cultural and social traditions of Japan: "They recognize that, after all, truth is relative. Yet, since deeper than the idea of truth there is in Japan the idea of the gods as constituting tradition, all must submit themselves to them." Even though the "age of the gods" created by Motoori to contest the intrusion of politics and institutions into the wholeness and rhythm of everyday life was conceived during the Tokugawa period, Kamei finds it even more timely in the modern society of early twentieth-century Japan. He urges his contemporaries to retrace Hanzō's steps along the Kiso road until they too find that "to return to ancient times means to return to nature. And to return to nature means to discover a new past."[44]

Kamei adds that Motoori's doctrine of a return to nature was not well understood by the ideologues of early Meiji Japan. By and large, these advocates of modernization either saw Motoori's thought in light of the political interpretation given it by the Restorationists (who then quickly abandoned it) or sided with a merchant interpretation, which also assisted in the rise of a modern bourgeoisie. In opposition to these two interpretations and, Kamei holds, closer to Motoori's original intent, is the "political-spiritual" interpretation given it by men such as Hanzō. Ironically, the last interpretation is the only one not to survive in post-Meiji Japan, as it was sacrificed during the transitional period immediately following the Restoration. In the narrative of *Before the Dawn*, the death of the "political-spiritual" interpretation of the Restoration is represented by Hanzō's increasing alienation from society, his resignation from his position in the Ministry of Religious Affairs, and his service as the head of a small, rural Shinto shrine. Kamei notes that this is Hanzō's happiest time, when he can devote himself entirely to self-purification and service to the gods (*itsuki no michi*). But when his term expires, he returns to his village only to discover that he no longer feels at home there. His ravings against his "invisible enemy" (which Kamei calls "civilization") earns him a madman's cell, where he ends his days in loneliness and madness, "the image of one who has completely lost his home town," a sacrificial victim to the forces of history.[45]

Kamei's conclusion to "On *Before the Dawn*" is a concise summary of why he is moved by this work as well as what relevance it has for the future of Japan. It is difficult to grasp the connection of *Before the Dawn* to Kamei's criticism of civilization without it. In the conclusion, Kamei suggests a coming, second dawn in Japanese history that, if the lessons from the first dawn have been learned well enough, might rectify the evils of modernity:

Japan has passed through its first dawn [the Meiji Restoration], and even while we still cannot yet say that it has been completed, Japan now faces the beginning of its second dawn. At this point, the question raised by Tōson is quite deep indeed. How can a real dawn be possible in present-day Japan? Tōson tried, through his exhaustive historical research and then through the tragic will that lived in that history, to sketch a new direction. We are quite moved by his efforts. But what will this new direction be like? What must the final words to *Before the Dawn* be? This is, of course, something that I am unable to say. But I can, I believe, offer the following:

While the present requires a new self-sacrifice, this sacrifice must progress beyond Hanzō's corpse. In other words, it is destined to become a faithful executor of Hanzō's last will and testament. But will this executor, like Hanzō, be satisfied merely with yearning to teach ideals in the face of what mercilessly frustrated them? Will it not, more likely, attempt revenge for modern capitalism's complete destruction of the pure will to "return to nature"? At such time, it will no longer abstractly brandish concepts like faith and will, but will proceed directly to a criticism of the very modern capitalism that destroyed it. Then, owing to this criticism, it will feel shame to be defeated again, like Hanzō, and will begin the battle that should deliver the final blow to the decadence of the modern age that mocked its defeat. Does not the glory of modern writers lie precisely in the insanity of such a struggle?[46]

This new self-sacrifice refers to the perceived need to readdress the unfinished business of the Meiji Restoration. Kamei believes that while the Meiji Restoration introduced a thoroughly modern way of life to the Japanese, transforming them from their feudal slumber to active participants in world politics, its effect on their spirit and culture have yet to be taken into full account.

The spiritual crisis left by the incomplete Meiji Restoration is the subject of a short essay Kamei wrote less than a year later, "The Future of Japaneseness."[47] In it he describes two results of the Restoration: the emergence of the masses in Japanese history and the "disorderly" state of culture. The meaning of the emergence of the masses, he argues, can only be determined through a thorough investigation of "Japaneseness." But not so the state of culture. For the source of the chaotic state of Japanese culture, one needs only to look at the introduction of foreign literature. While this is a perennial problem (Kamei recognizes the existence of foreign influences on Japanese culture as far back as the *Man'yōshū*), with the overwhelming interest in Western literature that followed the Restoration, Japanese intellectuals tried to develop a world-class literature based solely on Western models. It is high time, he argues, for Japanese to recognize this attempt as a mistake and to return to their own tradition as the basis for a Japanese world-class literature. The key to the success of both projects rests on how they are carried out within the context of the war on the Asian continent:

> I believe one can say that the focus of my interest in modernity is first and foremost related to the problem of the war. It is not an exaggeration to say that everything else emanates from it. For example, the special nature of Japanese ethnicity and the tradition of Japanese literature that recently have begun to be debated are, in the final analysis, heartfelt investigations into how best to overcome the crisis of the war (the crisis of Japan as a whole). Naturally, one may say that they originate from knowing and loving Japan and everything Japanese.[48]

Kamei's use of the words "the crisis of the war" should not be misconstrued as a form of protest against the war. Rather, he means to describe the war in broad terms as a spiritual crisis on which the Japanese have staked their culture and their blood, a crisis that they must successfully overcome if they are ever to realize their own cultural and spiritual independence from the West. In order to understand this independence, Kamei next attempts to clarify what is signified by "Japan and everything Japanese."

THE ETHICS OF ETHNICITY

By late 1937 Kamei's thought already had begun to show a clear and close relationship to the war effort. Events in the months following "The Future of Japaneseness" supported this tendency and contributed to the rise of Kamei's influence in intellectual circles. One such event was the establishment by the Konoe cabinet in October of the People's Spiritual Mobilization Movement (Kokumin Seishin Sōdōin Undō) as a branch of the National Mobilization Movement (Kokka Sōdōin Undō). Kamei's cooperation became especially valuable as General Araki Sadao began to expand the war effort into the realm of culture and literature in later years under the rubric of "the unity of mind and matter" in the construction of a New Order. On December 14, only two months after the people's spirit was officially mobilized, a large-scale repression and intimidation of intellectuals was carried out, which became known as the Popular Front Incident (*Jinmin sensen jiken*). In February 1938, this pogrom reached a new height with the arrest of more than four hundred intellectuals and university professors. At the same time, the dissolution of the Proletarian Party and the National Labor Union Council (Nihon Rōdō Kumiai Zenkoku Hyōgikai) signaled a radical tightening of the bounds of permissible discourse. Kamei was not in the least adversely affected by these developments. But the turn of events did help in his decision to redirect his analysis on the ego from the subject of action to the possibility of a collective subject represented by Japanese ethnicity.

The meaning of Kamei's move can be gleaned from an article he wrote on Shimazaki Tōson in 1939 called "Thoughts on Wandering."[49] In this essay he asserts that the whole of Tōson's oeuvre can be summed up in Hagiwara Sakutarō's concept of the wanderer (*hyōhakusha*). He returns to the problem he raised earlier of Tōson's failure to synthesize the Western tradition of "the wanderer" with the Japanese tradition of "*tabibito*" as expressed by

Matsuo Bashō (1644–94) and others. The solution can only be found, he concludes, in the war, which not only offers a way out for each individual modern wanderer but also holds out the promise of rebirth through the destruction of the existing order of things.

> The will to separate oneself from all of the past and to volunteer for the crisis of death is a sad and touching business bestowed only on human beings. At the border between life and death there is a pure, chaotic life. It is the long river of life, filled with screams, courage, and wild dreams, whose source and mouth cannot be known. There is no more noble an ordeal than to entrust oneself to it and to gain inspiration from the inconstancy [*mujō*] implicit in the defiance of death. This is also the place where the idea that life is a journey is violently forged. All existing principles must die once.[50]

"Wandering" here means not merely the adventurous spirit of a traveler on a bright, sunny day but also the thrill Kamei conjures out of the dangers of a long and arduous trip like that of Bashō on dark, rainy days as well. The Japanese must become such courageous, wandering soldiers, he argues, because "while the Black Ships that represented the material might of the West have left, a hundred years later the Black Ships of thought are still threatening us."[51] From 1939 until the end of the war, and especially during the 1942 debates on overcoming modernity, Kamei was increasingly haunted by the Black Ships of thought.

In October 1940, the Imperial Rule Assistance Association (Taisei Yokusankai) was organized as the nucleus of the Konoe cabinet's "New Structure Movement" (Shin Taisei Undō). In the same year, Kamei traveled to the ancient capital of Nara, where he indulged a recently acquired interest in Buddhism, and particularly in Shinran (1173–1262). His new interest in this religion culminated in the publication in June 1942 of *On Faith*, a collection of essays Kamei had written in 1941–42.[52] Through his study of Buddhism, Kamei was able to clarify the role nature played in his critique of modernity. Nature, he argues, is more than a pristine, preindustrial space; it constitutes the common denominator of all life, shared equally by all classes of Japanese, if not all races: "What we Japanese have provisionally called nature—that which is shared equally by sage and layman alike and which embodies constancy, the creative power of the origin that absorbs all and forsakes none—this is the first principle of all things. Even our own lives did not originate with us but were given to us by this first principle."[53] As the underlying principle for a new collective subjectivity, nature thus displaces the individual as the source of life while suggesting that individual judgment also must be suspended in favor of an intuitive, collective harmony with the pulse of life.

Kamei sees individuals as totally helpless in the face of nature to alter their own fate by either relying on their own initiative or praying for help from the gods. Specifically, Kamei notes his disagreement with Shinran's doctrine of reliance on "outside help" (*tariki*) for the salvation of the individual, arguing that ultimately it too is just another folly of the modern ego:

> From the point of view of pure faith, there is no self-help [*jiriki*] or outside help [*tariki*]. Rather, at its core is a self-awareness of, and conversion to, the immortal soul [*hosshin*], which is already present within self-help. This immortal soul is nothing but the self-evident truth that no one can escape from nature. Thus, if we stretch to the limit the meaning of the prayers to this immortal soul, then we can say that all faith is oriented toward outside help. Humans are far stronger when they rely on outside help than when they rely on self-help. This is because they lose their own insignificant egos and only nature-life [*shizen-seimei*] is revealed.[54]

Although Kamei never defines precisely what he means by nature-life, it is at least clear that it does not refer to the biological life of the individual. He rejects the importance of the individual's life, noting that "what has recently come to interest me more than anything else is the forceful dissolution of the ego. I believe that this is directly related to the rebirth of our ethnicity. It is not a question of how we should live; it is a question of *how we should die*."[55] Needless to say, Kamei is not suggesting the death of the Japanese people as a whole. Rather, his argument is for the return of each individual through his or her own death to the source of life, nature, as experienced in the eternal Japanese ethnic group.

This rediscovery of nature also suggested an answer to the question of ethical action, which had concerned Kamei since his youth. Although he first tried to attack the evils of civilization through an appeal to morality and the good, his disillusion with proletariat literature and his discovery of Shestov's *Philosophy of Tragedy* ultimately led him to a consideration of evil as an alternative foundation for ethical action. Through his study of Shinran, however, he concludes that both good and evil are equally insufficient as guidelines for morally correct behavior.

> If "I" decide to do some good deed, that good immediately becomes artificial in nature. Artificial things are made to be seen by others. The nonredemptive nature of action is lost. But again, if I intentionally do evil deeds thinking that evil is not to be feared, that too, along with artificial good, becomes a kind of vainglory. While the vainglory of evil is even more enticing than the vainglory of good, to the extent that it sways the good sense and discretion of others, the difference is really insignificant. No evil can measure up to the all embracing nature-life force (*shizen-seimei ryoku*). Thus, it is best not to discriminate between good and evil but silently to place all one's trust in what comes from the heavens.[56]

Abandoning the idea of individual ethical action, whether based on notions of good or notions of evil, Kamei is left with the nature-life force as realized in the Japanese ethnic group as the object of historical action. As a consequence, his use of faith to criticize modern civilization converges with the ideology of the Japanese state.

The significance of Kamei's new emphasis on ethnicity stems from the historical circumstances of early Shōwa Japan. He does not turn to faith merely to escape from historical problems, but in order to discover a more appropriate response to them. What characterized his interest in faith from as early as his initial studies of the ego and *Before the Dawn* was a growing confidence that he had at last found the way out of the confusion and chaos of modern life. His study of faith ultimately leads him to the concept of individual self-abandonment (*sutemi; shashin*) as the solution to this chaos:

> For the past year or two my chief concerns have all dealt with the problem of faith.... Education, knowledge, learning, and information about current affairs seem to me incapable of offering quietude and peace of mind. In order to escape from the confusion we have suffered during the hundred years since Meiji, it is only necessary

hereafter to rid ourselves of the spirit of private existence: that is, to die and be reborn, to rise from the dead and be resurrected. Not for the purpose of protecting ourselves from the chaos of these hundred years; rather, in order to gain the best possible remedy by abandoning ourselves [*sutemi*] to this chaos and knowing precisely what all the symptoms of this disease are. Sometimes it is necessary to dilute the poison of civilization with poison.[57]

This passage implies, in addition to an encouragement to volunteer for the imperial army, that there is no hope of overcoming the chaos of civilization while clinging to one's own individual life. The chaos of the West can only be overcome through the solidarity offered by Japanese ethnicity.

Kamei's interest in the Pacific War as the historical manifestation of the endemic faith of the Japanese people appears in his essay "Crisis and the Search for Faith."[58] In this essay, more than ever, Kamei makes explicit the relationship in his thought between Japan's historical crisis and his interest in faith. Japan, he argues, is both cursed and blessed by its geographical location. In ways reminiscent of Watsuji Tetsurō's *A Climate*, Kamei seeks to depict Japan in a precarious geographical location, between the "world's largest continent" and "the world's largest ocean." It is Japan's historic role to serve as a knot (*musubime*) tying the world together that gave rise to an identification of Japan with the mythical creator-god (*musubi-no-kami*).[59] As the creator-god, Japan represents the only world power capable of transcending the limitations of both East and West through an inspired eclecticism. Kamei sees this eclecticism at the heart of the Pacific War, a war fought like none before with modern technology and weaponry. Thus, his statement that "the war replicates our classics"[60] can only mean the perceived necessity of drawing on both the evils of modernity and the moral energy of Japanese tradition to preserve Japanese ethnicity in the present. But since Kamei believes that this eclecticism will eventually exclude any form of modernity, he increasingly intones the cry of "overcoming modernity."

On June 18, 1942, in the same month that Kamei published *On Faith*, the Japan Literary Patriotic Society (Nihon Bungaku Hōkokukai) held its first public meeting. In its organizational meeting held nearly a month earlier on May 26, Kamei was named the group's secretary for criticism and essays. The purpose of the organization was to create a central forum for writers to assist in the war effort by disseminating the state's propaganda and ideology. Perhaps more than anything else, what best reveals the nature and significance of this organization is the fact that the society was addressed at its opening meeting by Premier Tōjō Hideki, Director of Intelligence Tani Masayuki, and Minister of Education Hashida Kunihiko. While one could also argue that the participation of these high-level officials put extreme pressure on all writers to join regardless of their own political stances, it is hard to argue along the same lines that Kamei was therefore compelled to accept one of the most prominent positions of the society. On the contrary, his position within this ideological organization was anything but coerced and was merely a logical extension of his hopes for a "Japanese rebirth" to be accomplished through the war.

One month later, Kamei expounded the themes of *On Faith* in the debates on overcoming modernity. He emphasized that the war against Anglo-American forces was also a war against the insidious effects of modern civilization on the Japanese spirit. But he also had strong words for those who would simplify the struggle against modernity: "I have often seen the following sort of thing passed off as intellectual warfare. The good guy, 'Japanese Spirit,' and the bad guy, 'Foreign Thought,' exchange insults and begin to fight. Then, lo and behold, just like toppling a doll, the good guy knocks down the bad guy and basks in applause. It really seems as though people's minds have been completely taken over by this sort of childish drama."[61] The longing for an easy victory, fueled by early reports of Japan's military successes, was attributed to the egoism of modern man. Rather than repeat Kamei's views on egoism here, suffice it to note that his dissatisfaction with these attacks on foreign thought stemmed from his desire to replace the ego as the subject of history and did not imply any significant degree of tolerance for "foreign thought."

Kamei maintained his belief in overcoming modernity beyond the debates and down to the end of the war. Supported by a negative evaluation of Western civilization, he was able to sustain his belief in Japanese tradition even while military defeat became more and more a certainty in the years following the debates. He increasingly turned for consolation to Buddhism and ancient Japanese history, as evident in his 1943 study *Records of the Landscape of Japanese Ancient Temples* (*Yamato koji fūbutsu shi*). Nevertheless, Japan's final military defeat and the end of the war came as a deep shock to him and, immediately on hearing the news of surrender, he reportedly went out with Hayashi Fusao and Kobayashi Hideo and got quite drunk.[62] After the war he proved himself one of Japan's most durable intellectuals with his second "conversion" (*tenkō*), which claimed to disavow all his previous connections with the Japanese state.

In retrospect, it seems that this was hardly a conversion for Kamei, who had already begun a redefinition of political action as early as 1934. While he certainly cooperated with the state during the war and accepted positions of authority within it, his own interests lay primarily in formulating the basis for a Japanese subjectivity in contradistinction to that of the West. This interest continued into the postwar years through such works as *The Ideal Image of Twentieth-Century Japan* (*Nijisseiki Nihon no risōzō*) and *Studies in the Spirit of the Japanese* (*Nihon no seishinshi kenkyū*), the latter receiving the Kikuchi Kan Prize in 1965 and contributing to Kamei's brief postwar resurgence in popularity. While in the end Kamei may have failed to overcome modernity, his attempt to establish a Japanese subjectivity through cultural practice is still being carried out today by others, especially under the rubric of "what it means to be a Japanese" (*Nihonjinron*).

5

The Production of a Culture
of the Same

> There was a common struggle for a common stake, German
> unity, the only progressive ideal evolved by the early Op-
> position. Our defeat is perhaps a blessing.... As brothers in
> arms we should have fought loyally at each other's side, we
> should have been firmly united in battle, even in the hour
> of victory ... but the next morning irreconcilable differ-
> ences would have appeared which could only be settled
> by the *ultima ratio popularum*, that is, the foreign decapitat-
> ing machine.
>
> Heinrich Heine, *Ludwig Börne*

The three years from 1932 to 1935 marked a short period of intense
activity in Japanese intellectual history known as "the period of
cultural renaissance" (*bungei fukkō ki*). Although explicit discussions of a cultural renaissance gained an ascendancy during these
years, the problem of culture itself, especially the deeply felt need
for a reexamination of the status of culture in modern Japan, was a
strong and constant undercurrent throughout the prewar years
and may be traced to the form of culturalism (*kyōyō-shugi*) prevalent during the Taishō period. As the cultural renaissance took
shape in the early 1930s, however, it was formulated within, and
ultimately against, the leading Marxist organizations that were
active in early Shōwa years. Thus, any serious analysis of the
origins of the cultural renaissance must first address a host of
related issues, including the dissolution of the All-Japan Federation of Proletarian Arts (NAPF), the problem of "ideological conversion" (*tenkō*), the relationship of politics to art, and the rise of
romanticism in Japan during the early 1930s.

The term "cultural renaissance" was first coined by Hayashi
Fusao in an attempt to describe his reasons for certain misgivings
with the direction taken by the leadership of NAPF.[1] The leaders

of NAPF, Kobayashi Takiji (1903–33) and Miyamoto Kenji (b. 1908), had begun a lengthy series of debates in 1929 on "the value of politics and the value of art." Ultimately, they successfully established as the organization's position their own view that art was to be completely subordinated to politics, in spite of the objections of Hayashi and others who had argued for a broader view of literary production.[2] Hayashi, in particular, foresaw that the subordination of art to politics was not merely a theoretical issue concerning the relationship of superstructure to base but was also designed to bring the Japanese proletarian movement to the position adopted by the Comintern and, eventually, with the foreign policies of the Soviet Union. In attempting to reassert the value of literary practice in the face of the proletarian movement's denunciation of it as "apolitical," Hayashi was attacking the federation's Achilles' heel. Raising the issue of culture in the context of the internationalization of the proletarian movement, he implied not only that the leaders of the movement were less than patriotic but also that a more radical program of change could best be found elsewhere. This led him to conclude that meaningful change could only be carried out through a cultural renaissance that would eventually restore ancient Japanese culture.

Hayashi began to articulate this concept in a series of articles published between May and September of 1932. The first, "For the Author," is a stinging rebuttal of the widespread belief within NAPF that literature, apolitical by nature, ought merely to reflect external political reality.[3] Hayashi argues that what is of paramount importance is "the completion of the internal world of the author." This world is not an interiority that remains free from the political. Instead, it signifies a place where the author "completes a new world within himself," where the concerns of politics and literature are synthesized. Hayashi insists that it is the duty of literary theory to raise the consciousness of the author until he becomes an "aware individual" (*jikakujin*) who "can penetrate like rays of sunlight into mysterious aspects of reality that scholars, politicians and journalists cannot see even when they try, which they are quite content to overlook." The establishment of the author's internal world—a world of political literature and literary politics—breaks the bounds of all previous history, what Hayashi describes as the "prehistoric period of humanity," and "ushers in a true history and life ... by recuperating a political consciousness that has been lost."[4]

Here we find a clue to the meaning of Hayashi's break from the proletarian movement and his subsequent "ideological conversion" to Japanism. It is not coincidental that Hayashi's own *tenkō* is supposed to have occurred in 1932, the same year when he penned "For the Author." This article suggests that the problem of *tenkō*, at least in Hayashi's case, is not best conceived as a set of objective procedures or steps that lead from Marxism to nationalism, but rather in terms of the creation of something recent critics have called the "subject-work."[5] This concept has been developed recently by Philippe Lacoue-Labarthe and Jean-Luc Nancy to describe the romantic subject's auto-production in the literary work.[6] For Hayashi, although the author is excluded from the proletarian theory of literature, he is both the source and object of artistic production. As the author of a work on the author, Hayashi himself is caught up in a self-conscious turn from the production of goods for society to the production of the self for the self, thus implying that society can be fundamentally altered by restoring a logic of self-sufficiency.[7]

The force of auto-production was defeated in the early years of the Meiji period when, Hayashi observes, bourgeois realism gave up its defense of traditional realism (identified with Ihara Saikaku [1642–93]) in the face of the wholesale importation of foreign literature and accommodated itself to the bureaucratic politics of Yamagata Aritomo (1838–1922) and Katsura Tarō (1847–1913). Following Naturalism's surrender to bureaucratic politics, a half-hearted attempt was made by the "aristocrats" of the Shirakabaha (a group of writers associated with the *Shirakaba,* or "white birch," journal) against the new order but they failed, according to Hayashi, because their own elite class consciousness precluded any unification with the proletarian masses. Consequently, for Hayashi, the bourgeoisie had ceded its role as the promoter of culture to the proletariat. But this analysis, with its use of Marxist terminology, obfuscates rather than clarifies what Hayashi expected from the "proletarian" movement. By displacing the question of production from a consideration of social needs and utility, Hayashi does not, in spite of such terminology, remain true to a Marxist analysis of class conflict. Instead, "proletarian" begins to signify the idealized locus of a social essence; it marks a shift from a society composed of competing political interests to one in which a single interest represents a harmonious whole. This "proletariat," the common masses of Japan, who are largely untouched by the culture of the Other, will set in motion and sustain a process of auto-production: the cultural renaissance will come about through the same producing the same.[8]

In anticipating this cultural rebirth, Hayashi still adhered in 1932 to a belief in future progress. He located this belief in a highly eccentric understanding of Marx. To Hayashi, all great thinkers, Marx included, were either representatives of their age or prophets of the future. By overlooking Marx's deep involvement in the social conditions of his time and his penetrating analysis of his contemporary society, Hayashi was able to discard everything that did not coincide with his own interest in Marx as a prophet of the future. Thus, one must be careful in attributing statements such as the following to a Marxist ideology:

> What I want to make loud and clear is a challenge to the entirety of the writing of Japanese civil literature, not just the kind of reform of writing that emphasized popularization [*tsūzokuka*], as has been done up to the present. That is, I want to see our writers commit themselves to the same type of undertaking as that of Yamada Bimyō and Hasegawa Futabatei [Shimei] who, representing industrial-capitalist culture, succeeded in challenging and defeating the culture of the townspeople of the Tokugawa period.[9]

Language such as "industrial-capitalist culture" is loaded with specific connotations and implications, many of which Hayashi seems happy to ignore. What he means by this phrase may be determined to some extent by his comments a few lines later in the passage:

> The class that they [Yamada Bimyō and Futabatei Shimei] represented was the industrial bourgeoisie, which the Meiji Restoration had gradually brought to the forefront of society. Readers will probably find much too much of the West in these two, especially in Yamada at certain times. Indeed, an undigested West. This will then reveal that the class that they represented was already by that time the "much-too-much Western," the unavoidably Western, industrial bourgeoisie. What they brushed aside was the townspeople literature of the Tokugawa period.[10]

The "same type of undertaking" that Hayashi wants from his contemporaries is not the same unadulterated adoration of the West to which Yamada and Futabatei allegedly were obligated by their own historical conditions. Hayashi wants to see his contemporaries in intellectual and literary positions of influence commit themselves to an identical *type* of undertaking, a Shōwa Restoration, which will this time represent the common masses (the descendants of the Tokugawa townspeople) and expunge the baneful influence of the West. By employing such Marxist terms as *class* and *bourgeoisie*, Hayashi seeks to predict the historically inevitable triumph of Japanese culture over Western utilitarianism and thus to inaugurate a cultural renaissance.

The vehicle for this renaissance was the journal *Literary World* (*Bungakkai*), which was founded by Hayashi, Kobayashi Hideo, and Takeda Rintarō (1904–46) and published by the Institute for Cultural Review (Bunka Kōronsha) in October 1933.[11] The new journal created a sensation in intellectual circles at the time and, as the issues began to be widely discussed, other voices joined with Hayashi in defining the nature of the renaissance. Beginning with a 1933 conference, "A Colloquium on the Cultural Renaissance," led by Kikuchi Kan (1888–1948), a long list of articles on the subject by leading intellectuals appeared, including essays by Aono Suekichi (1890–1961), Hayashi Tatsuo (1896–1984), Hirotsu Kazuo (1891–1968), Takeda Rintarō, Tanigawa Tetsuzō (b. 1895), Togaeri Hajime (1914–63), Yamamoto Sanehiko (1885–1952), and Yasuda Yojūrō. A second conference was held in July 1934, entitled "The Essence of the Cultural Renaissance," and was headed by Nakamura Murao (1886–1949). Few of these intellectuals were sanguine about Hayashi's interpretation of the renaissance, and most adopted a wait-and-see attitude toward it. Even fewer yet, however, condemned the renewed interest in culture outright. Most were content to recognize the success of the cultural renaissance in restoring art to a prominent place in intellectual discourse and to redefine their own work in relation to it.[12]

It was, perhaps, Yokomitsu Riichi's essay, "A Theory of the Pure Novel," that provided the most theoretical power to the cultural renaissance. Yokomitsu does not share Hayashi's rejection of "popularization" (*tsūzokuka*) but seeks through his concept of the "pure novel" (*junsui shōsetsu*) to reconcile the populists with those who still adhere to the elite culture of "pure literature" (*jun bungaku*). He writes in the opening lines, "If there is something that can be called a 'cultural renaissance,' I now believe it totally impossible to achieve through any means other than the popular novel within pure literature." What Yokomitsu hopes to accomplish through the synthesis of the two major divisions within Japanese literary theory in the 1930s is the unification of all Japanese intellectuals around a single position as a precondition to the cultural renaissance. He writes that "if this pure novel does not come forth from Japan as a Japanese product, then we writers should give up writing."[13]

This new, unifying position is promised by the concept of an ethnic people (*minzoku*), a conclusion which Yokomitsu arrives at by reflecting on Japanese historical conditions. Yokomitsu argues that because the Japanese are different from Europeans, European rationality is not compatible with Asian sentiments. Yet Yokomitsu read widely from European writers in reaching this conclusion and, ironically, it was the work of the French author André Gide (1869–1951) that was most instrumental in his theoretical development. Specifically, it was Gide's investigations into self-consciousness and the liberation of the ego that led Yokomitsu to his concept of a grammatical "fourth person," which he describes as "the self viewing the self" (*jibun o miru jibun*).[14] The "fourth person" not only avoids the narrow individualism of the first person of realist novels but opens the possibility of a cultural renaissance by suggesting a new way of writing that conforms with Japan's "specificity" (*tokushusei*). By invoking closure around Japanese ethnicity, Yokomitsu believes that the cultural renaissance will achieve an elusive goal—the unification of the proletarian writers with the *Literary World* and other such "apolitical" writers. "I believe the moment has finally arrived," he writes, "to think about ethnicity that up until now has mostly been overlooked."[15]

Yokomitsu's invocation of ethnicity was answered by Kobayashi Hideo in his seminal essay, "On the I-Novel." This essay, more than any other work, influenced the direction of the cultural renaissance.[16] For Kobayashi, the I-novel is neither an accidental development in Japanese literary history nor a transparently Western phenomenon. Rather, it reveals a fundamental problem in modern Japanese culture. Although Kobayashi traces the origins of the I-novel to Rousseau's *Confessions*, it only appeared in Japan, he argues, in the modern civil society of the Meiji period, when the Naturalist writers imported it from the West. What they failed to understand, he continues, is that "the extraneous circumstances that gave birth to the I-novel in the West were completely lacking in our own country."[17] Moreover, these extraneous circumstances can only be known within the context of the relationship of the "I" and society.

Kobayashi argues that the reason for the growing dissatisfaction among consumers of Japanese literature with the I-novel may be found in the cultural differences between Japan and the West. Attempts like that of Yokomitsu merely to replace the I-novel with a "pure novel" are bound to fail until Japanese intellectuals understand that Gide and Marcel Proust (1871–1922), unlike Tayama Katai (1872–1930) and the Meiji Naturalists who imported the I-novel, lived in a Western culture where the "I" was already a "socialized I" (*shakaika shita watakushi*).[18] Thus, whereas for Gide, the I-novel provided an opportunity to investigate the "problems of the I," for the Japanese it remains little more than a celebration of literary techniques or "the forms of the I." It is possible that Kobayashi drew this concept of the "socialized I" from Marx's argument in his *Critique of Hegel's Philosophy of Right* that the bourgeois state, based on private property and its separation of *citoyen* and *homme* (à la Rousseau), could finally be overcome by a return to "socialized man."[19] But Kobayashi remains a staunch critic of all "isms," including Marxism, and nowhere more so than in "On the I-Novel."[20] Rather, his use of the "socialized I" in the context of the cultural renaissance signifies that the displacement of the political subject by an individual (*kojin*) ultimately is realized only through a tentative reidentification of the individual with society.

Although a critic of Marxism, Kobayashi concedes that it has, for the first time in Japanese intellectual history, introduced a philosophy from the West, rather than mere techniques. In doing so, he argues, it killed all attempts to resuscitate the I-novel in terms of Japanese everyday life by its replacement of the idea of an everyday life with the concept of "historicity." However, Marxism failed as a literary method, he notes, since its unrelenting insistence on the Marxist perspective refused to recognize other views. In contrast, "the great I-novels in our country express the plain face of the individual. What they [Marxists] have erased is this face."[21] Yet, even though Kobayashi rejects Marxism for its limited perspective, he also recognizes the failure of Gide's I-novel (and by extension, Yokomitsu's "pure novel") to adopt any point of view.

In the end, Kobayashi calls for a "new arena" in which the discourse on culture can be carried out in terms of a "social tradition" (*shakai-teki dentō*). But he seeks to prevent this tradition from absolute closure around a specific position by arguing for a concept that incorporates a multiplicity of individual perspectives without favoring any one. This kind of tradition can only be realized by constantly deferring any fixed definition of the self from which one can metonymically construct a similar definition of society. Instead, Kobayashi suggests a dialectic relationship between self and society in which they are mutually defining and therefore never fully disclosed. By positing what he calls a "mysterious" social tradition, Kobayashi hopes to displace the current argument over whether a return to tradition is desirable by simply suggesting that it is beyond one's power to understand the whole of which one is, after all, merely a part. What is more important, at any rate, is that "if an author's material lives within a social tradition, the author will win the sympathy of his readers without even attempting to do so."[22] In this new arena, contradictions between production and consumption, along with the conflict between self and Other, will give way to a culture in which the "I" will have been completely displaced. But Kobayashi leaves open the question of how this new culture is to be produced. Although he makes it clear that he does not believe that Japanese writers can return to the I-novel, or resort to Yokomitsu's "pure novel," as an expressive measure of a cultural renaissance, he intimates that certain private Japanese experiences may have survived Marxist ideology in the social tradition.

In light of Kobayashi's analysis, the subsequent direction of the cultural renaissance was fundamentally altered.[23] By situating identity in a social tradition that resists the model of society derived from Western theories, Kobayashi effectively shifted the axis of the discourse away from critics such as Aono Suekichi and Hayashi Tatsuo, who had tried to interpret culture in universalist terms. For Hayashi Fusao, this emphasis on social tradition not only validated his focus on auto-production as the function of culture, but it also made it all the more necessary to identify the historical forces that had displaced this cultural principle in the early Meiji years. After Kobayashi's essay, it was increasingly clear to many that the discourse on the cultural renaissance had to discard momentarily the language of literary production in favor of a broader, historical analysis of the origins of the loss of culture.

THE IDEALS OF HISTORY

In 1931, while serving time in prison as a suspected communist collaborator, Hayashi began a study of the Meiji Restoration that culminated eight years later in a lengthy work of historical fiction, *Youth* (*Seinen*). Although he first began publishing *Youth* in serial form in *The Central Review* (*Chūō kōron*, August 1932–September 1933), the entire work, encompassing both the first half, "Youth," and the second half, "Manhood" ("Sōnen"), was not completed until 1939. Throughout this period, Hayashi focused his study on the role of the Chōshū domain in the Restoration, and in particular on its role in the Battle of Shimonoseki, as a key to understanding the failure of Japanese culture to survive in vibrant form in modern society. Chōshū had played a pivotal role in the Restoration, and the policy debates within the domain between the younger and older samurai factions provided Hayashi with a key interpretive strategy for understanding why culture in post-Meiji Japan had lost out to the politics of internationalization. *Youth* represented, then, not only a work of literary value but, through its attempt to rewrite history, an ideological tract as well.

One of the first questions the text presents to its readers is that of form. Why did Hayashi choose to encode his history in a work of fiction, and particularly in a historical novel? Although it is difficult to answer this question fully, it is at least clear that by 1935, when Hayashi published his *A Romanticist's Handbook*, he had formed a romantic view of literature as constitutive of history. "Literature," he writes, "creates the character of the next historical period."[24] By thus subordinating history to literature, Hayashi reveals a prejudice common to romantics: literature is seen not merely as a signifying practice, as one genre among many; rather, it is seen as the privileged site of production in general. It becomes what Lacoue-Labarthe and Nancy call "the literary absolute," which is the result of a thought process that is ultimately

> less concerned with the production of literary things than with *production*, absolutely speaking. Romantic poetry sets out to penetrate the essence of poiesy, in which the literary thing produces the truth of production in itself, and thus ... the truth of the production *of itself*, of autopoiesy. And if it is true ... that auto-production constitutes the ultimate instance and closure of the speculative absolute, then Romantic thought involves not only the absolute of literature, but literature as the absolute. Romanticism is the inauguration of the *literary absolute*.[25]

As a historical novel dealing with the birth moment of modern Japanese society and culture, *Youth* is, by these standards, a romantic work. In it, Hayashi accepts the closure of the speculative absolute but only to the extent that it can be transformed into a new principle of production. In order to do so, however, it is first necessary to turn the tables on established history, which covered up its own fictitiousness by presenting an alternative view of history as fiction. Thus, it is not merely the suspicion of literary genres as such that informs Hayashi's historical project, but the suspicion of a history that cannot be reduced to literature and auto-production.

In his classic study of the historical novel, Georg Lukács shows that this form lends itself particularly well to expressing a collective consciousness, usually of a group that has been excluded from history. Although in the end Lukács concludes that the historical novel is antiromantic, he admits that for Sir Walter Scott, the first of the great authors of the historical novel, historical authenticity means "the quality of inner life, the morality, heroism, capacity for sacrifice, steadfastness etc. peculiar to a given age."[26] A more accurate description of romanticism would be hard to find! Certainly Hayashi, in *Youth*, tries to recoup the "historical authenticity" of the late Tokugawa period through his two "heroes," Shiji Bunta (Inoue Kaoru) and Itō Shunsuke (Itō Hirobumi). In keeping with Lukács's description of the hero of a historical novel, these two impressionable young men seem more like antiheroes—men whose very mediocrity "renders visible the generally progressive features of the whole of society, of the whole age."[27] Like Sir Walter Scott, Hayashi wants to tell the story of those who have been excluded from history, the victims of modernization. But since for Hayashi the ultimate victim is Japanese culture, his literary work, as a cultural product itself, unwittingly becomes its own story.

Hayashi's story focuses on the struggles of Shiji and Itō as they return to their domain of Yamaguchi after a secret trip to the West where they had studied technology. Armed with this new knowledge, they attempt to intervene in the revolt against the *bakufu* that is being carried out under the banner of "Revere the Emperor, Expel the Barbarians" (*Sonnō jōi*). The opening passage of the novel illustrates the essential conflict between East and West that underlies Hayashi's interpretation of the political fight between Chōshū and the *bakufu*:

> It was summer in the first year of Genji. One July afternoon, two young Portuguese, led by the official interpreter for the English embassy, Ernest Satow, stood in front of Shibaya Hatsugorō's inn in the Benten district of Yokohama. The head clerk was completely taken aback. The two young Portuguese simply looked too much like Japanese.
>
> The first year of Genji corresponds to 1864 in the Western calendar, and it was already ten years since Perry had arrived. It was seven years since Yokohama had been declared an open port. During these seven years, the city had developed from a decaying fishing village built on dank swampland to an international city where one could not avoid meeting foreigners on the streets. And since Shibaya Hatsugorō had watched these developments up close, he no longer felt foreigners were such a novelty, and would not even be surprised to hear that one or two of them had yellow skin. There were even black ones among these foreigners....
>
> Hatsugorō knew that the Portuguese, with their black eyes and black hair, looked just like Japanese from their short stature right down to their skin color. It had gotten to the point where lecherous foreigners would take pleasure in giving Spanish or Portuguese names to the women of Yokohama's brothels. But, even so, these two young Portuguese just looked too much like Japanese!...
>
> Hatsugorō merely sensed it. Like a dog senses a dog, like a cat senses a cat, he sensed an undeniable Japaneseness in these two young Portuguese.
>
> Ernest Satow mentioned their nationality and briefly explained

that they had come from Hong Kong on business and then, in fairly good Japanese, asked

"Do you have a room?"

"A room, you say? Hmm."

Groveling in the dirt and rubbing his hands together in an obsequious manner, Hatsugorō seemed the experienced innkeeper, and with a stubborn pride in his judgment of guests gleaming in his eyes, he returned the gaze on the interpreter's face. But his adversary did not flinch.

"These two gentlemen would like to spend the night."

"Oh yes, that ... indeed."

Since words failed him, Hatsugorō tried scratching his head. An uncertain anger overcame him and he stared at the two youths. The two youths were clearly uneasy.

It was unmistakable! But somehow or other, the sense of the victory of a direct hit eluded him. As he gradually realized that they were Japanese, an inexplicable fear seized him.

"Well, I am so sorry, but ..."

"You don't have a room?"

Satow fired this back with a haughtiness full of the self-confidence common to all foreigners in a colonial land. The tone of his words clearly were meant to communicate that simply because we are at the height of antiforeign sentiment and foreign businessmen are not to be out and about does not force you to say you have no rooms.

"Well, that's, you see ..."

Hatsugorō's rhombi-form face became even more rhombic, his eyebrows were knitted, and in general he looked rather pathetic.

"What's the matter?"

What's the matter, indeed! The nerve to bring along these two monsterish guests![28]

Needless to say, the three travelers do not get their room. They return to the foreign section where Satow has them put up in a hotel designated for foreigners. In what seems to be a simple request for a night's lodging, interactions between East and West are not only rife with misunderstandings but essentially informed by considerations of rivalry and power. Yet Hayashi's primary focus in *Youth* is not on the dynamics of the relationship between East and West; he assumes this relationship to be antagonistic from the beginning. Rather, his ultimate concern is with the Japanese and their response to the imposition of the West.

Of course, the two "Portuguese" are indeed Shiji Bunta and Itō Shunsuke. As Japanese, they do not belong in the foreign section, so they must exercise prudence to avoid detection by the staff and residents of the foreign hotel. Hayashi's point here is quite clear: modernized Japanese like Shiji and Itō have lost their home and now drift about in a world where they never belong. His scorn in the passage cited above is directed at the innkeeper, who grovels before Westerners, but also, and even more, directed at pro-Western Japanese like Shiji and Itō, who have betrayed their own people and culture for Western technology. (Hayashi wrote elsewhere, "I say there is no need to wear Western helmets. They give us a disagreeable feeling, don't they?")[29] *Youth* follows the lengthy development of Shiji and Itō as they initially try to convince the Chōshū elders that war with the Western powers is foolish and futile and that England, in particular, can be counted on for assistance in the battle against the *bakufu*. Eventually, the two realize that a battle with the West is inevitable and prove their loyalty to their domain (and thus to the emperor) by removing their "Western helmets" and fighting against their former Western friends in the Battle of Shimonoseki. Even when the strategies adopted by Shiji, Itō, and their domain change, the two youths remain steadfast in their belief that Japan must be united if it is to survive. Indeed, the ideal of a unified Japan, more than any technology, is the most valuable souvenir the two bring back with them from the West. Although in the beginning of the story Shiji and Itō are not aware of this fact, as *Youth* unfolds it becomes increasingly clear that for Hayashi the history of the Meiji Restoration is reducible to the development of an understanding of this ideal by the two youths.

Of equal importance to the signified of this ideal—a unified Japan—is what Hayashi conceives as the proper understanding of the relationship between ideals, men, and history. Negating the influence of ideology in history, Hayashi argues that men do not mobilize ideals to bend history in the direction they choose, but rather, ideals mobilize men and compel them to act in a preordained, often incomprehensible, way. Nowhere does Hayashi's view of history gain clearer articulation than through the words of the Swiss Dr. Pruyn, who is sympathetic to the cause of the two youths and argues in their defense against the bellicose Lieutenant Tracey. When Dr. Pruyn mentions the name of Heinrich Heine, the British lieutenant explodes in outrage: "Heinrich Heine! The German Jew who reviled us Englishmen as egotists who will not admit that they are destroying the globe for profit! We Englishmen have no reason to show any sympathy for even one of his words."[30] In response, Dr. Pruyn tries to convince Lieutenant Tracey that Heine understood patriotic sentiments and shaped a view of history and action based on the motivating power of such ideals:

> Only when possessed by ideals can men, though weak and ugly by nature, discover their true reality. The call of ideals wells up from an unknown place, perhaps from the base of history.... The secret of those men who are thought weak and ugly and yet who appear from time to time in history with the beauty and courage of a god is to be found here. For example ... Heinrich Heine expresses the feelings of one who is dragged along by these ideals. He does not necessarily seem to be the type of person who would take a special interest in politics or social struggles.... Yet when, inside the room where he had secretly run in search of tranquillity and escape, he heard outside the voices singing the Marseillaise, he was dragged unwillingly out of his room by the ideals that compelled him to abandon his poetry and rush out into the streets. He confesses with honest lamentation that although people believe that men grasp ideals, it is really ideals that grasp men.[31]

If Lieutenant Tracey remains unconvinced by such ideals, Hayashi did not. In fact, Hayashi paid tribute to the German romantics by including an essay on Heine, the only Western writer so honored, in his *Romanticist's Handbook*. In this essay, Hayashi repeats his belief that ideals move men to action but focuses on a man—Heine—as a "poet-revolutionary" who fought against the imperialism of Napoleonic France. With the Western navies (including French, but not German, ships) bombarding the port at Shimonoseki, the historical context that Hayashi places his two youths in was very similar to Heine's Germany.

A crucial point in the story arises when, having failed in their effort to convince the senior counselors of Chōshū of the futility of a military engagement with the West, Shiji and Itō withdraw into seclusion and begin to question the power of their ideals. It is only after an encounter with their spiritual leader, Takasugi Shinsaku, that they are able to regain a sense of optimism and confidence in their project. Takasugi chides Itō for self-pity at a time when his abilities are most needed by his domain. Although the argument takes place as a discussion of the merits of Itō's poetry (which Itō sees as inferior to the work of his idol, the late Tokugawa martyr Hashimoto Sanai), there is no question that the stakes are much larger:

> "Master Sanai's work reveals hope, but mine does not."
> "You're wrong."
> "But ..."
> "I said you're wrong." Shinsaku sat up. "Master Sanai's poems sing of a quiet resignation that comes from a thorough understanding of his fate. A deeper resignation that wells up from the depths of a bitter disappointment. But yours, what shall I say, they're merely fretful. They're like a child worried that no one will sympathize with his worries. There is no disappointment in them.... They are good because they have no disappointment. What kind of a mess would it be if at this time you indulged in the kind of resignation that Master Sanai felt in prison? Master Hashimoto Sanai and Master Yoshida Shōin lived in a time when the force of events [*ikioi*] was not favorable to us.... But now the force of events has begun to change. Looking just at the situation in our own domain, I see this war as an opportunity for a change in our favor. That is why I say that while your poems seem gloomy, they are not gloomy in the slightest."[32]

Takasugi's praise for Itō's poetry is meant to convey a sense of optimism to the young patriot by pointing out that Itō, unlike Hashimoto, does not face immediate execution. All is not lost, he argues, only the force of events has changed. He convinces Itō and Shiji to return to the service of their domain and do what they can to continue the struggle against the *bakufu*.

The "force of events" represents for Hayashi the fundamental law of historical change. Along with ideals that motivate men to act, it signifies the set of conditions that limits the possibilities for human intervention in the process of historical and social change. Ideals and the force of events share a nature that transcends human knowledge and can only be understood once made manifest in concrete form or, in other words, once it is already too late for contestation. By placing the contingency of the force of events and ideals above the intentionality of human agency, Hayashi seeks to portray history as a process of self-unfolding rather than as the object of production. Kobayashi Hideo, Hayashi's colleague in *Literary World*, criticized Hayashi for ignoring the role of the author in producing history, citing the following passage from *Youth*:

> History often seems to favor this kind of accident. If this [a chance meeting of Shiji, Itō, and Takasugi] were the result of the author's artifice ... it would be too vulgar and the effect would be instead quite dull.[33]

Kobayashi points out that Hayashi's disclaimer itself reveals the fictitiousness of his history. But in a paradoxical way Kobayashi's criticism works not to undermine his fellow romantics' project but to support it. Kobayashi's remarks are directed not at revealing the conditions of historical production but at the subjective mirror of writing in general. His summary of all other criticism of *Youth* into the aphorism "This Is Hayashi Fusao" attempts a metonymical substitution of the author for the work, the producer for the product, and in so doing to erase all traces of the process of production.

If Hayashi did not write *Youth* from a belief in historical objectivity, neither did he write it out of a need to express his own unique psyche. Somewhere between the two extremes of history and fiction lay a conception of the historical novel as a motivating force for social intervention in the historical present. Recalling that Hayashi was engaged in an attempt at a cultural renaissance, one immediately senses the relationship that Hayashi sought to forge between the view of the Meiji Restoration that emerges in *Youth* and the contours of ideological discourse in the Japan of the 1930s. By focusing on the Battle of Shimonoseki as a catalyst in the struggle for national unity, and especially by describing as "native" such phenomena as the *kiheitai*, or "shock troops," Hayashi sought to accomplish something quite similar to what Michel de Certeau calls bringing "scientific practices and language back toward their native land." As Michel de Certeau shows, this involves a recuperation of what science rejects as its remainder as a new "whole" that is now signified by culture. Furthermore, he maintains that knowledge of this new whole is most accessible to the "common man" in the realm of fiction. Hayashi, too, believed that the novel was best suited to present the historical struggle for this "whole," and he envisioned the "common man" in a new "class-less Japan" as the hero of the cultural renaissance.[34]

Hayashi argues that the antiforeign slogan (*jōi*) of the late Tokugawa years only became a part of the anti-*bakufu* movement after the Battle of Shimonoseki, when it became obvious that the old feudal regime must fall before any progress could be made toward expelling the foreign powers. Patriots such as Shiji Bunta and Itō Shunsuke had to sacrifice this ultimate goal for the immediate ideal of national unification. It is this deep sense of resignation and unfinished business that lends thematic unity to *Youth* and goes the farthest in explaining why Hayashi turned to a study of Japanese history at a crucial moment in the search for a new Japanese culture. Certainly when he began outlining *Youth* in prison, he himself shared this resignation and frustration and may have envisioned the work as a release from his own personal loneliness. But in the process of writing the novel, he produced a text that would not be contained within the bounds of auto-production but went beyond to signify a history of cultural defeat and to promise the future possibility of a cultural renaissance.

THE CULTURE OF THE EMPEROR

Two roughly simultaneous events, the completion of *Youth* in 1934 and the publication of Kobayashi's essay on the I-novel in 1935, saw a transformation of the problem of culture and the end of the first phase of the cultural renaissance. A general consensus among Japanese intellectuals greeted Hayashi and Nakamura Mitsuo when each declared in 1935 that the cultural renaissance was dead.[35] These declarations were in response to the changes in cultural discourse brought about by Kobayashi's article, which foregrounded the issue of the West in cultural formulations, and by Hayashi's historical novel, which traced the origins of modern Japanese culture to an aborted battle against the West. But to declare the cultural renaissance "dead" did not necessarily mean that the issue of culture finally had been settled, or that it no longer informed a major part of the intellectual activity of the day. Such declarations were meant to convey a sense of closure to prevailing cultural practices (especially proletarian literature) that were grounded in a view of society as contestation and to suggest a resurrection of the cultural renaissance based on a view of society as a harmonious whole.

Writing from prison, Hayashi outlined a short history of the first phase of the cultural renaissance and suggested how the second phase would be carried out:

> This time, as soon as I finish the first installment of *Manhood*, I intend to attack the capital and let loose rage in all its fury for the sake of the second phase of the cultural renaissance.... The first phase was a time of literature's self-assertion, a movement that distinguished the literary from the nonliterary. The group associated with the journal *Literary World* represented this phase. During this time, there can be no doubt that over the course of a year or so, as new people came forth and old ones were revitalized, those who framed various theories called forth a new consciousness from men of letters. The second period takes its beginnings here.... I believe it is the movement of the Japan Romantic School that signifies the beginning of this phase.[36]

As Kamei Katsuichirō has revealed, it was Hayashi who suggested such language as "exalted spirit," "violent rage," and "noble isolation" in the initial stages of conceptualizing the character of the Romantic School.[37] For Hayashi, the Japan Romantic School, with its emphasis on "friendship" (*yūjō*) and exclusivity, was ideally situated to carry on the mission of the cultural renaissance through its palingenesis of Heine's use of culture to protest against foreign aggression.

In the second phase of the cultural renaissance, Hayashi continued to reject any appeal to politics, maintaining instead the essentially romantic belief that what was most inherently political could be represented as apolitical. Thus, he argues with equal emphasis that the purpose of literature is "to cultivate the sentiment and spirit of the *Nationalvolk* (*kokumin*) on the level of everyday life" and that "the motivating force of literature is not to be found within the policies of the government ... [but] within the writer himself." To those who object that the cultivation of the "spirit of the *Nationalvolk*" is itself highly ideological and political, Hayashi would reply that they have failed to understand that the power of the author "towers above the clouds of politics ... [and] when angered, casts thunderbolts down to smash politics." Here Hayashi reveals his view of literature as excess, existing beyond the rules of production and consumption and yet able to intervene at crucial moments to change radically the course of everyday life. The Japan Romantic School embodies this view of literature best, he argues, by calling for a transcendence of the lowly and vulgar and by adhering to the principles of faith (*shin-nen*) and determination (*ketsui*) as its method of intervention.[38]

At the heart of Hayashi's view of literature is a view of society as a homogeneous whole. Already in *Youth*, Hayashi foresha-dowed this view by suggesting the ideal of a class-free Japan. Initially conceived as a negation of politics, this utopian view became the positive definition of a society whose members can all be reduced to a single commonality. In this sense, Hayashi's view closely approximates Georges Bataille's definition of homo-geneity as "the commensurability of elements and the awareness of the commensurability: human relations are sustained by a re-duction to fixed rules based on the consciousness of the possible identity of delineable persons and situations."[39] In Hayashi's view, Japanese social relations are sustained by the realization that all members of society first and foremost belong to the *Nationalvolk*. "Fortunately, no Japanese writer is not [part of the] *Nationalvolk*," he writes, in an attempt to reduce individual differences of opinion to a natural basis of identity and thereby to displace the political agendas of "liberal" intellectuals.[40]

If Hayashi envisions Japanese society as a homogeneous whole, it is not because he shares Yokomitsu's primary emphasis on ethnicity (*minzoku*) as the basis of this whole. Certainly, his focus on the *Nationalvolk* involves elements of ethnicity, but Hayashi is less concerned with the *Nationalvolk* in and of themselves than he is with using it to construct a social homogeneity that contrasts with his ultimate concern, the emperor as the principle of hetero-geneity. He conceives of this relationship in a manner similar to that described by Bataille: "Since the king [emperor] is the object in which homogeneous society has found its reason for being, maintaining this relationship demands that he conduct himself in such a way that the *homogeneous* society can exist *for him*. In the first place, this requirement bears upon the fundamental *het-erogeneity* of the king, guaranteed by numerous prohibitions of contract [*sic*] (taboos)."[41] For Hayashi, the *Nationalvolk* do not exist as subjects themselves, but only for the emperor, who be-

longs to a heterogeneous world. Ironically, Hayashi seems happy
to ignore the fact that such an opposition implies a functional
equivalence between the emperor, as the excess of society, and
foreign cultures that were also extraneous to the homogeneous
Nationalvolk. His purpose, of course, is to displace any rival principle of difference, specifically foreign cultures, through this imagination of a radically different emperor.

By relegating the emperor to a realm beyond homogeneous
society and human knowledge, Hayashi also implies that the emperor is the only true agent of production. Divine by nature, the
emperor transcends the limitations of human knowledge and time,
penetrating the clouded myths of the past as well as the mysteries
of the future. But the emperor is also human and therein lie certain
possibilities for social and cultural change. Existing both at one
with the *Nationalvolk* in time and removed from them in space,
the emperor serves to mediate the timeless essence of the *Nationalvolk* and the cultural and political chaos introduced by modernity. As this mediating presence, "the emperor" (*tennō*) signifies
not merely the living emperor, Hirohito, but simultaneously all
emperors throughout and beyond Japanese history when reduced
to their shared difference from the whole of Japanese society.
Consequently, the immediate problem facing Hayashi is how
best to shape the consciousness of his fellow Japanese so that they
will understand the role of the emperor in history and work in
accordance with (supposed) imperial desires.

In 1941, Hayashi published two works that suggest how he
believed the goal of grounding the homogeneity of the *Nationalvolk* in the heterogeneity of the emperor could be achieved. The
first, *On Ideological Conversion* (*Tenkō ni tsuite*), was offered as an
innocent, autobiographical account of what led Hayashi to make
his "conversion" from Marxism to romanticism. Regardless of
how he hoped the work would be received, the very fact that this
"self-reflection" was penned nearly ten years after his conversion
supposedly occurred is persuasive evidence that the problem of
tenkō is not necessarily synonymous with the act. As Hayashi
writes in the opening lines of this work,

> The time has come to rethink what is called *tenkō*. It seems that a
> time when it can be reconsidered has finally ripened. . . .

But *tenkō* is not a simple change of direction. It is a rebirth of the entire man. It is not enough simply to get naked. It is not enough to wash one's skin in cold water. One must wash out one's bone marrow. It is not a matter of external form. It is a problem of one's innermost thoughts.[42]

Certainly, as this passage suggests, the problem of *tenkō* re-emerged for Hayashi in the early 1940s in the context of the problematic of auto-production and the emperor. Shimizu Shōzō notes that unlike Kamei's approach to the problem of *tenkō*, which stemmed from the question of ethnicity, Hayashi's understanding was largely formed in light of his interest in the emperor.[43] For Hayashi, *tenkō* provided a way, based on the mechanics of auto-production (as distinguished from production), to reshape the self in conformity with the perceived desires of the emperor and thereby provide a sense of direction to the new culture, a culture of the emperor.

The second work was explicitly titled "An Introduction to a Theory of Literature of Loyalty to the Emperor" ("Kinnō bungaku ron josetsu") and appeared in serial form in the pages of the newspaper *Asahi* in early June 1941. These short articles, along with the longer essay Hayashi submitted the following year to the debates on overcoming modernity called "The Spirit of Loyalty to the Emperor" ("Kinnō no kokoro"), represent some of his most widely read and influential works. Loyalty to the emperor, he argues, should not be confused with the more mundane patriotism practiced by even the most barbaric of foreigners. Rather, it is based on the realization that "Japan's *Nationalvolk* serves no one other than the divine emperor made incarnate (*arahitogami*)."[44] This loyalty means not merely the self's production of itself (*tenkō*) but ultimately the destruction of the self in a rapture of the beauty of the battlefield. "The literature of loyalty to the emperor began on the battlefields of the continent. Japan's battles are beautiful."[45] This literature, represented by the writings of such hawkish writers as Saitō Ryū (1874–1953), Hino Ashihei (1907–60), and Kageyama Masaharu (1910–79) is summarized in the ancient poem, "I would die by your side, My Lord / and never look back."

Of crucial importance in this theory is the assertion that the death of the self is not the end of literature but the precondition of a new literature that will overcome the failure of modern culture to articulate a vision of full (Japanese) humanity. Hayashi argues that modern writers have abandoned their own humanity by forsaking their culture for an illusion of universal humanity:

> Modern writers have gone too far in trying to be independent of popular goals and suffered under the illusion that literature has its own goals. At that moment they ceased being servants of the gods, ceased being human, and finally degenerated into human beasts....
> With the appearance of "war literature," Japanese literature ... for the first time became humane literature and now approaches a literature of the gods.[46]

By arguing for a "humane" (*ningen rashii*) literature as a way of regaining access to the emperor, Hayashi repeats his romantic interest in displacing questions of politics with a quest for personal development. Writ large, personal development translates into the cultural development of the *Nationalvolk*. In both cases, a sense of self-identity realized through a confrontation with the "Other" on the battlefields underlies and makes possible this displacement. "War literature" reinforces this concept of identity by erasing any trace of difference between the individual and the literary, on the one hand, and the social and the ideological, on the other. All are subordinated to the service of the emperor as the only remaining locus of difference and, therefore, of culture.

Hayashi's arrival at a view of the emperor as the locus of production stemmed from his earlier interest in the relationship between culture and politics in modern Japan. His involvement with proletarian writers had taught him the political utility of assertions of "apolitical" art and helped lay the foundation for his romantic view of history. Of course, his insistence on the value of "apolitical" culture was anything but apolitical itself, as it implicated Hayashi in various attempts, both theoretical and nontheoretical, to construct a model of society based on the concept of homogeneity.[47] According to this model, all contestatory claims to power will be displaced by a shared set of commensurable elements that stand in contrast to the emperor as the sole source of difference and power. This romantic view of society is buttressed by an equally paradoxical attempt to erase history through the production of historical novels that reduce change to certain timeless ideals, chiefly the ideal of a unified Japan whose "essence" will counter the baleful influence of foreign culture (modernization) on Japan. It is thus within the context of the problem of modernity and the alienation implicit in the loss of past traditions and cultural practices that Hayashi's valorization of the emperor must be placed.

In the 1942 debates on overcoming modernity, Hayashi most clearly articulated the reasons for his renewed interest in the emperor. He rejects the theory of progress, which he calls a study of fads, and holds it responsible for "turning [my] eyes away from the existence of that which is immutable."[48] This theory was born in the days immediately following the Meiji Restoration, when bureaucrats distorted the Restoration into a self-serving aping of the West. Hayashi strongly denies that the Meiji Restoration was informed by a desire for modernization and even argues that the "freedom and people's rights movement" (*jiyū minken undō*) was not a forerunner of modern political parties but was actually an attack on the bureaucracy's policy of "civilization and enlightenment" (*bunmei kaika*).[49] The Meiji Restoration was, he argues, an attempt to return to the ancient age, "a classless period when the *Nationalvolk* could face the emperor directly and worship him."[50] By reestablishing a direct link between a homogeneous people and a heterogeneous emperor, Hayashi hopes to overcome the alienation of modern life by transferring alienation from the process of production to the realm of culture.

The Pacific War offered Hayashi concrete proof of the continuation of the aborted struggle against the fads of the West. Hayashi greeted the attack on Pearl Harbor with special enthusiasm, for it represented not only a preemptive strike against the West but also a return to the true, holy purpose of the war, which had been mired for ten years in more complex, intra-Asian hostilities. As a war in defense of Japanese culture, the Pacific War could be seen as the extension of a conflict that began as early as the 1840s, when—Hayashi claimed—the first Western ships penetrated Japan's proud isolation.[51] Hayashi believed that the failure in the Meiji and Taishō periods to preserve culture against historical change was due in a large part to the inability of Japanese intellectuals to articulate an indigenous principle of imperial rule. Thus, Hayashi's conception of the emperor as the sole agent of production, supported by his call for writers to engage in a spontaneous "auto-production" of literature as a means of representing imperial desires, was concerned in the final instance not with Japan as much as with the perceived cultural threat posed to Japan by the West.

Epilogue
Romanticism Rehabilitated

This study began with the assumption that the historical significance of the Japan Romantic School was to be found in its articulation of a critical response to modernity. We have seen how that
response was articulated in five distinct moments that, collec-
tively, constituted the core of the school's attempt to escape from
the constraints of the modern world. Yasuda's aesthetics, Hagiwara's poetic ambiguities, Tanaka and Itō's attack on narrative,
Kamei's ethics, and Hayashi's new historicism all suggested alternative ways of establishing a Japanese identity that rejected the
universalistic claims of modernity. We have also seen how this
critique risked implication in certain forms of modern politics
while ironically claiming exemption from politics. Before any final assessment of the historical role of the Japan Romantic School
can be made, it is necessary to gain a broader view of how such
arguments outlived the prewar years and how they were ultimately reformulated in postwar Japan.

What follows is not an attempt to provide a conclusive, or even
comprehensive, account of postwar Japanese intellectual history.
Rather, I intend merely to sketch out some relevant issues and
perspectives from the postwar years that I believe have contributed to a reappraisal of the Japan Romantic School and its critique
of modernity. It is an incomplete and highly subjective history,
but one that is essential in appreciating how (and why) the Japan
Romantic School has been largely redefined to fit the needs of the
vastly transformed intellectual landscape of postwar Japan. Once
this redefinition has been grasped in its historical conditions, we
can see how the issues it raised, through intersections with and
incorporation into other cultural and political concerns, have
transcended the lives of the individual members of the school.

One key aspect of the postwar rehabilitation of romanticism and of the Japan Romantic School in particular was a redefinition of the relationship between Japan and modernity. Before the war modernity was seen by and large as something that Japan had either too much or too little of; either way, modernity was not always or exclusively identified with the West. Indeed, the widespread criticism during the 1930s of the fads of *modanizumu*, represented by the *mobo* and *moga*, can be seen as a rebellion against the attempt to assert a specific modern culture, through the process of "Americanization," as the final definition of modernity within Japanese culture. This trend was supported by the Meiji "success" with modernization, which promoted a decontextualized view of modernity, as many Japanese took pride in being the only Asians to have modernized by the turn of the twentieth century through their amalgamation of various aspects of modernity from several cultures. Certainly, there were those in the prewar period who were critical of modernity. The whole debate over "leaving Europe and re-entering Asia" (*datsu-Ō nyū-A*) attests to their presence. But the adherents of "leaving Europe" shared with modernists an assumption that Japan had already been modernized, thoroughly so, if perhaps too much so. This was precisely the position of the members of the Japan Romantic School, who began their investigation into the conditions of Japanese modernity with the belief that European, especially German, contributions to the critique of modernity were at least as pertinent and valuable as American modernity. Their point of origin, the belief that a critique of modernity involved a critique of the self, led the members of the Japan Romantic School to focus their energies on the problem of imagining new identities.

This redefinition of Japan's relation to modernity was greatly facilitated by the underlying paradox of the Pacific War as a war of conquest and Asian liberation, of antimodern rhetoric and modern weapons. While the war was fought, undeniably, with the most modern means of warfare available, there was also an undeniable attempt to portray the war as a struggle against modernity.[1] This meant that modernity was no longer seen merely as a natural component of Japanese "official nationalism" (*kokka-shugi*), the source of Japanese national pride, but was projected as essentially foreign and evil and therefore antithetical to the goals of ethnic nationalism (*minzoku-shugi*).

The climax of this wartime reevaluation was the symposium on overcoming modernity held in Kyoto in 1942 under the direct auspices of the Japanese state. As the participants of the symposium hotly debated the proposal that "modernity" could be overcome, it became increasingly clear that "modernity" here was intended to refer to the West, a proposition that some, nonetheless, tried to resist. Still, while all agreed that the symposium ended in failure because of its inability to establish a consensus concerning the identification of modernity with the West, it did succeed in establishing the terms for a postwar reevaluation of the concept.

Overall, the postwar discourse on modernity has been marked not so much by a break with, as a continuation of, the wartime project. After the implementation of General Douglas MacArthur's mission to complete Japan's interrupted progress toward modernization, it could no longer be doubted by even the most stalwart holdout that Japan was a modern society. Assured that Japan was now thoroughly and unquestionably back on the road to modernity, postwar Japanese intellectuals who were not preoccupied with reinforcing modern values over remnants of a feudal, traditional consciousness could finally return to their unfinished business of partaking in the modern tradition of attacking modernity. Ironically, because modernity in the postwar period was intricately connected to the dominant American culture and, specifically, to the American policy of converting Japan into its own self-image of a capitalist democracy, the wartime effort to portray modernity as synonymous with the West was only further validated, if more narrowly focused on the United States. The identification of modernity with the United States was, in turn, closely related to the political developments of the "reverse course" of 1947–52. While the "reverse course" in Occupation policy was directed at returning to office political leaders considered most favorable to American foreign policy goals, it also carried the potential of undermining the Occupation's claim that modernity served the cause of impartial justice and consistent progress for all.

With the lifting of the Occupation in 1952, the stage was set for a reconception of what modernity meant in the Japanese historical context. As the Japanese state, now assuredly modern by all accounts, began to use its newly gained autonomy to repress its own citizens and to support American intervention in Korea and later in Vietnam, critical voices from both the left and the right began to call for a rejection of modernism and the West (particularly United States policies in Asia) and for a return to Asia. Clearly, what these intellectuals meant by a return to Asia was quite different from what wartime ideologues had termed a "Greater East Asia Co-Prosperity Sphere." Indeed, much of their criticism was directed at postwar Japanese policies that in effect created a relationship of Japanese economic dominance over the rest of Asia. Drawing on the popularity of Maoist celebrations of "the people," many of these antimodernists focused their attentions on ethnicity, or the "folk" (*minzoku*), all the while condemning prewar and postwar excesses of Japanese state power in Asia. It was precisely this renewed interest in the possibility of a new social identity grounded in ethnicity to resist the universalism of modernist notions of "humanity" or "citizen" that led the antimodernists and neo-nationalists of the late 1950s and early 1960s to reconsider the critical possibilities inherent in the Japan Romantic School.

OVERCOMING MODERNITY

Perhaps the single most important catalyst in ensuring the survival of this critique of modernity in postwar Japan was the symposium on overcoming modernity held at the height of the war years. These talks, conducted on July 23 and 24, 1942, and published in the September and November issues of *Literary World*, brought together leading members of Japan's scientific, literary, and artistic communities. The Kyoto School of philosophy was represented by Nishitani Keiji (1900–1990) and Suzuki Shigetaka (a.k.a. Seikō; 1907–88), while the Japan Romantic School was represented by Hayashi Fusao and Kamei Katsuichirō.[2] As a leading member of the Japan Literary Patriotic Society, Kamei had called for such a symposium earlier in the year and played a major role in the actual planning of it.[3] Yet he declined an offer to serve as the moderator of the symposium in favor of Kawakami Tetsutarō who, it was generally agreed, could lend a greater sense of impartiality and legitimacy to the task.

The target of the symposium may be seen in Kawakami's concluding remarks. Kawakami confessed that he had patterned the symposium after an earlier one held under the auspices of the League of Nations' Institut International de Coopération Intellectuelle and chaired by Paul Valéry. This symposium met nine times between 1932 and 1938 in various countries in Europe and South America and some of its early proceedings were recorded in two monographs, *The Future of the European Spirit* and *The Formation of the Modern Man*, which were translated into Japanese in 1936 and 1937, respectively.

The participants in the league's symposium, including such luminaries as Aldous Huxley, Johan Huizinga, Jules Romains, Julien Benda, Georges Duhamel, and Thomas Mann, sought to address the question of the universality of European culture. Underlying their rhetoric was a deep concern over the growth of nationalism, especially in Africa, Asia, and Latin America, which rejected the applicability of a "European spirit" to diverse cultures and peoples. In short, it was a symposium that, in Kawakami's poetic words, "appeared at first glance to be quite stunning, all decked out in the finery of intellectual propriety, but in its beautiful melody, which skipped the most essential intervals, the voices of the chorus rang hollow."[4] The failure of the league's symposium represented for Kawakami the end of the intellectual authority and prestige of Western civilization and reaffirmed his belief in a Japanese tradition distinct from the humanism of the West. It was his hope that the symposium on overcoming modernity, sponsored by the Japanese Council on Intellectual Cooperation (Chiteki Kyōryoku Kaigi) would be able to succeed where Valéry and the West had failed.

The immediate precursor to the symposium on overcoming modernity may be found in a series of similar symposiums centered on the Kyoto School philosophers and held during the early 1940s, beginning with "The World Historical Position and Japan" (held November 26, 1941) and followed by "The Ethical and Historical Nature of the East Asia Co-Prosperity Sphere" and "The Philosophy of Total War." As the issues in these symposiums were published a few months afterward in the prominent journal *Chūō kōron*, they served as an influential and popular harnessing of main currents of Nishida Kitarō's philosophy in an ideological support of the wartime Japanese state. The participants in the first symposium were such well-known figures of the Kyoto School as Kōsaka Masaaki (1900–1969), Koyama Iwao (b. 1905), Nishitani, and Suzuki. Their primary contribution to the critique of modernity was already present here in their attempt to provide a "philosophy of world history" that would "both account for Japan's current position and disclose the course of future action [but which ultimately was] a thinly disguised justification, written in the language of Hegelian metaphysics, for Japanese aggression and continuing imperialism."[5] Given the importance of the Kyoto School in shaping the wartime critique of modernity, a brief look at some of its key concepts is helpful in gaining a better sense of this debate, as well as in discerning the position of the Japan Romantic School in the symposium on overcoming modernity.

World history, as articulated by the members of the Kyoto School, is fundamentally a process of competition among nation-states. The nation-state is seen as the embodiment of Nishida's paradoxical insight that history is a continuous unfolding of discontinuity. In Kōsaka's writings this paradox is manifested in the nation-state as the synthesis of "culture" (blood) and "place" (soil). Consequently, he rejects an attempt to depict ethnic nationalism as distinct from the state and concludes that "ethnic subjectivity, that is the consciousness of the absoluteness of the state, is the hidden foundation [of war]."[6] Representing ethnicity and culture, a nation-state becomes not merely a historical or political construction but the embodiment of the "moral energy" of a people, one of the ways Kōsaka represents Nishida's concept of absolute nothingness. Far from something to be avoided, war is simply the competition between various forms of moral energies, and only victory in war can determine which form is virtuous and which is not.

Such sanguine assessments of the role of the state and war in the process of overcoming modernity also characterized the comments of Nishitani and Suzuki in their dialogue with Hayashi, Kamei, and others at the 1942 symposium. From the first day of the debates, it was clear that there was very little agreement even on the central problem of how to define modernity. "Modernity" was referred to both as "civilization and enlightenment" (*bunmei kaika*) and "modernity" (*kindai*). Some such as Hayashi wanted to keep the focus on modernity as a product of the West, whereas Yoshimitsu Yoshihiko (1904–45) suggested that it could be found in the "universal" problem of atheism. Nishitani and Suzuki revealed a subtle difference from other members of the Kyoto School, such as Kōsaka, in their acceptance of some aspects of modernity, particularly the contribution of the formation of the modern Japanese state in preventing colonization by the West.[7] Yet in the end such subtle disagreements within the Kyoto School were absorbed within a broader consensus that the solution to overcoming modernity in the present lay, as Nishitani noted, in the fusion of moral qualities and state politics, a fusion that submerged individual interests into the collectivity of the state while the state promoted the construction of a new world order by waging war.

Kamei and Hayashi represented the Japan Romantic School's position. (Kamei's essay, "A Memorandum on the Modern Spirit" ["Gendai seishin ni kansuru oboegaki"] also opened the proceedings as they were published in monograph form the following year by Sōgensha.) Kamei argued as his central theme that the war against the Anglo-American forces was actually part of a general struggle against the insidious effects of modern civilization on the Japanese spirit. He cautioned against expectations of an easy victory, fueled by reports of Japan's initial military successes. He attributed these expectations to a residual, modern egoism and, repeating his condemnation of egoism as the root of modern civilization, suggested its replacement by a devotion to the Japanese gods as the true subjective force of history.

Kamei lamented that the introduction of civilization had brought about the loss of the native Japanese spirit. "Spirit" signified here the creation of a Japanese identity unfettered by the claims of Western rationality. According to this view, the battle for a modern Japanese identity was fought first by Uchimura Kanzō (1861–1930) in the Meiji period, when Japan was inundated with Western civilization. Uchimura, who foresaw the necessity of a Japanese response to modernity based on spirit, ultimately failed in his goal by locating his "spirit" in the Christian god of the West. Kamei agreed with Uchimura that the modern Japanese "lost sight of their gods [*kami*]," but he left the question of how to restore this faith to the Catholic philosopher Yoshimitsu. Needless to say, Kamei did not agree with Yoshimitsu as to which gods are worth restoring.[8]

As we saw in Chapter 4, Kamei sought the rediscovery of the power of the traditional Japanese creator-god, the *musubi-no-kami*. When he argued, "If a power to overcome modernity exists, it is none other than the belief in the gods [*kami*],"[9] he was referring to the world-renewing power of the indigenous *musubi-no-kami*. Moreover, the significance of his belief that "the war replicates our classics" was elucidated by his statement that "the spirit of our classics may be taken as the best antidote to the poisons of civilization."[10] A return to the spirit of these classics (Kamei used both the more common *koten* and *shinten*, or "divine classics") would provide the Japanese with the epistemological basis—in Kamei's words, the faith—to fight a war of aggression as a war of cultural liberation. Thus, he argued, "The current hostilities are part of a war fought for this deeper war, and on these battlefields a clarity of mind that sweeps away all delusions and a steadfast faith that knows no fear will determine the fate of our ethnic people. Rather than the peace of slaves, give us the war of kings!"[11]

Kamei's belief that overcoming modernity meant a revolt against the West was supported by his fellow member of the Romantic School, Hayashi Fusao. Hayashi also grasped the problem of overcoming modernity as a struggle against the West and rejected outright Nishitani's suggestion that modernity was a universal problem that stemmed from the French Revolution, if not from the Renaissance. Rather, drawing from his historical novel *Seinen*, he argued that modernity in the Japanese context referred to the legacy of a great world-historical conflict between East and West that resulted in the Meiji Restoration. At that time, the East emerged victorious, he claimed, as Japan survived as a political and cultural entity, but the adoption of Western civilization that was thought necessary to compete with the West soon turned the victory into a Pyrrhic one.[12] When Kawakami, Kobayashi, Miyoshi Tatsuji, Suzuki, and Yoshimitsu joined Nishitani in an extended discussion of "the West within us," Hayashi maintained an absolute silence, broken only when the topic of conversation turned to

"Americanism and modernism." Here, Hayashi came forth with the opinion that American democracy was really nothing more than the movies that it exported for mass consumption throughout the world.

Ultimately, Hayashi's concern during the symposium was not with an investigation of the conditions of modernity, but with the production of a new Japanese identity that might circumvent the kinds of dangers he saw posed by modern civilization. This new identity would begin with an awareness of the edifying powers of the ancient Japanese classics, which formed an enduring substratum of Japanese culture. The problem of modernity, he insisted, was really a problem of how Japanese culture had become tainted with the influence of the West. Everything from Western science, theology, movies, and even styles of singing was blamed for corrupting the purity and solidarity of the Japanese people. Discussing "the possibilities for Japanese today," the last of the topics addressed by the symposium, Hayashi bemoaned the fact that Japan was "a country that merely absorbs influence [from foreign countries]." What he hoped the symposium might lead to, he confessed, was the discovery of a Japanese people who had not been touched by foreign influences. It was clear from the context that "foreign" here meant Western, especially American, culture.[13]

There were, of course, those who strongly disagreed with the romantics' equation of modernity with the West. Kobayashi Hideo, for one, rejected the argument, labeling it and all such attempts to mobilize Japanese classics for overtly ideological purposes as disingenuous and vain.[14] Instead of such positive assessments of the possibilities of overcoming modernity, Kobayashi offered only a pessimistic evaluation of social change, which sought to substitute an individualistic aesthetics for history. Kobayashi's pessimism was shared by Nakamura Mitsuo (1911–88), who stated, "To speak of 'overcoming modernity' without paying particular attention to our unique 'modernity' appears to us to be at the very least a meaningless, idealistic game."[15] Nakamura went on to explain that Japanese modernity was unique in that, as a chaotic whole, it incorporated both native traditions and foreign adaptations. This view, of course, became increasingly popular later in the postwar years, but it cut against the grain of the symposium on overcoming modernity and the hopes of its organizers. Such critical assessments, however, did prevent the more sanguine voices from declaring a premature triumph over modernity.

At the conclusion of two days of discussion, the general consensus was that the symposium had failed in its declared goal of suggesting ways of overcoming modernity. As moderator, Kawakami tried to take personal responsibility for this failure, although he was merely attempting to gloss over the deeper reasons for it, which had more to do with the task itself than with any selection of intellectual strategies. And yet, while the symposium may have failed as a body to arrive at an agreement about what modernity was, let alone how it might be overcome, it was an important moment in Japanese intellectual history that helped to set the terms for, and define the boundaries of, the Japanese discourse on modernity, which continued into the postwar years and up to the present. It also revealed how completely the earlier attempt by some in the Romantic School to establish a distinction between "ethnic nationalism" and the state had faded from view.

MODERNITY REVISITED, 1945–1952

When General Douglas MacArthur stepped out of his plane at Atsugi airfield on August 28, 1945, armed only with his corncob pipe, he was inaugurating more than a transfer of political power in Japan. Ostensibly concerned with "demilitarization and democratization," that is to say, with the completion of an aborted Japanese attempt at modernization, the Occupation had a deep and lasting impact on postwar Japanese culture. This is not to say that the Occupation completely displaced prewar concerns or that it was merely an "American interlude." Rather, it was a sustained and rather skillful attempt to redirect Japanese culture in ways that largely reflected American foreign policy goals.[16] But as an instance of cultural intervention, it soon became implicated in the very culture it was supposed to manipulate and, ironically, was reformulated by the Japanese in ways that surely were not intended by the Supreme Commander of the Allied Powers. In later years, Shin'ichirō Nakamura recalled that "as a result of the defeat, the Japanese government has declared that Japan will be reconstructed as 'a cultural nation.'... After the defeat many young men and women who had lost their 'national goal' now very seriously pursued the goal of culture. And literary men ('men of culture,' so-called) ... were now called upon to speak at 'cultural meetings' throughout the country."[17] While some of these "men of culture" initially joined in the defense of modern culture, others soon began to doubt whether this second modern revolution was ever intended to accomplish anything at all for the Japanese themselves.

From the very beginning of the American Occupation, it was obvious that more was involved than simply reaping the spoils of a long and bloody war—although the booming "pan-pan" (prostitution) trade offered plenty of evidence of that. Rather, Japan was to be the object of a highly self-conscious, American experiment in social and political restructuring on an unprecedented scale.[18] The hatred and scorn for the Japanese "enemy" that had been carefully inculcated in the American people during the war was to be transformed overnight into affectionate paternalism. Indeed, SCAP reforms in such areas as civil rights, labor relations, land ownership, and education did succeed at first in winning the approval and loyalty of many Japanese. At the same time, the reforms of the early Occupation were not merely an integral part of an altruistic mission to transform Japan into a modern nation, bereft of its semi-feudalistic militarism. Some Japanese also saw them as expressions of an arrogance and moral conceit as only a nation of unchallenged world dominance, such as America in the early postwar period, could imagine. This was evident as early as December 1945, when the Occupation ordered NHK to broadcast the American view of the war in a radio program called "This Is True."[19] Initially, the Occupation's arrogation of the positions of judge and liberator was passively accepted because many Japanese had suffered greatly from, and were exhausted by, the long and costly war. In the midst of terrible privation and starvation, many Japanese did hope (insofar as they thought about such matters at all) that SCAP and its call for the primacy of universal rights over arbitrary privilege would indeed lead to a greater respect for the rights of the individual and increased political and cultural freedom. But such hopes, perhaps too idealistic from the beginning, were soon abandoned in the face of events that followed.

Two moments in particular stand out: the war crimes trials and the outbreak of war in Korea. The first involved SCAP's decision to prosecute many of the Japanese wartime leaders at the Tokyo War Crimes Trials (formally, the International Military Tribunal for the Far East). From the day the court opened on May 3, 1946, until the death sentences were carried out on December 23, 1948, the war crimes trials represented the most obvious example of the Occupation's self-arrogation of the right to decide matters of justice, even of life and death, for the Japanese people. Badly flawed from a legal standpoint, the trials seriously undermined the American claim that justice could be impartially determined by its understanding of Western jurisprudence.[20] Especially revealing was the decision by the Occupation officials not to indict the emperor, a step that Tsurumi Shunsuke points out "was considered a denial of the very logic of the trial for war crimes."[21] Of course, there was little popular support for prosecuting the emperor, but Tsurumi is identifying what later was recognized as a serious, theoretical problem with the "justice" of the war crimes trials. If, as chief prosecutor Joseph B. Keenan argued, the seven leaders had to sacrifice their lives because of their personal responsibility in bringing Japan to war, then it was quite obvious to many Japanese that, theoretically, the same logic should have been applied even more so to the emperor, who was the source of all wartime commands. If, on the other hand, the main responsibility for Japan's path to war lay in an impersonal social structure that suffered from a latent semi-feudalism, as MacArthur maintained in arguing the need for reforms and many Japanese were quick to agree, then it was cruel and unjust to hold any individual personally responsible for what were, after all, structural problems. This disparity between what was said and done by the Occupation led many ordinary Japanese to conclude that the justice of the Americans was simply "victor's justice," and it brought into greater relief the culturally bound nature of the "modernity" that the Occupation imposed on postwar Japan.

Yet, in retrospect, it is clear that this was not the first instance of the exercise of power in the Occupation that belied any innocent belief that the experience was to be essentially a benign one. While historians of postwar Japan generally note a shift in SCAP's policy after 1947 away from experiments with social reform and toward a greater concern with security and Japan's economic rehabilitation, this change can be traced to an incident that occurred nearly one month before the war crimes trials began. On April 7, 1946, SCAP mobilized its military and police forces to crush a popular demonstration by the League of the Democratic People (Minshu Jinmin Renmei) against the Shidehara Cabinet.[22] Nearly a year later, on January 31, 1947, MacArthur suddenly rescinded permission for a nationwide, general strike, thereby dealing a serious blow to the reconstruction of the Japanese labor union movement.[23] This shift in Occupation policy had a direct impact on the discourse on modernity by undermining the claim that the modernity of the West would liberate the Japanese people. Taken together, these two events left a strong doubt in the minds of many Japanese as to whether, regardless of all the rhetoric of democracy, the Occupation was placing the interests of the Japanese people first. Thereafter, claims by the Occupation that it was simply serving the cause of justice for all began to ring hollow.

Yet, the case for modernity had strong support among some intellectuals. In the immediate postwar years, this position was articulated by a group of intellectuals who shared the belief that increasing amounts of "modernity" were the solution to the problems that had led to the disastrous war. These writers, often referred to as the Modern Literature School (Kindai Bungakuha), included Honda Shūgo (b. 1908), Hirano Ken (1907–78), Yamamuro Shizuka (b. 1906), Haniya Yutaka (b. 1910), Ara Masahito (1913–79), Sasaki Kiichi (b. 1914), and Odagiri Hideo (b. 1916). In their journal *Modern Literature* (*Kindai bungaku*), which they published from January 1946 to August 1964, they called for an investigation into why culture had failed to prevent the horrors of the war, and they especially excoriated what they called "Art for Art's Sake." They sought to implant firmly within Japanese culture a universalized concept of "ego" that would serve as the basis for a "democratic" society. Underneath this progressive rhetoric, however, lay a refusal to confront the issues that had animated the prewar debates on modernity, a refusal that stemmed from their belief that history (at least the history that mattered) in Japan had ground to a halt in 1931.

When Ara and Hirano criticized Marxism's contempt for individual human subjectivity (*ko no ningen-teki shutaisei*) and insisted

on the importance of a reinstatement of the individual's own feelings (*jikkan*) as an integral part of the rebirth of egoism, they
sparked one of the most important debates in the history of postwar Japanese thought. The debate on subjectivity, which took
place from 1946 to 1948, pitted the supporters of modernity (including members of the Association for Research into the Science
of Thought [Shisō no Kagaku Kenkyūkai] such as Ōtsuka Hisao,
Maruyama Masao, Kawashima Takeyoshi, and Shimizu Ikutarō)
against both the Communist Party and traditionalists.[24] The latter
two groups argued that the modernists were guilty of an elitist
outlook that, as a result of a preoccupation with their own over-
blown sense of self-worth, snubbed the people (conceived as the
"masses" or the "folk") as politically impotent, if not irrelevant.
The Communists were especially harsh, condemning the modernists as "petit bourgeois individualists who served the imperialist
ideology of monopoly capitalism by aestheticizing modernism and
capitalism."[25] Officially denounced by the Communist Party, the
debate on subjectivity was abruptly terminated, although the
issues involved were merely transformed and absorbed into the
ongoing debate on modernity.

Although generally aligning themselves with the position of the
Occupation, the modernists were not able to silence their oppo-
nents. In June 1947, while the debate on subjectivity still raged,
nineteen members of the prewar *Literary World*, including such
participants at the 1942 symposium on overcoming modernity as
Hayashi Fusao, Kamei Katsuichirō, Kawakami Tetsutarō, and
Miyoshi Tatsuji, came together and reissued the group's journal,
Bungakkai. In the inaugural issue, Kamei reflected on how the
prewar journal dealt with a wide variety of cultural topics. It is
now time, he suggests, for a similar journal that will encompass
religion, philosophy, and natural science while "maintaining the
loftiness that resists politics."[26] Given the sociopolitical conditions
of Japan in 1947, it should be clear that *politics* here signifies none
other than the reality of the Occupation and its enforcement of a
modernist theory over the prewar discourse on culture. Culture,
for the members of the *Literary World*, represented an attempt to
preserve some basis for a collective identity that could remain
distinct and apart from the onslaught of modernism.

Support came from a number of organizations that were beginning in the late 1940s to publish their own journals attacking modernism. One such group, centered on the journal *Kokoro*, which began publishing in July 1948, strongly opposed modernism as a form of facile Eurocentrism and adopted a culturalist or traditionalist position. Composed mainly of such intellectuals as Abe Yoshishige (1883–1966), Tsuda Sōkichi (1873–1961), Watsuji Tetsurō, and Yanagita Kunio, the *Kokoro* group did not completely reject modernization but argued that a return to true Japanese tradition was a necessary element in an indigenous (*naihatsu-teki*) modernization.

In contrast, the journal *Sokoku*, which was published from 1949 to 1955 and centered on Yasuda Yojūrō, grasped the struggle against modernization as a struggle for Asian freedom and autonomy. In a dialogue published in the journal, Yasuda denounces the "ethics of peace" that are maintaining the postwar political order and, while generally adopting a negative position on the rearmament of Japan, argues that the problem is deeper than simply the issue of rearmament: "One cannot maintain, morally speaking, that armaments preserve the freedom of the folk. It is time for the Japanese to show the world the truth that, at present, only the Japanese understand that this cannot be said. Even Mr. Nehru does not grasp this. This is the intellectual significance of Asia today.... We are not saying that war is bad or that armaments are bad. We are saying that 'modern' life is bad."[27] Yasuda makes it clear that he holds no sympathy for the advocates of a conditional peace who argue that a realistic appraisal of modernism leads to the conclusion that it is a necessary, if unfortunate, compromise for the future survival of Japan. The choice is not between the "democracy" of the United States and the "communism" of the Soviet Union: Japan, he argues, must reject such alternatives and choose the position of an Asia that remains absolutely peaceful, eternally unchanged, and beyond the pale of history and modernity.[28] In short, in a manner reminiscent of his earlier, prewar thought, Yasuda tries to suggest that the solution to the major political issues of postwar Japan can only be found in totalizing cultural perspectives that displace modern political and historical modes of action.

In the process of discrediting modernity, the outbreak of the Korean War in 1950 was an important moment that was second, perhaps, only to the ambiguities of life under Occupation policy. From the perspective of proponents of an Asian ethnic unity, the intervention of the United States in the Korean conflict looked too much like a painfully familiar form of white imperialism in Asia. Indeed, if the Japanese had been guilty during the Pacific War of egregious violations of international law, human rights, and common decency, and paid for it with their military defeat and occupation, how much more indefensible were claims that the United States had a right to cross the ocean to defend what it called its interests in the Pacific. Following on the heels of the Communist victory in China, the Korean war gave new form, and a new sense of urgency, to the expression of the long-stewing Asian discontent with modernity. Thus, in April 1951, while Yasuda and the *Sokoku* circle were calling for the adoption of an "Asian position" apart from the modern, Western world, the *Literary World* group issued a summons for new members, published a new column in the journal devoted exclusively to the membership's suggestions for it, and opened the journal to writers such as Yoshiyuki Junnosuke (b. 1924) and Ōe Kenzaburō (b. 1935), who brought with them new talents as well as new concerns. Many of these younger writers did, however, share the general sense of malaise with modernity and the resurgence of interest in the "people," however broadly defined, as the focus of political action. No doubt, the little magazines that the noted publishing house Bungei Shunjū brought out in 1950 for popular consumption contributed to this trend.[29] As a result, one finds throughout the 1950s a general trend toward intellectual polarization and pluralization, in which the "people" emerged not only as a powerful ideological weapon against modernity but also as a very real, political force that challenged the Japanese state in the form of a variety of popular movements.

ROMANTICISM REHABILITATED, 1960–1990

Given the events described above and the role they played in the reemergence of ethnic populism as a critical force, we can now consider the rehabilitation of the Japan Romantic School in the postwar period. This rehabilitation was largely the result of the efforts of two men, Hashikawa Bunzō (1922–83) and Takeuchi Yoshimi (1910–77). From 1957 to 1959, Hashikawa began publishing a series of essays on the Romantic School in the journal *Contemporaneity* (*Dōjidai*). These essays, which later formed the core of his justly famous study *An Introduction to a Criticism of the Japan Romantic School* (1965), try to explain why the Japan Romantic School was so influential among members of Hashikawa's generation, while avoiding a reduction of the Romantic School to ultranationalism or "the aestheticization of fascism." Hashikawa takes as his point of departure a comment made by Takeuchi Yoshimi who, in his essay "Modernism and the Problem of Ethnicity" ("Kindai-shugi to minzoku no mondai"; 1951), complains that the dominance of modernism in postwar Japanese intellectual discourse has prevented a fuller treatment of the issues raised by the wartime romantics. As one who was personally influenced by the romantics, Hashikawa argues, he is ideally situated to see both the risks and advantages of the romantics' project, and he takes it upon himself to meet the challenge posed by Takeuchi.

In Hashikawa's analysis, the Japan Romantic School encapsulated the three most important sources of radical thought during the Shōwa period: Marxism, nativism, and German romanticism. All three shared a critical orientation toward modern rationality and were fused together in the Japan Romantic School through the concept of irony. Irony, as conceived and used by the members of the school, was nothing less than an attempt to displace the claims of similitude posed by the modernist, bureaucratic state in its ideology of a "family-state" and to suggest new sources of creative thought and action. In this sense, Hashikawa, who largely reduces the Romantic School to the writings of Yasuda, finds Yasuda's description of "the irony of a Japan free to simultaneously ensure destruction and construction" to be closely related to Carl Schmitt's view that "the reservation of all infinite possibilities lies in irony."[30] From this reading of the function of romantic irony, Hashikawa is able to conclude that the historical role of the Japan Romantic School was not that of serving the interests of the militarist state, as the modernists claimed. Rather, he notes, the critical possibilities inherent in their task were merely frustrated by the personal failings of "complete cowards" such as Yasuda.[31]

Hashikawa's restoration of romanticism as a critical force was given additional support by Takeuchi's seminal essay "Overcoming Modernity," which he wrote in November 1959 for the seventh volume of the "Lectures in the History of Modern Japanese Thought" series ("Kindai Nihon shisōshi kōza"). Developing themes suggested in his earlier essay on "Modernism and the Problem of Ethnicity," this study broadens the focus from romanticism to the issue of modernity itself. In the section on "the role of the Japan Romantic School" in the project to overcome modernity, Takeuchi suggests that the issues raised by the Romantic School could not be reduced only to those explicitly treated by the men who wrote for the school's journal, but were part of a broader cultural and aesthetic criticism of modernity, which he sees as the most powerful underlying current of modern Japanese intellectual history. He roundly criticizes modernists such as Odagiri Hideo for their failure to recognize that inherent in the Japan Romantic School's criticism of modernity was a concept of ethnicity that could serve as a powerful critique not only of the West but of the Japanese state as well.[32] The historical significance of the "ethnic revival" becomes apparent in light of the fact that Takeuchi wrote his article in the months of intense debate leading up to the unprecedented massive protest over the revision of the U.S.-Japan Security Treaty in May and June 1960. In this new, postwar context, the significance of the Japan Romantic School is not how it was used by the Japanese state during the war but how its critique of modernity might be resuscitated to reveal Japanese complicity in a modernism that is now identified with the West, particularly with the United States.

Takeuchi concedes that the antimodern rhetoric of the romantics led to a justification of an imperialistic war in Asia and he criticizes that aspect of it. But more important, he notes, it was a profound articulation of a colonized people's longing for independence and autonomy, and it is this aspect of the attempt to overcome modernity that Takeuchi finds most relevant for a Japan torn apart by the Security Treaty crisis. According to Takeuchi, the participants of the 1942 symposium on overcoming modernity tried to articulate a basis for Japanese culture independent from prevailing European forms of culture. Here, Takeuchi is clearly equating modernity with the West. He defines modernity as the "self" of Europe, and interprets modern history as the unfolding of a process that preserves the "self" through a form of self-expansion that transforms its "Other" into an image of itself.[33] Thus, he calls for a reawakening of Asian consciousness as the method of preserving this cultural distinctiveness against the claims of similitude posed by modernism. He lauds the Japan Romantic School for the role it played in exposing the "aporia" of Japanese modernity by urging a consideration of ethnicity as the foundation of this new cultural identity.[34] In the end, he suggests that the Japanese, in solidarity with other Asian peoples, should replace their Western-based modernity with an Asian form drawn from a Chinese model.

Takeuchi's proposal for overcoming modernity and the National Literature movement it spawned were immediately challenged by Hanada Kiyoteru (1909–74) in his own study, *Overcoming Modernity*, which was published in December 1959, just one month after Takeuchi's essay appeared. Without mentioning Takeuchi by name, Hanada suggests that it is meaningless to talk of overcoming modernity through an ethnic identity that rejects modernity, and he seeks to return the issue of popular culture to the discourse. A self-avowed communist, Hanada calls for the practice of an avant-garde art form as a precondition for a new concept of the masses as inheritors of a premodern "sensory culture" (*shichōkaku bunka*). This is not literally a return to a premodern or "nonmodern" position, such as Takeuchi's concept of Asia as a spatial challenge to historical development, but an attempt to overcome the contradictions of history and class consciousness through the strategy of a dialectic rhetoric based on a concept of language as fiction. Through the production of fictitiousness, Hanada hopes to resuscitate the romantic emphasis on aesthetics and thereby create a space for new forms of cosmopolitan culture that might truly transcend modernity, without appealing to ethnicity or race.

The debate between Takeuchi and Hanada centers on different evaluations of the significance of history and language. Takeuchi rejects Hanada's emphasis on language as symbolic fiction in favor of a view of language as utterance (*hatsugo*).[35] Here, language as utterance is one means of portraying the unity and authenticity of ethnic identity prior to modern notions of signification and the alienation of word and thing. Consequently, for Takeuchi the central problem ultimately rests on the historical conditions that qualify the subject to speak. But for Hanada, to overcome modernity requires a willingness to abandon the certainty provided by historical knowledge in favor of the direct experience of the contradictions of life and livelihood. While he shares Takeuchi's analysis of history as an interplay of contradictory forces, he rejects Takeuchi's identification with Asia as an ethnic (racial?) whole and, instead, insists on working within the contradictions of life, labor, and language in order to overcome modernity. Reversing Takeuchi's formula, Hanada defines the issue as how "to change national things from an international point of view."[36]

With the success of Japan's policy of high-growth economics in the 1960s and early 1970s, the discourse on modernity underwent further challenge and change. Newly acquired wealth not only enabled increasing numbers of Japanese to travel overseas but also led many Japanese intellectuals to rethink their relationship with the rest of Asia. Japan was now emerging as one of the world's most economically powerful nations, while serving as a major military base for the American involvement in Vietnam, a war that appeared to many as merely the latest in a series of Western (read "modern") interventions in Asia. With the beginning of major U.S. bombing raids on North Vietnam in the spring of 1965, a resurgence of mass political protest in Japan surprised many conservatives who might otherwise have been tempted to believe that Prime Minister Ikeda's policy of substituting economic growth for political debate had succeeded.[37] As had happened during the Security Treaty crisis five years earlier, this awakening of political protest was accompanied by a renewed interest in the critical possibilities of romanticism.

Led by Ōkubo Tsuneo (b. 1928), these writers and critics self-consciously described the object of their interest as "revolutionary romanticism," thus suggesting ties with the Chinese Cultural Revolution that was just getting underway.[38] For them, the Japan Romantic School offered a moral basis for individual action in a world where politics seemed totally corrupt and devoid of any possibility for shaping new, critical responses to the threat of modernity. The prewar concern with producing various forms of cultural subjectivity to replace the modern "ego" was therefore largely translated into the question of forming an "ethical subject" that might act according to norms established by an autonomous "folk" or race. With the growth in the postwar years of a general distrust of grandiose language concerning culture writ large, the focus on romanticism shifted to how the individual could preserve an ethical basis for action against, or separate from, a state that seemed hopelessly divorced from traditional norms of morality and ethics. Hence, "revolutionary" romanticism often has turned to Kobayashi Hideo and his search for an ethical basis in the thought of Motoori Norinaga, or Kamei Katsuichirō and his research into the aesthetics of Japanese spirit, or Yasuda Yojūrō and his exploration of traditional art and ways of life. Unlike the earlier discourse on romanticism, much of the critical impulse in this recent reappropriation of the Japan Romantic School has retreated from an explicit engagement with issues of modernity and the West and has been redirected to provide a cultural framework for the affluent postwar generation.

Because this revitalization of romanticism is still going on, it may be premature to pronounce final judgment on its possibilities as a critical force. One question that remains to be answered is whether the new postwar reading of the Japan Romantic School can resist tendencies to convert its critical orientation into familiar forms of ethnocentrism and racial bigotry, especially in light of the recent treatment of foreign laborers in Japan. We have yet to see if postmodernism, with its close ties to romanticism's reevaluation of the relationship of culture to politics, will merely provide a more compelling effacement of the critical possibilities of ethnicity by incorporating it into a resurgent "official" nationalism in contemporary Japan.[39] It is worth remembering that those involved in the postwar rehabilitation of the Japan Romantic School who have focused on its discovery of ethnicity as a critical and historical basis of identity have remained closest to the romantics' original project. For it was the Japan Romantic School's forceful articulation of a shared cultural identity that formed its most powerful critique of modernity and, at the same time, represents yet another reminder of the incomplete nature of the modernist project.

Appendix A
Members of the Japan Romantic School

Listed in chronological order of membership.
Boldfaced type indicates a founding member.
*indicates a contributor to the journal *Nihon rōmanha*.

Name	Dates	Sponsor	Miscellaneous
Yasuda Yojūrō*	1910–81		leader of school; former member of *Genjitsu*, *Cogito*
Kamei Katsuichirō*	1907–66		member of *Shinjinkai*
Nakatani Takao*	b. 1901		member of *Seki*
Nakajima Eijirō*	1910–45	Yasuda	member of *Cogito*; war casualty in Luzon
Jinbō Kōtarō*	1905–90	Kamei(?)	Kamei's friend from Yamagata Higher School
Ogata Takashi*	1905–38	Nakatani	member of *Seki*; novelist; died of TB
Itō Shizuo*	1906–53	Kamei/Nakatani	poet laureate of JRS
Itō Sakio*	1910–71		novelist
Iwata Kuichi*	b. ?–d. ?		resigned from JRS August 1935
Ima Uhei*	1908–84		a.k.a. Harube; born Takasaki Hideo
Haga Mayumi*	1903–91		member of *Shiki*
Ōyama Teiichi	1904–74	Jinbō	trans. Goethe, Rilke, T. Mann
Watanabe Kan*	b. ?–d. ?		

Yodono Ryūzō*	1904–67		real name, Sankichi; trans. Gide
Dazai Osamu*	1909–48		novelist
Dan Kazuo*	1917–76		novelist
Yamagishi Gaishi*	1904–77		joined JCP after Pacific War
Kiyama Shōhei*	1904–68		novelist
Kitamura Kenjirō*	b. 1901		novelist
Kōriyama Hiroshi*	b. 1902		a.k.a. Nakahara Ryūki-chi; poet
Midorigawa Mitsugu*	b. 1912		born Naitō; novelist
Yukiyama Toshiyuki*	b. ?–d. ?		novelist

JOINED AFTER JULY 1935

Nakamura Chihei*	1908–63		born Jihei

JOINED AFTER JANUARY 1936

Sakamoto Etsurō*	1906–69	Kamei	poet
Satō Hiroshi*	b. 1907		
Sawanishi Susumu*	b. ?–d. ?		died before 1972; a.k.a. Banzai (?)

JOINED AFTER JUNE 1936

Ishinaka Shōji*	1900–1981		trans. Nietzsche, Rilke
Inoue Tōru*	b. ?–d. ?		
Tamura Gorō	b. ?–d. ?		
Takita Masaru	b. ?–d. ?		
Takahashi Sachio*	b. 1912		
Tachibana Yoshikazu	b. ?–d.?		
Tsuneki Minoru	b. 1913		student of German literature
Kubota Shōbun	b. 1912		(professor, Risshō U.)
Matsuyama Takeo*	b. ?–d. ?		
Funabashi Hanirō*	b. ?–d. ?		

Fukuda Minoru	1912–1985		
Kondō Harufumi	b. ?–d. ?		
Asakura Yasuhira*	b. ?–d. ?		
Saitō Makoto*	b. ?–d. ?		
Kon Kan'ichi*	1909–83		novelist

JOINED IN AUGUST 1936

| Hayashi Fusao* | 1903–75 | | born Gotō Toshio; member of *Shinjinkai* |

JOINED AFTER JANUARY 1937

Hagiwara Sakutarō	1886–1942		well-known poet
Satō Haruo*	1892–1964		well-known writer, Yasuda's "mentor"
Nakagawa Yoichi*	b. 1897		
Banshōya Eiichi	1895–1966		professor of German, Rikkyō University
Miyoshi Tatsuji	1900–1964		member of *Shiki*; poet and translator
Tomura Shigeru*	1902–1961		

JOINED BY MARCH 1938

Hirabayashi Eiko*	b. 1902		married to Nakatani Takao
Wakabayashi Tsuya*	b. 1905		born Sugiyama Mitoe; member of *Genjitsu*
Yokota Fumiko*	1909–85		
Masugi Shizue	1901–55	Nakamura Chihei(?)	lived with Nakamura 1933–42
Hara Tamiki	1905–51		poet and novelist
Komada Shinji	b. 1914		
Koyama Yūshi	1906–82		playwright
Togaeri Hajime	1914–63		

TOTAL MEMBERS: 56

CONTRIBUTORS AND AFFILIATES

Maeda Makoto	b. ?–d. ?		publisher and editor of *NRH*
Makabe Jin*	1907–84	Jinbō	Jinbō's friend from primary school
Mori Takeshi*	b. ?–d. ?		
Nakamura Takesa-burō*	b. ?–d. ?		
Asano Akira*	1901–90		member of *Shinjinkai*
Asami Fukashi*	1899–1973		
Tachihara Michizō*	1914–39		member of *Shiki*
Tanaka Katsumi	b. 1911		member of *Cogito*
Yoshida Makoto*	b. ?–d. ?		
Nomura Takuichi*	b. ?–d. ?		
Shida Fumoto*	1913–84		
Mori Michio*	b. ?–d. ?		

TOTAL AFFILIATES: 12

TOTAL MEMBERS AND AFFILIATES: 68

SOURCES: Nitta Mitsuo, ed., *Nihon rōmanha to wa nanika* (Tokyo: Yūshōdō sho-ten, 1972): 169–76; Amano Keitarō and Fukai Hitoshi, eds., *Nihon zasshi sōmokuji yōran* (Tokyo: Nichigai asoshiētsu, 1985); Odagiri Susumu, ed., *Nihon kindai bungaku daijiten* (Tokyo: Kōdansha, 1977), s.v. "Nihon rōmanha," by Ōkubo Tsuneo; Saegusa Yasutaka, *Nihon rōmanha no undō* (Tokyo: Gendaisha, 1959), 247–62; Tanisaki Akio (personal correspondence).

Appendix B
Subjective Positions in Itō Shizuo's
Laments to My Person

Title of Poem	Position	Original Source
On a Clear Day	I	*Cogito*, Aug. 1934
Song of the Prairie	half-self	*Cogito*, Apr. 1935
I Am Compelled	half-self	*Cogito*, Feb. 1934
Frozen Valley	half-self	*Bungakkai*, Apr. 1935
Cinema in the New World	I	*Ro*, July 1933
On a Country Road	I	*Cogito*, Feb. 1935
A Noon Rest	half-self	*Nihon rōmanha*, Apr. 1935
The Homecomer	I	*Cogito*, Apr. 1934
Envoy	I	*Ro*, Oct. 1932
In a Cold Place	half-self	*Cogito*, Dec. 1934
Sea Bathing	I	*Ro*, Nov. 1933
Laments to My Person	half-self	*Cogito*, Nov. 1934
A Quiet Xenie*	I	—
A Recitation	half-self	*Ro*, Nov. 1932
April Winds	I	*Ro*, June 1934
Improvisation	half-self	*Shii no ki*, Apr. 1935
Without Flying, the Mud Hen	I	*Shiki*, Apr. 1935
A Recitation	half-self	*Ro*, Nov. 1932
Memories of the Ariake Sea	I	*Cogito*, Mar. 1935
(Anonymous)	half-self	*Ro*, Nov. 1932
I'll Call That Smiling Person	half-self	*Nihon rōmanha*, July 1935
Song of a Hospital Patient	I	*Ro*, June 1933

Begone, Your ...	I	*Cogito*, June 1935
A Riverside Poem	I	*Cogito*, Oct. 1934
Wandering	half-self	*Cogito*, Aug. 1935
Rather They Shall Sing of My Today	I	*Cogito*, Jan. 1935
Nightingale	an old man	*Ro*, Feb. 1934
(Anonymous)	(an old man)	*Ro*, Dec. 1932

*Believed to be the most recent of the poems.

SOURCE: Sugimoto Hidetarō, *Itō Shizuo* (Tokyo: Chikuma shobō, 1985), 275.

Notes

PROLOGUE

1. Representative of the renewed interest in the problem of nationalism are Anderson, *Imagined Communities*; Breuilly, *Nationalism and the State*; Gellner, *Nations and Nationalism*; Hobsbawm, *Nations and Nationalism Since 1780*; and Smith, *Theories of Nationalism*. An especially thoughtful analysis of nationalism and literature is Berlant, *Anatomy of National Fantasy*. For a recent study on nationalism in postwar Japan, see Yoshino, *Cultural Nationalism in Contemporary Japan*.

2. Bloch, "Nonsynchronism and the Obligation to Its Dialectics."

3. For a detailed and powerful analysis of the failure of class-based analyses of the problem of nationalism, see Breuilly, *Nationalism and the State*, especially 21–28.

4. The classic expression of this explanation is Reischauer, "What Went Wrong?"

5. Pyle, *The New Generation in Meiji Japan*.

6. Ishida, *Nihon no seiji to kotoba*, 160–61.

7. Ibid., 166–68.

8. Pyle, *New Generation in Meiji Japan*, 19–20.

9. Gluck, *Japan's Modern Myths*, 23.

10. Yasuda, "Meiji no seishin," especially 223–29.

11. Habermas, "Modernity," 142.

12. Ibid.

13. Anderson, *Imagined Communities*, 80–128.

14. Storry, *Double Patriots*, is a classic example of the *kokka-shugi* focus, which Anderson uses in his comments on Japanese nationalism in *Imagined Communities*; Pyle, *New Generation in Meiji Japan*, focuses on culture and identity but from the overall perspective of constructing a modern nation-state. One of the dominant trends in scholarship on Japan has been "modernization theory," which often congratulates Japan for successfully building a powerful and wealthy nation. The best example is Reischauer, *Japan*. An important recent study of Japanese nationalism, White et al., *Ambivalence of Nationalism*, touches on some themes relevant to ethnic-nationalism but does not develop them as distinct from "official nationalism."

15. Harootunian, "Commentary on Nationalism in Japan," 57 (emphasis mine).

16. Those who resist translating *minzoku-shugi* (literally, ethnic-ism) as "nationalism" should consider that Stalin's *Marxism and the National and Colonial Question* was translated into Japanese as *Marukusu-shugi to minzoku mondai* (Marxism and the minzoku question). See Nagashima, "Minzoku narabi ni minzoku undō ni tsuite," for a discussion of Stalin's text in the context of nationalist movements in Europe.

17. Anderson, *Imagined Communities*, 106–9.

18. Yasuda, "Bōrudōin shushō," 95–96.

19. Nairn and Hechter's "theory of internal colonialism" is discussed in Smith, *Ethnic Revival*, 4 and also 26–44.

20. Ibid., 25.

21. Karatani, "Kindai Nihon no hihyō," 18.

22. See Harootunian, "Introduction." There were, of course, still labor strikes and other political struggles, but the concept of the individual political subject was more frequently subsumed within collective identities as the new subjects of political action.

23. For a comparative look at the problem of creating tradition in modern societies, see Hobsbawm and T. Ranger, *Invention of Tradition*, especially Hobsbawm's "Introduction: Inventing Traditions."

24. Hobsbawm extends the period of high nationalism until 1950 and looks at the complex problems posed by post–World War II anti-imperial 'national' movements of the Third World. See his *Nations and Nationalism Since 1780*, 131–62. These problems are less relevant to my study of pre–World War II Japanese nationalism, as I share his view that Japan in the 1930s should "be considered an honorary western imperial power, and thus a national and nationalist state somewhat like its western models" (151).

25. Anderson, *Imagined Communities*, 104 (emphasis in original).

26. Miki, "Fuan no shisō to sono chōkoku," 14. Cf. Gadamer, *Philosophical Hermeneutics*, 124: "Jaspers contrasted the concept of certain knowledge, 'world-orientation,' as he called it, with the illumination of existence, which comes into play in the boundary situations of the scientific as well as every human capacity for knowledge. According to Jaspers, boundary situations are those situations of human existence in which the possibilities of being guided by the anonymous powers of science break down, and where, for that reason, everything depends upon oneself."

27. Miki, "Fuan no shisō to sono chōkoku," 11.

28. Smith, *Japan's First Student Radicals*, 40–45, 77–88.

29. Roden, "Taishō Culture and the Problem of Gender Ambivalence," 39–40 (emphasis added); internal quotes are attributed to George Mosse, *The Culture of Western Europe* (New York: Rand McNally, 1965), 227–78.

30. [Miki], "Henshū yōroku."

31. Miki, "Kagaku hihan no kadai," 16.

32. Yasuda Yojūrō discusses the influence of the "New Science" group on his thought in his postwar reflections *Nihon rōmanha no jidai*, especially 16–17.

33. Iwamoto, "Aspects of the Proletarian Literary Movement in Japan," 156–57.

34. Shea, *Leftwing Literature in Japan*.

35. One Marxist literary critic who tried to address these concerns with exceptional rigor was Nakano Shigeharu. See Silverberg, *Changing Song*.

36. Kakuzo Okakura, *Ideals of the East, with Special Reference to the Art of Japan* (Rutland, Vt.: Tuttle, 1970); cited in Najita and Harootunian, "Japanese Revolt Against the West," 715. Much of the following discussion of contemporary attempts by other culturalist groups to overcome modernity is, except where otherwise noted, indebted to Najita and Harootunian's masterful essay.

37. Nishida Kitarō, *Hataraku mono kara miru mono e* (1927); cited in Arakawa, *Shōwa shisō shi*, 170–71.

38. Tosaka Jun, "Kyōto gakuha no tetsugaku," (September 1932); cited in Arakawa, *Shōwa shisō shi*, 168–69. Arakawa explicitly calls Nishida's philosophy "Romantic."

39. Arakawa, *Shōwa shisō shi*, 190.

40. Tanabe Hajime, *Shu no ronri no benshōhō*; cited in Arakawa, *Shōwa shisō shi*, 174.

41. Najita and Harootunian, "Japanese Revolt Against the West," 751.

42. Tanizaki Jun'ichiro, *In Praise of Shadows*, trans. Edward Seidensticker and Thomas Harper (New Haven: Leete's Island Books, 1977), 8; cited in Najita and Harootunian, "Japanese Revolt Against the West," 753.

43. Yasuda, *Nihon rōmanha no jidai*, 42.

44. For those who still want to know more about Yasuda's life, there is an exhaustive chronology with a comprehensive listing of his publications in *YYz* appendix 5:85–212.

45. The editors of *Hoshu handō shisōka ni manabu hon* believe Yasuda did have experience in left-wing movements (283). In fact, Yasuda's memoirs of this period deserve the same degree of skepticism that all retrospective accounts do.

46. Yasuda, *Nihon rōmanha no jidai*, 16–17, 100–125.

47. Smith, *Ethnic Revival*, 125.

48. Rabinow and Sullivan, "Interpretive Turn," 9.

49. Smith, *Ethnic Revival*, 88. But see his full discussion of the relationship of historicism to ethnic movements, 87–107.

50. [Yasuda], "Henshū kōki."

51. Lacoue-Labarthe and Nancy, *Literary Absolute*, 11.

52. See the brief treatment of the Japan Romantic School ("the Romanha writers") in Najita and Harootunian, "Japanese Revolt Against the West," 754–58.

53. Seyhan, *Representation and Its Discontents*, 4 (emphasis mine).

54. [Yasuda], "'Nihon rōmanha' kōkoku," 173.

55. Seyhan, *Representation and Its Discontents*, 60.

56. Schmitt, *Political Romanticism*, 12–14.

57. Ibid., 10–11.

58. Heine, *Die romantische Schule*, 10. I am indebted to John M. Jeep, who located and translated this passage for me.
59. [Yasuda], "Sōkan no ji."
60. Bachelard, *Poetics of Space*, xiv–xviii.
61. Ibid., xi.
62. Anderson, *Imagined Communities*, 132.
63. For an analysis of the use of the fragment by German romantics to create desire, see Lacoue-Labarthe and Nancy, *Literary Absolute*, 39–58.
64. Seyhan, *Representation and Its Discontents*, 37.
65. Karatani, "Fūkei no hakken," 30–31.
66. Lacoue-Labarthe and Nancy, *Literary Absolute*, 52. See also "Overture: The System-Subject," 27–37, in the same book.
67. Easthope, *Poetry as Discourse*, 123.
68. [Yasuda], "'Nihon rōmanha' no kōkoku," 173.

1. TOWARD AN IRONIC PRAXIS

1. See Harootunian, "Introduction."
2. Yasuda, "Hyōgen to hyōjō," 29.
3. Smith, *Ethnic Revival*, 127.
4. Oketani, *Yasuda Yojūrō*, 13.
5. Yasuda, "'Hihyō' no mondai," 179–80.
6. Yasuda, "Kiyoraka na shijin," 213.
7. Carroll, *Subject in Question*, 95.
8. Yasuda, "Sento Herena," 219–20.
9. Ibid., 221–56.
10. Ibid., 251.
11. Kawamura, "Yasuda Yojūrō ron," 142.
12. Yasuda, "Sento Herena," 253.
13. Yasuda, "Bungaku no aimaisa," 62.
14. Cf. Ōoka Makoto's argument that decadence for Yasuda is rooted in the loss of nature, not God (as it is for Kamei). See his *Jojō no hihan*, 56.
15. Edwards, *Encyclopedia of Philosophy*, s.v. "Hans Vaihinger," by Rollo Handy.
16. Yasuda, "Bungaku no aimaisa," 55.
17. Oketani, *Yasuda Yojūrō*, 28. For Yasuda's views on the Shinkankakuha writers, see his "Hyōgen to hyōjō," and "Kawabata Yasunari ron."
18. See Worringer, *Abstraction and Empathy*, 9.
19. Pierrot, *Decadent Imagination*, especially 166–90.
20. Yasuda, "Bungaku no aimaisa," 61.
21. Yasuda, "Sento Herena," 281.
22. Yasuda, *Taikan shijin no goichininsha*, 20.
23. Ibid., 24–25.
24. Ibid., 40–41.
25. Ibid., 20.

26. Yasuda, "Hakuhō-Tenpyō no seishin," 96.
27. Yasuda, *Taikan shijin no goichininsha*, 23–27.
28. Yasuda, *Nihon no hashi*, 10–17.
29. Adorno, *Aesthetic Theory*, 95.
30. Ibid., 95–96.
31. Ibid., 95.
32. Yasuda, " 'Nihon-teki na mono' hihyō ni tsuite," 190–91.
33. Ibid., 204.
34. Ibid., 206.
35. Ōkubo, *Shōwa bungaku no shokumei*, 82; Ōka, cited in Kawamura, "Yasuda Yojūrō ron," 144; Matsumoto, "Yasuda Yojūrō oboegaki," 140.
36. In an article published early in 1937, Kamei berates Yasuda as the "Greek of the Orient" while characterizing himself as "the Israelite of the Orient" (cited in Kurihara, *Nihon rōmanha*, 97). Whatever Kamei may mean in terms of the differences between the two romantics, his choice of metaphors may have stemmed from a perspective similar to that presented by Anthony D. Smith, who argues that "the Greeks and Jews of antiquity evinced a fervent sense of ethnicity and resisted isolation and tyranny with a passionate, if intermittent, sense of solidarity" (*Ethnic Revival*, 19). The characterization may have been part of a personal struggle between Kamei and Yasuda for control of the Japan Romantic School, but within the broader problem of ethnic identity, it merely reinforced their shared agenda.
37. Yasuda, *Weruteru wa naze shinda ka*, 289. Yasuda's interpretation of *Werther* as an investigation of the conditions of modernity, rather than merely as a love story, is very close to Schiller's reading and may even have been indebted to it. See Schiller, *Naive and Sentimental Poetry*, and *On the Sublime*.
38. Yasuda, *Weruteru wa naze shinda ka*, 315.
39. Ibid., 305–6.
40. Ibid., 363.
41. Yasuda, "Meiji no seishin," 229–30.
42. Yasuda, "Masaoka Shiki ni tsuite," 20.
43. Yasuda, "Bunmei kaika no ronri no shūen ni tsuite," 13–15.
44. Yasuda, "Nihon no jōtai ni oite," 200–201.
45. Yasuda, "Waga kuni ni okeru rōmanshugi no gaikan," 302.
46. See Hashikawa, *Nihon rōmanha hihan josetsu*, 39–40; Matsumoto, "Yasuda Yojūrō oboegaki," 139; Kawamura, "Yasuda Yojūrō ron," 144–48; Ōkubo, *Shōwa bungaku no shukumei*, 82–83.
47. Oketani, *Yasuda Yojūrō*, 87–88.
48. Ōoka, *Jojō no hihan*, 63.
49. Yasuda, "Bungakushi-teki na kanmei," 563.
50. Yasuda, "Nihon rōmanha ni tsuite," 247.
51. See Romano Vulpitta's insightful comparison of Yasuda's concept of emperor with Mircea Eliade's myth of the eternal return in his "Yasuda Yojūrō to Mirucha Eriāde."

52. Yasuda, *Gotobain*, 16.
53. See Oketani, *Yasuda Yojūrō*, 87.
54. Yasuda, "Nihon bunka no dokusōsei," 270–71.
55. Yasuda, "Fūkei to rekishi," 377; 364–65; 373.
56. Ibid., 369–70.
57. Ibid., 383.
58. Lukács, "On the Romantic Philosophy of Life," 54.
59. Yasuda, "Tempyō no kofun ni tsuite," 14–15.
60. Yasuda, "Daitō-A sensō to Nihon bungaku," 212–13; Ōkubo Tsu- neo cites this passage in *Shōwa bungakushi no kōsō to bunseki* to support his belief that Yasuda sought to avoid West vs. Japan—in Ōkubo's mind, at least (288).
61. See Oketani, *Yasuda Yojūrō*, 92.
62. Kamiya, *Yasuda Yojūrō ron*, 108. On Tomobayashi's thought, see Harootunian, *Things Seen and Unseen*, 358–73, and, concerning Yasuda's text on Tomobayashi, 458 n. 22.
63. Harootunian, *Things Seen and Unseen*, 358.
64. Yasuda, "Jijo," 9–10.
65. Yasuda, *Nanzan tōunroku*, 95–124.
66. Yasuda, "Zadankai no kotoba ni tsuite," 480–81.

2. INDETERMINATE POETICS

1. Behler, "Foreword," xi.
2. [Yasuda], "'Nihon rōmanha' kōkoku," 172.
3. Ibid., 173.
4. [Yasuda], "Sōkan no ji," 92.
5. Odakane Jirō argues that although Jinbō was also a member of the *Shiki* group, his poetry was essentially different from that of other mem- bers such as Miyoshi Tatsuji and Tachihara Michizō. Odakane notes that because of Jinbō's "representation of a pristine side of the revolutionary romanticism ... that inhered in the Japan Romantic School, he may be classified as a representative poet of the Japan Romantic School rather than as a member of the *Shiki* group." Cited in Akitani, "Jinbō Kōtarō," 267.
6. Jinbō, "Atarashiki jikan no kakutoku," 86.
7. The similarities are striking between Jinbō's project and that of Watsuji Tetsurō and others who sought a new philosophy of space in the 1930s. See Watsuji, *A Climate*. Jinbō's own approach was to search for this logic of space in poetry.
8. Jinbō, "Nihon rōmanha shiron." In three segments: the first is sub- titled "On the Transformation of Poetry" (April 1935); the second, "In Search of a New Poem" (June 1935); and the third, "To My Critics" (August 1935).
9. Jinbō, "Nihon rōmanha shiron" (April 1935): 23.
10. "New Form Poetry" (Shintaishi) was a poetic movement founded

in 1882 by Toyama Masakazu (1848–1900), Yatabe Ryōkichi (1851–99), and Inoue Tetsujirō (1855–1944) and later developed by Kitamura Tōkoku, Shimazaki Tōson, Doi Bansui (1871–1952), Kanbara Ariake (1876–1952), and Susukida Kyūkin (1877–1945). It attempted a new style that rejected traditional Japanese poetry (*kanshi*) and, incorporating the form and spirit of Western poetry, insisted on a difference from the latter as well. It is regarded by many as the origin of modern Japanese poetry.

11. The New Prose Poetry Movement (Shin Sanbun Shi Undō) refers to a poetic movement inspired by the work of French surrealists and cubists, especially Max Jacob, that started in March 1929 with the publication by Kitagawa Fuyuhiko (b. 1900) of the group's manifesto, "The Road to New Prose Poetry" ("Shin sanbun shi e no michi") in *Shi to shiron*. Other members included Miyoshi Tatsuji (1900–1964), Anzai Fuyue (1898–1965), Haruyama Yukio (b. 1902), and Kanbara Tai (b. 1898). Kitagawa tried to organize the movement around the poetic ideal of New Realism in April 1930, along with Nakamachi Sadako (1894–1966), Tsujino Hisanori (1909–37), Takiguchi Takeshi (1904–82), and others, by publishing the journal *Time* (*Jikan*). The movement ended a few months later, in June, when Kitagawa, Kanbara, and Yodono Ryūzō (1904–67) left the group in disagreement over its increasing tendency toward Art for Art's Sake and an avoidance of reality, and instead joined the Proletarian Writers League.

12. The Proletariat Poetry Movement (Puroretaria Shi Undō) was formed in September 1930 with Hirasawa Teijirō (b. ?–d. ?) as chairman and Onchi Terutake (1901–67) as secretary. It was a very active movement and attracted nationwide interest until it dissolved into the Japan Proletarian Writers League (NALP) in November 1931.

13. Jinbō, "Nihon rōmanha shiron," 24.

14. Ibid., 25–26.

15. See Kristeva, *Revolution in Poetic Language*.

16. Jinbō, "Atarashiki poemu no tsuikyū," 30. This emphasis on spirit in poetry is reminiscent of Friedrich Schlegel's concept of the "representation of the impression," which also sought to focus attention not on "the poem about the poem" but on the impression that a poem should make on "any civilized person at any time." Cf. Behler, "Foreword," vii–xiii.

17. Jinbō, "Waga hihansha ni okuru," 19.

18. For example, see Yasuda, "Shijin Hagiwara Sakutarō," *YYz* 13: 435–39. See also Miyoshi, "Shi yo! Hagiwara Sakutarō."

19. Asano and Hiyama, *Zuibun*, 192.

20. Hagiwara, "Nihon rōmanha ni tsuite," 90.

21. Hagiwara, "Jo," in *Teihon aoneko*, 81.

22. Matsumoto, *Metsubō katei no bungaku*, 99.

23. Hagiwara, "Jijo," in *Teihon aoneko*, 264.

24. Ibid., 264.

25. Hagiwara, "Aoneko," in *Teihon aoneko*, 97–98.

26. Hagiwara, "Sharuru Bodoreru," in *Atarashiki yokujō*, 66.

27. Benjamin, *Charles Baudelaire*, 170.

28. Hagiwara, "Amanojaku," in *Atarashiki yokujō,* 19 (emphasis in original).

29. Matsumoto, *Metsubō katei no bungaku,* 132. Hagiwara's wife, the former Ueda Ineko, finally had enough of this life and ran off with a younger, and most certainly wealthier, man in 1929.

30. Ōoka, *Hagiwara Sakutarō,* 214–18.

31. Ibid., 218.

32. Ibid., 231.

33. Matsumoto, *Metsubō katei no bungaku,* 104.

34. Nakano Shigeharu, "'Kyōdo bōkeishi' ni arawareta fundo," *Roba* (October 1926): 4–14; cited in Matsumoto, *Metsubō katei no bungaku,* 121–22.

35. Hagiwara, "Ōwataribashi, in *Nihon no shika,*" 301.

36. Yasuda, "Bunmei kaika no ronri no shūen ni tsuite," 14.

37. Oketani, *Kindai no naraku,* 207.

38. There is some debate among Hagiwara specialists over which collection is the better work, *Howling at the Moon* or *The Iceland.* The debate began with the publication of Miyoshi Tatsuji's *Hagiwara Sakutarō* in 1963 with subsequent critics generally agreeing with Miyoshi that the later work is poetically inferior to the earlier one or arguing that *The Iceland* is the "fatalistic development of lyrical poetry" (Matsumoto Ken'ichi). Some, such as Ōkubo Tsuneo and Oketani Hideaki, have emphasized the historical significance of *The Iceland* in the development of Hagiwara's thought, thereby shifting the focus of the debate to emphasize that what is ultimately at stake is where one stands in regard to Hagiwara's nihilistic critique of modernity in the poem.

39. Oketani, *Kindai no naraku,* 218.

40. My discussion of Hagawara's use of classical language draws on Fukunaga Takehiko's analysis in "Shijin no shōzō," in Itō, *Hagiwara Sakutarō,* 399.

41. Hagiwara, "Jijo," *Hyōtō,* in Itō, *Hagiwara Sakutarō,* 306.

42. Hagiwara's view of a "lost home" is very closely related to Kobayashi Hideo's argument in "Kokyō o ushinatta bungaku," first published in *Bungei shunjū* May 1933, that his own generation was the first to have lost a sense of homeland and was thus the first truly modern generation in Japan. It is significant that both "Hyōhakusha no uta" and "Kokyō o ushinatta bungaku" were both published in a relatively close span of time.

43. Ōoka Makoto argues that Hagiwara suggests that only by not having anything can the Japanese have everything; that is, privation is a characteristic of Japanese culture (*Hagiwara Sakutarō,* 262–64).

44. Ibid., 238.

45. See, for example, Matsumoto, "Jojō no shukumei," in *Metsubō katei no bungaku,* and Ōoka, *Hagiwara Sakutarō.*

46. Hagiwara, "Eiyū to shijin o yomite," 52.

47. Ibid., 52.

48. To gain a sense of how widespread the issue of returning to Japan

and Japaneseness was, see the transcripts of a symposium attended by Miki Kiyoshi, Kobayashi Hideo, Abe Tomoji, Kawakami Tetsutarō, et al., "Gendai bungaku no Nihon-teki dōkō." See also Yokomitsu Riichi's novel *Ryoshū*.

49. Hagiwara, *Nihon e no kaiki*, 487.
50. Ibid.
51. Ibid.
52. Smith, *Ethnic Revival*, 19.
53. Hagiwara, *Nihon e no kaiki*, 579.
54. Benjamin, *Charles Baudelaire*, 171.

3. RETURN TO PARNASSUS

1. Asano and Hiyama, *Zuibun*, 191. The other poets were Jinbō and Kurahara Shinjirō (real name, Koretaka). Kurahara was a poet and novelist who studied French literature at Kēiō University and is best remembered for his collection of poems *Oriental Full Moon* (*Tōyō no mangetsu*), which is said to show the influence of Hagiwara's *Blue Cat*. Kurahara was a member of the *Shiki* group of poets (see note 2) and contributed both to that journal and to *Cogito*. He was a cousin of the proletarian critic Kurahara Korehito.

2. Tanaka was a member of the second *Shiki* (four seasons) group of poets, which was founded in 1934 with Hori Tatsuo (1904–53), Miyoshi Tatsuji, and Maruyama Kaoru (1899–1974) as the central figures. The group was influenced by modernism but criticized the intellectualism and formalism of the *Shi to Shiron* group led by Haruyama Yukio and Kitagawa Fuyuhiko, which it sought to replace with lyricism. Although some commentators have tried to distance the *Shiki* poets from the *Cogito* group and the Japan Romantic School by arguing that the *Shiki* group avoided associating lyricism with Japan, this distinction is not always easy to see. There was a close relationship among the three groups, and by January 1941 Hagiwara Sakutarō, Tanaka Katsumi, Itō Shizuo, and Yasuda Yojūrō were all members of the *Shiki* group. See Odagiri, *Nihon kindai bungaku daijiten*, s.v. "*Shiki*," by Niwa Yasuhiro.

3. Saegusa, *Nihon rōmanha no gunzō*, 64. Saegusa expresses his concern, however, over what he calls the dangers of emotional intoxication during a time of great social upheaval such as the one that followed the economic crisis in Japan after the First World War. The reference is to Nakano's poem "Uta." For a translation of and commentary on the poem, see Silverberg, *Changing Song*, 222–24.

4. Fukuchi, "Tanaka Katsumi," 369.

5. Cf., "Just as tradition no longer remains, or if it remains at all it only remains as form, [Tanaka's] poetry must always stand alone." Yasuda, "Futari no shijin," 59.

6. My discussion draws on the reprint of the poem in Fukuchi, "Tanaka Katsumi" and the excerpts in Nomura, *Gendai shijin zenshū*.

7. Yasuda, "Bungakushi-teki na kanmei," 561.

8. Ibid., 564.

9. Funakoshi, "Suguretaru shigyō no jōju," 98.

10. This poem, in the original German and with English translation, may be found in Hölderlin, *Selected Verse: Hölderlin*, 81–96.

11. Literally, "cove of many digressions." My rendering of this as "violent cove" is indebted to Fukuchi's gloss of this phrase as *hageshiku deiri shite iru [irie]* ("Tanaka Katsumi," 362).

12. "Tēburu supīchi," *Cogito* (November 1938): 24. *Mono no aware*, although often rendered "the pathos of things," is a particularly difficult phrase and deserves more expanded treatment than is possible here. A very useful analysis of the term may be found in Harootunian, *Things Seen and Unseen*, 94–98. See also Field, *Splendor of Longing in the Tale of Genji*, 297–302.

13. Tanaka, *Bungei bunka* (March 1940), cited in Fukuchi, "Tanaka Katsumi," 356.

14. This line was originally expressed as a *tanka* poem and appended at the beginning of *Sikang Province*. Cited in Fukuchi, "Tanaka Katsumi," 359.

15. Yasuda, "Futari no shijin," 63.

16. Ibid., 63–64.

17. Cited in Odagiri, *Kindai Nihon bungaku daijiten*, s.v. "Itō Shizuo," by Shōno Junzō.

18. On the evening of November 24, 1934, at a party sponsored by many future members of the Japan Romantic School in celebration of the publication of Itō's first work, *Laments to My Person*, Miyoshi Tatsuji took issue quite loudly with Hagiwara's preference for Itō's work over his own. Miyoshi, who had considered himself Hagiwara's favorite disciple, forced all in attendance to vote between him and Itō, only to find that the majority sided with Hagiwara in favor of Itō. Apparently, this caused a rift in the relationship between Miyoshi and Itō that continued until 1948, only five years before Itō's death, when the two poets finally came to a partial reconciliation. See Odakane, *Shijin*, 190–94.

19. Ogawa Kazusuke points out that the rise of these biographical approaches is directly related to the inclusion of Itō's poetry in middle school and high school textbooks. Whereas Itō's contemporaries shared Itō's educational experiences and world view, postwar school children did not. Thus, Ogawa argues, it was thought necessary to search Itō's life for models on which his poetry was supposedly based and to which his poetry could be reduced for easier comprehension. The most famous of these models is Sakai Yuriko, who is believed to have been the model for "Laments to My Person." See Ogawa, *Itō Shizuo ronkō*, 97. For an example of the approach Ogawa describes, see "Itō Shizuo," in Itō Shinkichi et al., *Nihon no shika*, vol. 23.

20. *Laments to My Person* (*Waga hito ni ataeru aika*) was published by Cogito Publishing and its formatting was done by Yasuda Yojūrō. The

title is believed to have been inspired by Hölderlin's "Menon's Laments for Diotima." See Itō Shinkichi et al., *Nihon no shika* 23:163–64. On Hagiwara's role in the awarding of the Bungei Hanron prize, see Ogawa, *Itō Shizuo ronkō*, 89.

21. Tanaka, "Shijihyō," 113.

22. Yasuda, "Itō Shizuo no shi no koto," 135.

23. Hagiwara, "Wagahito ni ataeru aika," 122.

24. Ibid., 125–26.

25. Tsujino, "Kyōmu no shijin," 47.

26. Ibid., 48. The wish to establish oneself as a king, i.e., to allow free reign to one's own desires and power in an ideal world, may well be an essential characteristic of exoticism. In such exoticized accounts, the enslavement of others inherent in the domination of exoticism is sublimated in favor of the freedom kingship bestows on the exoticizer. See Kipling, "Man Who Would Be King."

27. Itō, "Danwa no kawari ni," 222. Itō's concept of *xenie*, or epigram, is expressed in his poem "Shizuka na kusenie," in *ISz*, 34–36. I argue below that Itō's interest in these pointed, often antithetical, statements must be placed within his broader attempt to overcome the contradictions of self and world.

28. Takeda Chūya, *Noiu-zaharikaito bungakuron* (Tokyo: Kensetsusha, 1931); cited in Odakane, *Shijin*, 127.

29. Itō, "Danwa no kawari ni," 221.

30. Okaniwa, "Itō Shizuo to shōwa jūnendai," 94.

31. In addition to Sugimoto's study, *Itō Shizuo*, Yonekura, *Itō Shizuo*, which was published only two months later, also applies the "split-consciousness" approach, although with less theoretical rigor. But Yonekura's interpretation of "split consciousness" in Itō as resulting from an ambivalent emotional attachment both to metropolitan Osaka and to his home town of Isahaya is insightful.

32. Sugimoto, *Itō Shizuo*, 9.

33. Ibid., 6.

34. I call this phenomenon "discursive poetry" to distinguish the discourse within poetry that occurs in *Laments to My Person* from the "poetic discourse" described in Easthope, *Poetry as Discourse*, especially 19–29.

35. Sugimoto, *Itō Shizuo*, 12.

36. Ibid., 30–31.

37. There is an important play on words in line 7. Itō uses an archaic word for the fruit *tokijiku* (*Citrus tachibana*), so named because of its renowned ability to maintain a characteristic summer fragrance even in the autumn and winter frosts. Thus its name, *tokijiku*, or "timeless," suggests at once the deathly cold of the imaginary peaks and the temporality of mortal beings.

38. Odakane, *Shijin*, 194.

39. Yasuda, "Itō Shizuo no shi no koto," 137.

40. Itō, "Suichūka," 53. Itō explains in a short introduction to the poem

that a "water flower" (*suichūka*) is a toy flower that blooms when immersed in water. He puns on this in the poem by using the archaic name for the sixth month of the old calendar, *minazuki*, or "waterless month."

41. Ogawa, *Itō Shizuo ronkō*, 121.
42. Oketani, *Dochaku to jōkyō*, 121.
43. Itō, "Shokan," in *ISz*, 488.
44. Lacan, "The Mirror Stage as Formative of the Function of the I," 5.
45. Saigō, *Shi no hassei*, 51–54.
46. Lacan, "The Subject and the Other," 205.

4. THE ETHICS OF IDENTITY

1. Kamei, "Bunmei to dōtoku."
2. Kamei, "Nenpu," 517.
3. The Society for the Study of Marxist Art (Marukusu-shugi Geijutsu Kenkyūkai) was a student organization at Tokyo University founded in 1926 by Hayashi Fusao, Nakano Shigeharu, and Kaji Wataru as an outgrowth of the Shinjinkai. During its brief existence, it sought to investigate new developments in Marxist literary criticism. Within the year, the society gained control of the proletarian literary movement under the Japan Proletarian Arts League (Nihon Puroretaria Geijutsu Renmei), or JPAL. See Iwamoto, "Aspects of the Proletarian Literary Movement in Japan," 161–62.
4. The Japan Proletarian Writers League (NALP) was formed on February 10, 1929, under the aegis of the All-Japan Federation of Proletarian Arts (Nippona Artista Proleta Federacio, or NAPF). Along with Kamei, it included such noted writers as Hayashi Fusao, Kobayashi Takiji, and Nakano Shigeharu and was active in various forms until February 22, 1934, when, amid growing persecution by the state, it was finally disbanded.
5. The journal (*Puroretaria bungaku*) was published from January 1932 to October 1933 and served, along with *Literary News* (*Bungaku shinbun*; October 1931 to October 1933), as one of the two literary organs of NALP.
6. Kamei, "Kokyō e kaere," (emphasis mine).
7. Ibid., 289.
8. Kamei, *Tenkeiki no bungaku*, 12–13.
9. Ibid.
10. Ibid., 14.
11. Ibid.
12. Ibid., 15.
13. Ibid., 16–17.
14. Ibid., 17–18, 19.
15. Kamei, "Bungaku ni okeru ishi-teki jōnetsu," in *Tenkeiki no bungaku*, 23–55.
16. Valeri Iakovlevich Kirpotkin (b. 1898), Soviet literary historian and critic. Kirpotkin worked on the staff of the Central Committee of the All-

Union Communist Party (Bolshevik) and was secretary of the organizing committee of the Union of Writers of the USSR in 1932–34.

17. Maksim Gorkii (1868–1936), the famous Russian novelist and playwright.

18. Kamei, "Bungaku ni okeru ishi-teki jōnetsu," in *Tenkeiki no bungaku*, 22.

19. Ibid., 24.

20. Ibid., 23 (emphasis in original).

21. Ibid., 27 (emphasis in original).

22. Ibid., 45.

23. Kamei, "Geijutsu-teki kishitsu to shite no seiji yoku," in *Tenkeiki no bungaku*, 65–73.

24. Kamei uses the English words in his essay, following Hayashi Fusao's practice. Hayashi, who places the English terms *rebel* and *revolutionist* in parentheses after *hangyakusha* and *kakumeika*, argues that the difference between the two is that a rebel does not rely on reason to guide his actions. See Hayashi, "Seinen," 110–11.

25. Kamei, "Geijutsu-teki kishitsu to shite no seiji yoku," in *Tenkeiki no bungaku*, 72–73.

26. Kamei, "Seiji to bungaku ni tsuite," in *Tenkeiki no bungaku*, 74–81.

27. Ibid., 76.

28. Kamei, "Rōman-teki jiga no mondai."

29. Kawakami and Abe, "Fukyūhan jo," 1–2 (emphasis mine).

30. Kamei, "Ikeru Yuda (Shesutofu ron) 1" and "Ikeru Yuda (Shesutofu ron) 2."

31. Kamei, "Ikeru Yuda (Shesutofu ron) 1," 24.

32. Ibid., 25.

33. For a comparison with similar arguments in the West, see Pierre Klossowski, "Marquis de Sade and the Revolution."

34. Kamei, "Ikeru Yuda (Shesutofu ron) 1," 33, 34.

35. Ibid., 36.

36. Kamei, "Ikeru Yuda (Shesutofu ron) 2," 7 (emphasis in original). Quotations are by Kamei and refer to *Faust*.

37. Ibid. (emphasis is mine).

38. Ibid., 22, 22, 23.

39. Ibid., 24.

40. "*Yoakemae* gappyōkai."

41. This problematic was continued by the *Bungakkai* group in its Symposium on Overcoming Modernity (Kindai no Chōkoku Zadankai) held only six years later, in 1942. Although I discuss the symposium in more depth in the epilogue, it may be useful to note here that Kawakami served as the moderator of the symposium and Kamei played a leading role as both an organizer and a participant.

42. Kamei, "*Yoakemae* ni tsuite," 18.

43. Ibid., 13.

44. Ibid., 21, 20.

45. Ibid., 31.
46. Ibid., 32–33.
47. Kamei, "Nihon-teki na mono no shōrai."
48. Ibid., 118.
49. Kamei, "Hyōhaku no omoi."
50. Ibid., 193.
51. Ibid.
52. Kamei, *Shinkō ni tsuite* (Tokyo: Chikuma Shobō, 1942). Articles cited below with a double asterisk (**) were included in this work.
53. Kamei, "Shizen to shinkō,"** *Bungakkai* (June 1941): 4–5.
54. Ibid., 9.
55. Kamei, "Gendaijin no seikaku,"** *Bungei shunjū* (March 1942): 288 (emphasis in original).
56. Kamei, "Shizen to shinkō,"** 9.
57. Kamei, "Sensō to shinkō," 364.
58. Kamei, "Kiki to kyūshin." Much of this essay repeats arguments Kamei made earlier in "Sensō to shinkō."
59. Kamei, "Kiki to kyūshin," 18.
60. Kamei, "Tatakai no kokoro," in *Shinkō ni tsuite,* 200.
61. Kamei, "Gendai seishin ni kansuru oboegaki," originally published in *Kindai no chōkoku* (Tokyo: Sōgensha, 1943); cited here from Kawakami and Takeuchi et al., *Kindai no chōkoku,* 5.
62. Kamei, "Nenpu," 527.

5. THE PRODUCTION OF A CULTURE OF THE SAME

1. Hashikawa, "Tenkeiki no jiga," 127.
2. Odagiri, "Kaisetsu," 345.
3. "Sakka no tame ni," originally published in *Asahi shinbun* (May 1932). The other two sequels were "Bungaku no tame ni," originally published in *Kaizō* (July 1932); "Sakka to shite," originally published in *Shinchō* (September 1932). All three were later republished as the core of *Rōman-shugisha no techō.*
4. Hayashi, "Sakka no tame ni," in *HFc* 3:302–7.
5. See, for example, Steinhoff, "*Tenkō*," 147–55. This is a useful study. Steinhoff mentions the problem of the self but limits it to a source of weakness and a place of withdrawal and does not see it as a key concept intricately involved in the active production of a different sense of cultural identity.
6. See Lacoue-Labarthe and Nancy, *Literary Absolute,* especially 59–78.
7. Hayashi's *Tenkō ni tsuite,* published in 1941 at the height of militarism and nearly ten years after his *tenkō* allegedly occurred, is the most salient example of the subject-work. An attempt by Hayashi to produce himself in accord with subjective desire, it allows him the possibility to rewrite the reasons for his *tenkō* in the light of exigencies of the social conditions of 1941.

8. Hayashi, "Sakka to shite," in *Rōman-shugisha no techō*, 185–87.

9. Hayashi, "Bungaku no tame ni," in *Rōman-shugisha no techō*, 143.

10. Ibid., 147.

11. This is the *Second Literary World* (*Dai-ni bungakkai*); the first *Literary World* was published from 1893 to 1898 and associated with such intellectuals as Shimazaki Tōson, Kitamura Tōkoku, and Ueda Bin. In the postwar years, the third *Literary World* was organized in June 1947 by several members of the second *Literary World*, such as Hayashi Fusao, Kamei Katsuichirō, and Yokomitsu Riichi, and is still published today.

12. See the important essay by Takami Jun, "Bungei fukkō," in his *Shōwa bungaku seisuishi*, 306–35.

13. Yokomitsu, "Junsui shōsetsu ron," 71, 79.

14. Ibid., 76.

15. Ibid., 79.

16. Hashikawa, "Tenkeiki no jiga," 131.

17. Kobayashi, "Watakushi-shōsetsu ron," 122.

18. Ibid.; see also Hashikawa, "'Shakaika shita watakushi' o megutte," in *Nihon rōmanha hihan josetsu*, 101–26.

19. See Hoston, *Marxism and the Crisis of Development in Prewar Japan*, 136.

20. But see Kobayashi's important essay, "Samazama naru ishō."

21. *KHz* 3:132.

22. *KHz* 3:140.

23. Hashikawa, "Tenkeiki no jiga," 131.

24. Hayashi, *Rōman-shugisha no techō*, 202.

25. Lacoue-Labarthe and Nancy, *Literary Absolute*, 12 (emphasis in the original).

26. Lukács, *Historical Novel*, 50.

27. Ibid., 47.

28. Hayashi, *Seinen*, 5–6.

29. Hayashi, *Rōman-shugisha no techō*, 200.

30. Hayashi, *Seinen*, 34.

31. Ibid., 36.

32. Ibid., 16–17.

33. Kobayashi, "Hayashi Fusao no *Seinen*," 84–85.

34. See de Certeau, *Practice of Everyday Life*, 5–6.

35. Hashikawa, "Tenkeiki no jiga," 127.

36. Hayashi, "Gokuchūshin," 197–98; cited in Hashikawa, "Tenkeiki no jiga," 129.

37. Kamei, "Ongaku"; see also Takami, *Shōwa bungaku seisuishi*, 35–36.

38. Hayashi, "Bungaku to kokusaku," 89, 95, 92.

39. Bataille, "Psychological Structure of Fascism," 137–38.

40. Hayashi, "Bungaku to kokusaku," 95.

41. Bataille, "Psychological Structure of Fascism," 147 (emphasis in the original).

42. Hayashi, "Tenkō ni tsuite," 377.

43. Shimizu, "Hayashi Fusao," 108–9.
44. Hayashi, "Utsukushiki kodama."
45. Hayashi, "Risōsei no aware."
46. Hayashi, "Utsukushiki kodama," 4.
47. For example, as a member of the Writers Preliminary Committee for the New Organization (Bundan Shintaisei Junbi Iinkai), Hayashi willingly cooperated with the ideological state apparatus.
48. Nishitani et al., "Zadankai," 221.
49. Ibid., 242.
50. Ibid., 243.
51. Hayashi made this view most explicit in his postwar best-seller, *Daitōa sensō kōteiron*, especially 13–30; see also *HFc* 3:6–19.

EPILOGUE

1. See Dower, *War Without Mercy*, especially 203–33; also Najita and Harootunian, "Japanese Revolt Against the West."
2. As the acknowledged leader of the Romantic School, Yasuda Yojūrō was invited to the symposium but declined, citing poor health. In a brief essay on symposiums published the month the symposium on overcoming modernity was held, Yasuda decried the "journalistic" nature of all such gatherings. See "Zadankai no kotoba ni tsuite."
3. Watanabe Kazutami, "'Kindai no chōkoku' saidoku," in *Nashonarizumu no ryōgisei*, 206.
4. Kawakami Tetsutarō, "'Kindai no chōkoku' ketsugo," 166.
5. Najita and Harootunian, "Japanese Revolt Against the West," 741.
6. Kōsaka Masaaki, *Rekishiteki sekai*; cited in Arakawa, *Shōwa shisōshi*, 181.
7. A good, succinct discussion of the disagreements over the key problem of defining *modernity* in these debates is provided in Oketani, *Shōwa seishinshi*, 431–34; see also Watanabe Kazutami's close reading of the texts in his "'Kindai no chōkoku' saidoku."
8. Remarks attributed to Kamei, in Kawakami and Takeuchi et al., *Kindai no chōkoku*, 200. See also Yoshimitsu's contribution, "Kindai chōkoku no shingakuteki konkyo," 59–82.
9. Kawakami and Takeuchi et al., *Kindai no chōkoku*, 202.
10. Kamei, "Gendai seishin ni kansuru oboegaki," 16.
11. Ibid., 17.
12. Kawakami and Takeuchi et al., *Kindai no chōkoku*, 239–40.
13. Ibid., 264.
14. Ibid., 266–68.
15. Nakamura Mitsuo, "'Kindai' e no giwaku," 152. See also Watanabe, "'Kindai no chōkoku' saidoku," 214–17.
16. See Tsurumi, "Occupation."
17. Nakamura Shin'ichirō, *Sengo bungaku no kaisō* (Tokyo: Chikuma shobō, 1963); cited in Kosaka, *100 Million Japanese*, 20–21. Nakamura's remarks appear especially prescient in light of the announcement by the

Ohira government in 1980 of the establishment of an "age of culture." On the Ohira announcement, see Harootunian, "Visible Discourses / Invisible Ideologies."

18. See John Dower's classic essay, "Occupied Japan and the American Lake, 1945–1950."

19. Tsurumi, "Occupation," 9.

20. For a good synopsis of the major legal issues involved, see Itasaka, *Kodansha Encyclopedia of Japan*, s.v. "War Crimes Trials," by Richard Minear.

21. Tsurumi, "Occupation," 16.

22. Watanabe, "Genten to shite no 'sengo,'" 179.

23. See Gordon, *Evolution of Labor Relations in Japan*, especially 329–411.

24. On the debate on subjectivity, I have drawn freely from J. Victor Koschmann's essay, "The Debate on Subjectivity in Postwar Japan." See also Yoshida and Koyasu, *Nihon shisōshi dokuhon*, 248–52.

25. Yoshida and Koyasu, *Nihon shisōshi dokuhon*, 250.

26. Kamei Katsuichirō, *Bungakkai* (June 1947); cited in Odagiri, *Nihon kindai bungaku daijiten*, s.v. "Bungakkai," by Odagiri Susumu.

27. Yasuda, "Saigunbiron hihan," in *YYz* 27:591.

28. Yasuda, "Zettai heiwa ron," in *YYz* 25:82–84.

29. Watanabe, "Sengo shisō no mitori zu," 110–11.

30. Hashikawa, *Nihon rōmanha hihan josetsu*, 40–41. On Schmitt's views on Romanticism, see his *Political Romanticism*. In translating Hashikawa's citation from Schmitt, I have followed Oakes's translation; see Schmitt, *Political Romanticism*, 72.

31. Hashikawa, *Nihon rōmanha hihan josetsu*, 58–59.

32. Takeuchi, "Kindai no chōkoku."

33. Matsumoto, "Sengo shisō to Takeuchi Yoshimi," 231.

34. Ibid., 230.

35. Ueno, "Takeuchi Yoshimi to Hanada Kiyoteru," 137–38.

36. Hanada, *Nihon no runessansujin*,

37. On the impact of the Vietnam War on Japanese social and political discourse, see Havens, *Fire Across the Sea*.

38. These writers included Kageyama Masaharu, Kamiya Tadataka, Kawamura Jirō, Odakane Jirō, Oketani Hideaki, and Saegusa Yasutaka. Some representative works from the mid-1960s and early 1970s are Kawamura's "Yasuda Yojūrō ron" (1966); Ōkubo's *Tenkō to rōman-shugi* (1967); Izumi Aki's *Nihon rōmanha hihan* (1968); the collection of essays in the November 1971 issue of *Kaishaku to kanshō*, subtitled "Shōwa no rōman-shugi"; and, of course, *Nihon rōmanha* (1977), in the *Nihon bungaku kenkyū shiryō sōsho* series, which elevated the Romantic School to canonical status.

39. See Miyoshi and Harootunian, *Postmodernism and Japan*, especially Harootunian's discussion of Prime Minister Ohira's attempt to convert Japan into a cultural nation, 460–68.

Bibliography

Adorno, Theodor. *Aesthetic Theory*. Trans. C. Lenhardt and ed. Gretel Adorno and Rolf Tiedemann. London and New York: Routledge and Kegan Paul, 1984.

Akitani Yutaka. "Jinbō Kōtarō." In Itō Shinkichi, ed., *Gendai shi kanshō kōza*, vol. 10: *Gendai no jojō*. Tokyo: Kadokawa Shoten, 1969.

Anderson, Benedict. *Imagined Communities: Reflections on the Origin and Spread of Nationalism*. London: Verso, 1983.

Arakawa Ikuo. *Shōwa shisō shi: Kuraku kagayakeru 1930 nendai*. Tokyo: Asahi Shinbunsha, 1989.

Asano Akira and Hiyama Saburō. *Zuibun: Nihon rōmanha*. Tokyo: Chōei-sha, 1987.

Bachelard, Gaston. *The Poetics of Space*. Trans. Maria Jolas. N.p.: Orion Press, 1964; Boston: Beacon Press, 1969.

Bataille, Georges. "The Psychological Structure of Fascism." In *Visions of Excess: Selected Writings, 1927–1939*. Trans. Allan Stoekl et al., and ed. Allan Stoekl. Minneapolis: University of Minnesota Press, 1985.

Behler, Ernst. "Foreword." In A. Leslie Willson, ed., *German Romantic Criticism*. The German Library 21. New York: Continuum, 1982.

Benjamin, Walter. *Charles Baudelaire: A Lyric Poet in the Era of High Capitalism*. Trans. Harry Zohn. Norfolk, Engl.: Thetford Press, 1983.

Berlant, Lauren. *The Anatomy of National Fantasy: Hawthorne, Utopia, and Everyday Life*. Chicago: University of Chicago Press, 1991.

Bloch, Ernst. "Nonsynchronism and the Obligation to Its Dialectics." Trans. Mark Ritter. *New German Critique* (Spring 1977): 22–38.

Breuilly, John. *Nationalism and the State*. New York: St. Martin's Press, 1982.

Carroll, David. *The Subject in Question*. Chicago: University of Chicago Press, 1982.

Dale, Peter N. *The Myth of Japanese Uniqueness*. New York: St. Martin's Press, 1986.

de Certeau, Michel. *The Practice of Everyday Life*. Trans. Steven F. Rendall. Berkeley and Los Angeles: University of California Press, 1984.

Dower, John. "Occupied Japan and the American Lake, 1945–1950." In Edward Friedman and Mark Selden, eds., *America's Asia: Dissenting Essays on Asian-American Relations*. New York: Random House, 1969.

———. *War Without Mercy: Race and Power in the Pacific War*. New York: Pantheon Books, 1986.

Easthope, Anthony. *Poetry as Discourse*. New Accents. London and New York: Methuen, 1983.

Edwards, Paul, ed. *The Encyclopedia of Philosophy*. New York: Macmillan Company and Free Press, 1967.

Field, Norma. *The Splendor of Longing in the Tale of Genji*. Princeton: Princeton University Press, 1987.

Fujiwara Sadamu. "Fuan no bungaku." *Bungaku* (June 1933): 1–18.

Fukuchi Kuniki. "Tanaka Katsumi." In Itō Shinkichi, ed., *Gendai shi kanshō kōza*, vol. 10: *Gendai no jojō*. Tokyo: Kadokawa Shoten, 1969.

Funakoshi Akira. "Suguretaru shigyō no jōju." *Cogito* (November 1938): 96–99.

Gadamer, Hans-Georg. *Philosophical Hermeneutics*. Trans. and ed. David E. Linge. Berkeley and Los Angeles: University of California Press, 1976.

Gellner, Ernest. *Nations and Nationalism*. Oxford: Oxford University Press, 1983.

Gluck, Carol. *Japan's Modern Myths: Ideology in the Late Meiji Period*. Princeton: Princeton University Press, 1985.

Gordon, Andrew. *The Evolution of Labor Relations in Japan: Heavy Industry, 1853–1955*. Cambridge: Harvard University Press, 1988.

Habermas, Jürgen. "Modernity—An Incomplete Project." In Paul Rabinow and William M. Sullivan, eds., *Interpretive Social Science: A Second Look*. Berkeley and Los Angeles: University of California Press, 1987.

Hagiwara Sakutarō. *Atarashiki yokujō*. In *HSz* 4:5–237. Tokyo: Chikuma Shobō, 1975.

———. "Eiyū to shijin yomite." *Cogito* (January 1937): 52–55.

———. *Hagiwara Sakutarō zenshū*. 15 vols. Tokyo: Chikuma Shobō, 1975–78.

———. *Nihon e no kaiki*. In *HSz* 10:481–681.

———. "Nihon rōmanha ni tsuite." In *HSz* 10:90–92.

———. *Teihon Aoneko. Nihon no shika*, vol. 14. Chūō bunko, 1975.

———. "Wagahito ni ataeru aika." *Cogito* (January 1936): 120–25.

———. *Hagiwara Sakutarō: Bungei dokuhon*. Tokyo: Kawade Shobō Shinsha, 1976.

Hanada Kiyoteru. *Kindai no chōkoku*. Tokyo: Miraisha, 1959.

———. *Nihon no runessansujin*. Tokyo: Asahi Shinbunsha, 1975.

Harootunian, H. D. "Commentary on Nationalism in Japan: Nationalism as Intellectual History." *Journal of Asian Studies* (November 1971): 57–62.

———. "Introduction: A Sense of an Ending and the Problem of Taisho." In H. D. Harootunian and B. Silberman, eds., *Japan in Crisis: Essays on Taisho Democracy*. Princeton: Princeton University Press, 1974.

———. *Things Seen and Unseen: Discourse and Ideology in Tokugawa Nativism*. Chicago: University of Chicago Press, 1988.

———. "Visible Discourses / Invisible Ideologies." *South Atlantic Quarterly* (Summer 1988): 445–74.

Harootunian, H. D., and Tetsuo Najita. "Japanese Revolt Against the

West." In Peter Duus, ed., *The Cambridge History of Japan: Volume 6, The Twentieth Century*. Cambridge: Cambridge University Press, 1988.

Hashikawa, Bunzō. *Nihon rōmanha hihan josetsu*. Tokyo: Miraisha, 1965.

——. "Tenkeiki no jiga—'bungei fukkō' ki to gendai." In *Nihon rōmanha hihan josetsu*. Tokyo: Miraisha, 1965.

Hasumi Shigehiko et al. "Shōwa hihyō no shomondai: 'Bungaku-shugi no shihai' = bungei fukkōki kara 'tasha' to shite no Ajia e." *Kikan shichō* (October 1989): 30–68.

Havens, Thomas R. H. *Fire Across the Sea: The Vietnam War and Japan, 1965–1975*. Princeton: Princeton University Press, 1987.

Hayashi Fusao. "Bungaku to kokusaku." *Kaizō* (June 1938): 89–98.

——. *Daitō-A sensō kōteiron*. Tokyo: Banchō Shobō, 1975.

——. "Gokuchūshin." In *HFc* 3:194–239.

——. *Hayashi Fusao chosakushū*. 3 vols. Tokyo: Yokushoin, 1968–69.

——. "Kinnō no kokoro." In *HFc* 3:414–38.

——. "Kyō no junsuiha—kinnō bungaku ron josetsu 2." *Asahi shinbun*, June 3, 1941, p. 4.

——. "Risōsei no aware—kinnō bungaku ron josetsu 1." *Asahi shinbun*, June 2, 1941, p. 4.

——. *Rōman-shugisha no techō*. Tokyo: Sairensha, 1935.

——. "Seinen." *Chūō kōron* (November 1932): 80–127.

——. *Seinen*. In *Nihon no bungaku* 40:5–256, ed. Tanizaki Jun'ichirō et al. Tokyo: Chūō Kōronsha, 1968.

——. "Tenkō ni tsuite." In *HFc* 3:377–413.

——. "Utsukushiki kodama—kinnō bungaku ron josetsu 3." *Asahi shinbun*, June 4, 1941, p. 4.

Hayashi Fusao and Mishima Yukio. *Taiwa: Nihonjinron*. Tokyo: Banchō Shobō, 1966.

Heine, Heinrich. *Die romantische Schule*. Leipzig: Reclam, 1985.

"Henshū kōki." *Cogito* (March 1932): 103.

HFc. See Hayashi Fusao. *Hayashi Fusao chosakushū*.

Hirano Ken, Odagiri Hideo, and Yamamoto Kenkichi, eds. *Gendai Nihon bungaku ronsōshi*. 3 vols. Tokyo: Miraisha, 1956–57.

Hiromatsu Wataru. *"Kindai no chōkoku" ron*. Tokyo: Asahi Shuppansha, 1980.

Hobsbawm, E. J. *Nations and Nationalism Since 1780: Programe, Myth, Reality*. Cambridge: Cambridge University Press, 1990.

Hobsbawm, Eric, and Terence Ranger, eds. *The Invention of Tradition*. Cambridge: Cambridge University Press, 1983.

Hölderlin, Friedrich. *Selected Verse: Hölderlin*. Trans. and ed. Michael Hamburger. London: Anvil Poetry Press, 1986.

Hollier, Denis, ed. *The College of Sociology, 1937–39*. Trans. Betsy Wing. Minneapolis: University of Minnesota Press, 1988.

Hoshu handō shisōka ni manabu hon. Tokyo: JICC, 1985.

Hoston, Germaine A. *Marxism and the Crisis of Development in Prewar Japan*. Princeton: Princeton University Press, 1986.

HSz. See Hagiwara Sakutarō. *Hagiwara Sakutarō zenshū.*

Ishida Takeshi. *"Heiwa" to "kokka." Nihon no seiji to kotoba,* vol. 2. Tokyo: Tōkyō Daigaku Shuppankai, 1989.

ISz. See Itō Shizuo. *Itō Shizuō zenshū.*

Itasaka Gen, ed. *Kodansha Encyclopedia of Japan.* Tokyo: Kodansha, 1983.

Itō Shinkichi, Itō Sei, Inoue Yasushi, and Yamamoto Kenkichi, eds. *Hagiwara Sakutarō. Nihon no shika,* vol. 14. Tokyo: Chūō Kōronsha, 1975.

———. *Nakahara Chūya, Yagi Shigekichi, Itō Shizuo. Nihon no shika,* vol. 23. Tokyo: Chūō Kōronsha, 1974.

Itō Shizuo. "Byōin no kanja no uta." *Cogito* (August 1933): 92–95.

———. "Danwa no kawari ni." In *ISz:* 221–22.

———. *Itō Shizuo, gendaishi dokuhon,* vol. 10. Tokyo: Shichōsha, 1979.

———. *Itō Shizuo zenshū.* Ed. Kuwabara Takeo, Odakane Jirō, and Fuji Masaharu. Kyoto: Jinbun Shoin, 1969.

———. "Kyozetsu." *Cogito* (December 1935): 30–31.

———. "Suichūka." *Nihon rōmanha* (August 1973): 52–53.

Iwamoto, Yoshio. "Aspects of the Proletarian Literary Movement in Japan." In H. D. Harootunian and B. Silberman, eds., *Japan in Crisis: Essays on Taisho Democracy.* Princeton: Princeton University Press, 1974.

Jinbō Kōtarō. "Atarashiki jikan no kakutoku." *Nihon rōmanha* (August 1935): 86.

———. "Atarashiki poemu no tsuikyū: Nihon rōmanha shiron (II)." *Nihon rōmanha* (June 1935): 26–32.

———. "Nihon rōmanha shiron (I): Shi no henbō ni tsuite." *Nihon rōmanha* (April 1935): 22–26.

———. "Waga hihansha ni okuru: Nihon rōmanha shiron (3)." *Nihon rōmanha* (August 1935): 19–24.

Kageyama, Masaharu. *Minzokuha no bungaku undō.* Daitōjuku Shuppanbu, 1965.

Kamei Katsuichirō. "Bunmei to dōtoku." In *KKz,* appendix 3:13.

———. "Gendai seishin ni kansuru oboegaki." In Kawakami Tetsutarō and Takeuchi Yoshimi et al., eds., *Kindai no chōkoku.* Tokyo: Fuzanbō, 1979.

———. "Hyōhaku no omoi." *Bungakkai* (October 1939): 192–201.

———. "Ikeru Yuda (Shesutofu ron) 1." *Nihon rōmanha* (May 1935): 23–37.

———. "Ikeru Yuda (Shesutofu ron) 2." *Nihon rōmanha* (June 1935): 4–25.

———. *Kamei Katsuichirō zenshū.* 24 vols. Tokyo: Kōdansha, 1971–75.

———. "Kiki to kyūshin." *Bungakkai* (June 1942): 17–21.

———. "Kokyō e kaere." In *KKz* 1:287–92.

———. "Nenpu." In *KKz,* appendix 3:513–62.

———. "Nihon-teki na mono no shōrai." *Shinchō* (March 1937): 118–20.

———. "Ongaku." *Nihon rōmanha* (March 1935): 86–87.

———. "Rōman-teki jiga no mondai." *Nihon rōmanha* (March 1935): 14–21.

———. "Seiyō bunmei no higeki." In *KKz* 20:483–88.

———. "Sensō to shinkō." In *KKz* 19:362–65.

———. *Shinkō ni tsuite*. In *KKz* 6:177–266. Also published by Chikuma Shobō in 1942.

———. *Tenkeiki no bungaku*. In *KKz* 1:11–203.

———. "*Yoakemae* ni tsuite." *Nihon rōmanha* (June 1936): 12–33.

Kamiya Tadataka. "Yasuda Yojūrō ni okeru 'kindai no chōkoku.'" *Kikan shichō* (October 1989): 160–70.

———. *Yasuda Yojūrō ron*. Tokyo: Ganshokan, 1979.

Karatani Kōjin. "Fūkei no hakken." In *Nihon kindai bungaku no kigen*. Tokyo: Kōdansha, 1980.

———. "Kindai Nihon no hihyō." *Kikan shichō* (October 1989): 6–29.

———. *Nihon kindai bungaku no kigen*. Tokyo: Kōdansha, 1980.

Karatani Kōjin and Kasai Kiyoshi. *Posutomodanizumu hihan: Kyoten kara kyoten e*. Tokyo: Sakuhinsha, 1985.

Kawakami Tetsutarō. "Kindai no chōkoku ketsugo." In Kawakami and Takeuchi Yoshimi et al., eds., *Kindai no chōkoku*. Tokyo: Fuzanbō, 1979.

Kawakami Tetsutarō and Abe Rokurō. "Fukyūhan jo." In Lev Shestov, *Higeki no tetsugaku*. Trans. Kawakami and Abe. Tokyo: Shiba Shoten, 1936.

Kawakami Tetsutarō and Takeuchi Yoshimi et al., eds. *Kindai no chōkoku*. Tokyo: Fuzanbō, 1979.

Kawakami Tetsutarō et al. "*Yoakemae* Gappyōkai." *Bungakkai* (May 1936): 150–79.

Kawamura, Jirō. "Yasuda Yojūrō ron." *Tenbō* (September 1966): 135–148.

KHz. See Kobayashi Hideo. *Kobayashi Hideo zenshū*.

Kinmonth, Earl. *The Self-Made Man in Meiji Japanese Thought*. Berkeley and Los Angeles: University of California Press, 1981.

Kipling, Rudyard. "The Man Who Would Be King." In *Under the Deodars, The Phantom Rickshaw, Wee Willie Winkie*. New York: Macmillan, 1897.

KKz. See Kamei Katsuichirō. *Kamei Katsuichirō zenshū*.

Klossowski, Pierre. "The Marquis de Sade and the Revolution." In Denis Hollier, ed., *The College of Sociology, 1937–39*. Trans. Betsy Wing. Minneapolis: University of Minnesota Press, 1988.

Kobayashi Hideo. "Hayashi Fusao no *Seinen*." *KHz* 3:81–91.

———. *Kobayashi Hideo zenshū*. 12 vols. Tokyo: Shinchōsha, 1967–68.

———. "Kokyō wo ushinatta bungaku." In *KHz* 3:29–37.

———. "Samazama naru ishō." In *KHz* 1:11–27.

———. "Watakushi-shōsetsu ron." *KHz* 3:119–45.

Kobayashi Michinori. "'Kindai no chōkoku' to wa nani ka." *Jiyū* (July 1987): 10–23.

Kojiki. Trans. Donald Philippi. Tokyo: University of Tokyo Press, 1968.

Kosaka, Masataka. *100 Million Japanese: The Postwar Experience*. Tokyo and Palo Alto: Kodansha International, 1972.

Kosaka, Shūhei, ed. *New Japanology*. Tokyo: Gogatsusha, 1985.

Koschmann, J. Victor. "The Debate on Subjectivity in Postwar Japan: Foundations of Modernism as a Political Critique." *Pacific Affairs* (Winter 1981–82): 609–31.

Kristeva, Julia. *Revolution in Poetic Language*. Trans. Margaret Waller. New York: Columbia University Press, 1984.

Kurihara Katsumaru. *Nihon rōmanha: Sono shūhen*. Tokyo: Kōbunken, 1985.

Lacan, Jacques. "The Mirror Stage as Formative of the Function of the *I*." In *Écrits, a Selection*. Trans. Alan Sheridan. New York: W. W. Norton, 1977.

———. "The Subject and the Other: Alienation." In *The Four Fundamental Concepts of Psychoanalysis*. Trans. Alan Sheridan and ed. Jacques-Alain Miller. New York: W. W. Norton, 1978.

Lacoue-Labarthe, Philippe, and Jean-Luc Nancy. *The Literary Absolute: The Theory of Literature in German Romanticism*. Trans. Philip Barnard and Cheryl Lester. Albany: State University of New York Press, 1988.

Lukács, Georg. *The Historical Novel*. Trans. Hannah Mitchell and Stanley Mitchell. Lincoln: University of Nebraska Press, 1962.

———. "On the Romantic Philosophy of Life." In *Soul and Form*. Trans. Anna Bostock. London: Merlin Press, 1974 [MIT Press edition].

Matsumoto Ken'ichi. *Metsubō katei no bungaku*. Tokyo: Tōkisha, 1980.

Matsumoto, Sannosuke. "Sengo shisō to Takeuchi Yoshimi." *Sekai* (March 1986): 225–37.

Matsumoto Teruo. "Yasuda Yojūrō oboegaki." In Nihon Bungaku Kenkyū Shiryō Kankōkai, ed., *Nihon rōmanha*. Tokyo: Yūseido, 1977.

Miki Kiyoshi. "Fuan no shisō to sono chōkoku." *Kaizō* (June 1933): 26–41. Reprinted in Hirano Ken, ed., *Gendai Nihon bungaku ronsōshi* 3:9–18. Tokyo: Miraisha, 1957.

———. "Kagaku hihan no kadai." *Shinkō kagaku no hata no moto ni* (October 1928): 2–25.

———. "Henshū yōroku." *Shinkō kagaku no hata no moto ni* (November 1928): 146.

Miki Kiyoshi and Kobayashi Hideo et al. "Gendai bungaku no Nihon-teki dōkō." *Bungakkai* (February 1937): 202–30.

Miyoshi, Masao, and H. D. Harootunian, eds. "Postmodernism and Japan." *South Atlantic Quarterly* (Summer 1988).

Miyoshi Tatsuji. *Hagiwara Sakutarō*. Tokyo: Chikuma Shobō, 1963.

———. "Shi yo! Hagiwara Sakutarō." In *Hagiwara Sakutarō*. Tokyo: Kawade Shobō Shinsha, 1976.

Morely, James, ed. *Dilemmas of Growth in Prewar Japan*. Princeton: Princeton University Press.

Nagashima Matao. "Minzoku narabi ni minzoku undō ni tsuite." *Shinkō kagaku no hata no moto ni* (April 1929): 23–39.

Najita, Tetsuo, and H. D. Harootunian. "Japanese Revolt Against the West: Political and Cultural Criticism in the Twentieth Century." In

Peter Duus, ed., *The Cambridge History of Japan: Volume 6, The Twentieth Century.* Cambridge: Cambridge University Press, 1988.

Nakamura Mitsuo. "'Kindai' e no giwaku." In Kawakami Tetsutarō and Takeuchi Yoshimi et al., eds., *Kindai no chōkoku.* Tokyo: Fuzanbō, 1979.

Nihon Bungaku Kenkyū Shiryō Kankōkai, ed. *Nihon rōmanha.* Tokyo: Yūseido, 1977.

Nishitani Keiji et al. "Zadankai." In Kawakami Tetsutarō and Takeuchi Yoshimi et al., eds, *Kindai no chokoku.* Tokyo: Fuzanbō, 1979.

Nitta Mitsuo, ed. *Nihon rōmanha to wa nani ka.* Tokyo: Yūshōdō Shoten, 1972.

Noguchi Takehiko. "Ironī to kotodama: Nihon rōmanha ni okeru kindai no chōkoku to kaitai." *Kikan shichō* (October 1989): 70–86.

Nomura Shirō, ed. *Gendai shijin zenshū,* vol. 4, no. 4. Tokyo: Kadokawa Shoten, 1960.

Nomura Sōgō Kenkyūjō. *NRI Refarensu: Nihonjinron 2.* Kamakura: NRI, 1978.

Odagiri Hideo. "Kaisetsu." In Hirano Ken et al., eds., *Gendai Nihon bungaku ronsōshi,* vol. 2. Tokyo: Miraisha, 1956.

Odagiri Susumu, ed. *Nihon kindai bungaku daijiten.* Tokyo: Kōdansha, 1977.

Odakane, Jirō. *Shijin: Itō Shizuo.* Tokyo: Shinchōsha, 1971.

Ogawa Kazusuke. *Itō Shizuo ronkō.* Tokyo: Sōbunsha, 1983.

Okaniwa Noboru. "Itō Shizuo to shōwa jūnendai." In *Itō Shizuo gendaishi dokuhon.* Tokyo: Shinchōsha, 1976.

Oketani Hideaki. *Dochaku to jōkyō.* Tokyo: Kokubunsha, 1969.

———. *Kindai no naraku.* Tokyo: Kokubunsha, 1984.

———. *Shōwa seishinshi.* Tokyo: Bungei Shunjū, 1992.

———. *Yasuda Yojūrō.* Tokyo: Shinchōsha, 1983.

Ōkubo Tsuneo. *Shōwa bungaku no shukumei.* Tokyo: Tōjusha, 1975.

———. *Shōwa bungakushi no kōsō to bunseki.* Tokyo: Shibundō, 1971.

Ōoka, Makoto. *Hagiwara Sakutarō. Kindai Nihon shijin sen,* vol. 10. Tokyo: Chikuma Shobō, 1981.

———. *Jojō no hihan: Nihon-teki bi-ishiki no kōzō shiron.* Tokyo: Shōbunsha, 1961.

Passin, Herbert. *Society and Education in Japan.* Tokyo: Kodansha International, 1982.

Pierrot, Jean. *The Decadent Imagination, 1880–1900.* Trans. Derek Coltman. Chicago: University of Chicago Press, 1981.

Pyle, Kenneth B. *The New Generation in Meiji Japan: Problems of Cultural Identity, 1885–1895.* Stanford: Stanford University Press, 1969.

Rabinow, Paul, and William M. Sullivan, eds. *Interpretive Social Science: A Second Look.* Berkeley and Los Angeles: University of California Press, 1987.

———. "The Interpretive Turn." In Rabinow and Sullivan, eds., *Interpretive Social Science: A Second Look.* Berkeley and Los Angeles: University of California Press, 1987.

Reischauer, E. O. *Japan: The Story of a Nation*. 4th ed. New York: McGraw-Hill, 1990.

———. "What Went Wrong?" In James William Morley, ed., *Dilemmas of Growth in Prewar Japan*. Princeton: Princeton University Press, 1971.

Rimer, J. Thomas, ed. *Culture and Identity: Japanese Intellectuals During the Interwar Years*. Princeton: Princeton University Press, 1990.

Roden, Donald. "Taishō Culture and the Problem of Gender Ambivalence." In J. Thomas Rimer, ed., *Culture and Identity: Japanese Intellectuals During the Interwar Years*. Princeton: Princeton University Press, 1990.

Saegusa Yasutaka. *Nihon rōmanha no gunzō*. Tokyo: Yūshindō, 1967.

———. *Nihon rōmanha no undō*. Tokyo: Gendaisha, 1959.

Saigō, Nobutsuna. *Shi no hassei*. Tokyo: Miraisha, 1964.

Sakamoto Etsurō. "Tēburu Supīchi." *Cogito* (November 1938): 23–27.

Schiller, Friedrich von. *Naive and Sentimental Poetry, and On the Sublime*. Trans. Julius A. Elias. New York: Frederick Ungar, 1966.

Schmitt, Carl. *Political Romanticism*. Trans. Guy Oakes. Cambridge, Mass.: MIT Press, 1986.

Seyhan, Azade. *Representation and Its Discontents: The Critical Legacy of German Romanticism*. Berkeley and Los Angeles: University of California Press, 1992.

Shea, G. T. *Leftwing Literature in Japan*. Tokyo: Hōsei University Press, 1964.

Shestov, Lev. *Higeki no Tetsugaku*. Trans. Abe Rokurō and Kawakami Tetsutarō. Tokyo: Shiba Shoten, 1936.

Shimazaki Tōson. *Before the Dawn*. Trans. William E. Naff. Honolulu: University of Hawaii Press, 1987.

———. *Yoakemae*. 4 vols. Tokyo: Iwanami Shoten, 1962.

Shimizu Shōzō. "Hayashi Fusao." *Kaishaku to kanshō* (November 1971): 107–10.

Silverberg, Miriam. *Changing Song: The Marxist Manifestos of Nakano Shigeharu*. Princeton: Princeton University Press, 1990.

Smith, Anthony D. *The Ethnic Revival*. London: Cambridge University Press, 1981.

———. *Theories of Nationalism*. London: Cambridge University Press, 1983.

Smith, Henry D. II. *Japan's First Student Radicals*. Cambridge: Harvard University Press, 1972.

Steinhoff, Patricia G. "*Tenkō*: Ideology and Societal Integration in Prewar Japan." Ph.D. diss., Harvard University, 1969.

Storry, Richard. *The Double Patriots: A Study of Japanese Nationalism*. Boston: Houghton Mifflin, 1957.

Sugimoto Hidetarō. *Itō Shizuo*. *Kindai Nihon shijin sen*, vol. 18. Tokyo: Chikuma Shobō, 1985.

Takami Jun. *Shōwa bungaku seisuishi*. 2 vols. Tokyo: Bungei Shunjū Shinsha, 1958; reprinted, Bunshun Bunko, 1987.

Takeuchi Yoshimi. "Kindai no chōkoku." In Kawakami Tetsutarō and

Takeuchi et al., eds., *Kindai no chōkoku*. Tokyo: Fuzanbō, 1979.
Tanaka Katsumi. "Seikōshō—Dichtung und Wahrheit." *Cogito* (April 1934): 59–71.
———. "Shijihyō—1935 nen kaiko." *Cogito* (January 1936): 110–15.
———. "Tatōkai." *Cogito* (February 1935): 38–39.
Todorov, Tzvetan. "The Romantic Crisis." In *Theories of the Symbol*. Trans. Catherine Porter. Ithaca: Cornell University Press, 1982.
Tsujino Hisanori. "Kyomu no shijin (Itō Shizuo josetsu)." *Cogito* (February 1936): 41–48.
Tsurumi, Shunsuke. "Occupation: The American Way of Life as an Imposed Model." In *A Cultural History of Postwar Japan, 1945–1980*. London and New York: Kegan Paul, 1987.
Ueno Takashi. "Takeuchi Yoshimi to Hanada Kiyoteru." Kubo Akira and Fukushima Tadayuki, eds., in *Hanada Kiyoteru no sekai*. Tokyo: Shinpyōsha, 1981.
Vico, Giambattista. *The New Science of Giambattista Vico*. Trans. Thomas Goddard Bergin and Max Harold Fisch. Ithaca: Cornell University Press, 1970.
Vulpitta, Romano. "Yasuda Yojūrō to Mirucha Eriāde, I." *Shunjū shisha* (October 1984): 80–90.
———. "Yasuda Yojūrō to Mirucha Eriāde, II." *Shunjū shisha* (April 1985): 67–74.
Watanabe Kazutami. "Genten to shite no 'sengo.'" In *Nashonarizumu no ryōgisei*. Kyoto: Jinbun Shoin, 1984.
———. *Kindai Nihon no chishikijin*. Tokyo: Chikuma Shobō, 1978.
———. "'Kindai no chōkoku' saidoku." In *Nashonarizumu no ryōgisei*. Kyoto: Jinbun Shoin, 1984.
———. "Sengo shisō no mitori zu." In *Sengo Nihon no seishinshi*. Ed. Maeda Ai and Kamishima Jirō. Tokyo: Iwanami Shoten, 1988.
Watsuji Tetsurō. *A Climate: A Philosophical Study*. Trans. Geoffrey Bownas. [Tokyo?] Print Bureau, Japanese Government, [ca. 1961].
Wheeler, Kathleen, ed. *German Aesthetic and Literary Criticism: The Romantic Ironists and Goethe*. Cambridge: Cambridge University Press, 1984.
White, James, Michio Umegaki, and Thomas R. H. Havens, eds. *The Ambivalence of Nationalism: Modern Japan Between East and West*. Lanham, Md.: University Press of America, 1990.
Williams, Raymond. *Culture and Society, 1780–1950*. New York: Columbia University Press, 1983.
Willson, A. Leslie, ed. *German Romantic Criticism*. New York: Continuum Publishing Company, 1982.
Worringer, Wilhelm. *Abstraction and Empathy: A Contribution to the Psychology of Style*. Trans. Michael Bullock. London: Routledge and Kegan Paul, 1963.
Yasuda Yojūrō. "Bōrudōin shushō." *Nihon rōmanha* (April 1937): 92–99.
———. "Bungaku no aimaisa." *YYz* 3:49–67.
———. "Bungakushi-teki na kanmei." *YYz* 7:561–65.

————. "Bungaku-teki na kanmei." *Cogito* (November 1938): 100–103.
————. "Bunmei kaika no ronri no shūen ni tsuite." *YYz* 7:11–21.
————. "Daitō-A sensō to Nihon bungaku." *YYz* 19:205–24.
————. "Fūkei to rekishi." *YYz* 16:364–83.
————. "Futari no shijin—Tanaka Katsumi e no tegami." *Cogito* (December 1934): 58–64.
————. *Gotobain. YYz* 8:7–272.
————. "Hakuhō-Tenpyō no seishin." *YYz* 5:84–97.
————. "Hana no nagori." *YYz* 21:95–124.
[————]. "Henshū kōki." *Cogito* (March 1932): 103.
————. "'Hihyō' no mondai." *YYz* 2:179–92.
————. "Hyōgen to hyōjō." *YYz* 3:22–31.
————. "Itō Shizuo no shi no koto." *Cogito* (January 1936): 135–37.
————. "Jijo." *YYz* 21:9–12.
————. "Kawabata Yasunari ron." *YYz* 10:141–78.
————. "Kiyoraka na shijin." *YYz* 3:195–218.
————. "Konnichi no rōman-shugi." *YYz* 3:32–48.
————. "Masaoka Shiki ni tsuite." *YYz* 3:9–21.
————. "Meiji no seishin." *YYz* 5:193–251.
————. *Nanzan tōunroku. YYz* 21:9–356.
————. "Nihon bunka no dokusōsei." *YYz* 11:269–86.
————. *Nihon no hashi. YYz* 4:7–138.
————. "Nihon no jōtai ni oite." *YYz* 7:199–217.
[————]. "'Nihon rōmanha' kōkoku." *Cogito* (November 1934): 172–73.
————. "Nihon rōmanha ni tsuite." *YYz* 6:241–50.
————. *Nihon rōmanha no jidai. YYz* 36:7–354.
————. "'Nihon-teki na mono' hihyō ni tsuite." *YYz* 6:190–211.
————. "Sento Herena." *YYz* 3:219–83.
————. "Shijin Hagiwara Sakutarō." *YYz* 13:435–39.
[————]. "Sōkan no ji." *Nihon rōmanha* (March 1935): 92–93.
————. *Taikan shijin no goichininsha. YYz* 5:9–251.
————. "Tenpyō no kofun ni tsuite." *YYz* 11:9–24.
————. "Waga kuni ni okeru rōman-shugi no gaikan." *YYz* 11:287–304.
————. *Weruteru wa naze shinda ka. YYz* 3:287–376.
————. *Yasuda Yojūrō zenshū.* 45 vols. Tokyo: Kōdansha, 1985–89.
————. "Zadankai no kotoba ni tsuite." *YYz* 21:479–81.
Yokomitsu Riichi. "Junsui shosetsu ron." In Hirano Ken, Odagiri Hideo, and Yamamoto Kenkichi, eds., *Gendai Nihon bungaku ronsoōshi* 3:71–79. Tokyo: Miraisha, 1957.
————. *Ryoshū.* In *Yokomitsu Riichi zenshū,* vols. 8 and 9. Tokyo: Kawade Shobō Shinsha, 1982.
Yonekura Iwao. *Itō Shizuo: Yūjō no bigaku.* Tokyo: Sanbisha, 1985.
Yoshida Hikaru and Koyasu Nobukuni. *Nihon shisō dokuhon.* Tokyo: Tōkyō Keizai Shinpōsha, 1979.

Yoshimitsu Yoshihiko. "Kindai chōkoku no shingaku-teki konkyo: Ika ni shite kindaijin wa kami o midasu ka." In Kawakami Tetsutarō and Takeuchi Yoshimi, eds., *Kindai no chōkoku*. Tokyo: Fuzanbō, 1979.

Yoshino, Kosaku. *Cultural Nationalism in Contemporary Japan: A Sociological Enquiry*. London: Routledge, 1992.

YYz. See Yasuda Yojūrō. *Yasuda Yojūrō zenshū*.

Index

Godaigo, Emperor, 22
Goethe, Johann Wolfgang von, xvii, 7, 15–16, 55, 88, 93
Gondō Seikei, xxxv–xxvi, xxvii
Gorkii, Maksim, 84, 85
Gotoba, Emperor, 21–22
"Great Crossing Bridge, The" (Hagiwara), 41
Greater Asia Co-Prosperity Sphere, 134
Greece, 10, 53

Habermas, Jürgen, on modernity, xvi
Hagiwara Kyōjirō, 33
Hagiwara Sakutarō, xxx, xl, 3, 50, 52–53; and Itō, 60–61, 62, 67; poetics of, xli; on poetry as desire, 35–46; return from poetry, 46–49; on the wanderer, 100
Hakuhō-Tenpyō period, 10–11, 17
"Half-self, the" (*hanshin*), 68–71
Hanada Kiyoteru, 149–50
Hani Gorō, xxii, xxxi
Haniyu Yutaka, 143
Hannibal, 5
Harootunian, Harry, xvii, xxix
Hasegawa Futabatei (Shimei), 110
Hashida Kunihiko, 105
Hashikawa Bunzō, 146–47; on the Romantics, 147
Hashimoto Sanai, 121
Hayashi Fusao, xxiv, xxviii, xl, 95, 106, 131; on cultural renaissance, 107, 124; and Kamei, 88, 89; on modernity, 137, 138–139; on "a return to Japan," xlii–xliii, 48; in symposium, 134, 144; *tenko* of, 107–9, 126
Hayashi Tatsuo, 111, 114
Hechter, Michael, xviii
Hegel, Georg Wilhelm Friedrich, 136
Heine, Heinrich, xxvi, 51, 88, 119–20, 124; quoted, 107
Heroes and Poets (Yasuda), 35, 47
Hige Tsuneo, xxx
Hino Ashihei, 127
Hirabayashi Hatsunosuke, 3
Hirano Ken, 143
Hiranuma, Kiichirō, Baron (1926), Prime Minister (1939), 100
Hirohito, Emperor, 21, 126
Hirotsu Kazuo, 111
Historicism: on ancient and modern, xxxii; and Japan Romantics, xxxi, 51; Jinbō on, 55
History: and aesthetics, xi, 35; Hayashi on, 119–22; ideals of, 115–23; Kyoto School on, 136; and language, 149–50;

of modern Japanese poetry, 32; and the novel, 129; and Romantics, xxv, 75–76; Tanaka on, 56–57
Hobsbawm, Eric, xx
Hofmannsthal, Hugo von, 65
Hölderlin, Friedrich, 3, 5, 52, 54; and Itō, 59, 60, 76; quoted, 28
"Homecomer, The" (Itō), 63
"Homecoming, The" (Hagiwara), 43
Honda Shūgo, 143
Honorable Poet Laureate, An (Yasuda), 35
"Hopeful Views of the Homeland" (*Kyōdo bōkei shi*, Hagiwara), 29, 40–42
Howling at the Moon (Hagiwara), 35
Huizinga, Johan, 135
Huxley, Aldous, 135

I, the (*watakushi*), 68–71
I Am a Cat (Natsume), 37
I-Novel, the, 112–14, 123
Iceland, The (Hyōtō; Hagiwara), 42–46, 47
Ideal Image of Twentieth-Century Japan, The (Nijisseiki Nihon no risōzō; Kamei), 106
Identity, 78; collective notions of, xxiii; Hayashi on, 138–39; Itō on, xlii; and Japan Romantic School, xliii; Kamei on Japanese, 137–38
Ihara Saikaku, 109
Ikeda Hayato, Prime Minister, 150
Imperial Rule Assistance Association (Taisei Yokusankai), 101
Imperialism, 146; Kyoto School on, 136
"In Praise of Shadows" (*In'ei raisan*; Tanizaki), xxix
Individual, the: identity of, xxii; Kamei on, 81, 102; Modern School on, 143–44; and World War I, xxi; Yasuda on, 19
Industrialization, and Western modernization, xiv
Inoue Junnosuke, xxv
Inoue Nisshō, xxv–xxvi
"Inquietude et reconstruction" (Cremieux), xxi
Institute for Cultural Review (Bunka Kōronsha), 111
Introduction to a Criticism of the Japan Romantic School, An (Hashikawa), 147
"Introduction to a Theory of Literature of Loyalty to the Emperor, An" ("Kinnō bungaku ron josetsu"; Hayashi, 127
Inukai Tsuyoshi (1855–1932), Prime Minister (1931–32), xxv

Compositor: Asco Trade Typesetting Ltd.
Printer: Thomson-Shore, Inc.
Binder: Thomson-Shore, Inc.
Text: 10/13 Palatino
Display: Palatino